Lecture Notes in Computer Science 13204

More information about this series at https://link.springer.com/bookseries/558

Bo Luo · Mohamed Mosbah · Frédéric Cuppens ·
Lotfi Ben Othmane · Nora Cuppens ·
Slim Kallel (Eds.)

Risks and Security of Internet and Systems

16th International Conference, CRiSIS 2021
Virtual Event, Ames, USA, November 12–13, 2021
Revised Selected Papers

 Springer

Editors
Bo Luo
University of Kansas
Lawrence, KS, USA

Mohamed Mosbah 🔟
University of Bordeaux
Bordeaux, France

Frédéric Cuppens 🔟
Polytechnique Montréal
Montréal, QC, Canada

Lotfi Ben Othmane 🔟
Iowa State University
Iowa City, IA, USA

Nora Cuppens 🔟
Polytechnique Montréal
Montréal, QC, Canada

Slim Kallel 🔟
University of Sfax
Sfax, Tunisia

ISSN 0302-9743   ISSN 1611-3349 (electronic)
Lecture Notes in Computer Science
ISBN 978-3-031-02066-7   ISBN 978-3-031-02067-4 (eBook)
https://doi.org/10.1007/978-3-031-02067-4

This Springer imprint is published by the registered company Springer Nature Switzerland AG
The registered company address is: Gewerbestrasse 11, 6330 Cham, Switzerland

Preface

This volume contains the papers presented at the 16th International Conference on Risks and Security of Internet and Systems (CRISIS 2021). Due to the COVID-19 pandemic, CRISIS 2021 was held both virtually and onsite at Iowa State University, Ames, USA. It continued a tradition of successful conferences: Bourges (2005), Marrakech (2007), Tozeur (2008), Toulouse (2009), Montréal (2010), Timisoara (2011), Cork (2012), La Rochelle (2013), Trento (2014), Mytilene (2015), Roscoff (2016), Dinard (2017), Arcachon (2018), Hammamet (2019), and Online (2020).

In response to the call for papers, 23 papers were submitted. Each paper was reviewed by at least three reviewers. The Program Committee was composed of 54 members from 15 countries, completed by five external reviewers. The Program Committee selected nine regular papers and three short papers. The accepted papers cover the following research themes: cyber-physical systems, hardware security, network security, data security, attacks, responses, and security management. Ashfaq Khokar, chair of the Electrical and Computer Department at Iowa State University, USA, opened the conference and welcomed the participants and Bharat Bhargava from Purdue University, USA, gave the conference keynote.

We thank the people who contributed to the success of CRISIS 2021. In particular, we express our appreciation to the authors of the submitted papers, the Program Committee members, the external reviewers, and the organizing committee for the hard work they did locally at Iowa State University.

December 2021

Bo Luo
Mohamed Mosbah

Organization

General Chairs

Frédéric Cuppens	Polytechnique Montreal, Canada
Nora Cuppens	Polytechnique Montreal, Canada
Lotfi Ben Othmane	Iowa State University, USA

Program Committee Chairs

Bo Luo	University of Kansas, USA
Mohamed Mosbah	University of Bordeaux, France

Publicity Chairs

Reda Yaich	IRT SystemX, France
Slim Kallel	University of Sfax, Tunisia

Organizing Committee

Lotfi Ben Othmane	Iowa State University, USA
Jian Kai Lee	Iowa State University, USA

Program Committee

Saed Alrabaee	United Arab Emirates University, United Arab Emirates
Esma Aïmeur	University of Montreal, Canada
Michel Barbeau	Carleton University, Canada
Sébastien Bardin	CEA LIST, France
Lotfi Ben Othmane	Iowa State University, USA
Razvan Beuran	Japan Advanced Institute of Science and Technology, Japan
Anis Bkakria	IRT SystemX, France
Ismael Bouassida	LAAS-CNRS, France
Aymen Boudguiga	IRT SystemX, France
Ana Rosa Cavalli	Telecom SudParis, France
Frederic Cuppens	Polytechnique de Montreal, Canada
Nora Cuppens	Polytechnique de Montreal, Canada
Soufiene Djahel	Manchester Metropolitan University, UK

Bin Zhao   Pennsylvania State University, USA
Junwei Zhou   Wuhan University of Technology, China
Wei Zhou   Pennsylvania State University, USA

Additional Reviewers

Manh-Dung Nguyen
Congdong Lv
Farzaneh Abazari
Michael Schmid
David Harborth

Contents

Short Papers

CPS and Hardware Security

Threat Modeling of Cyber-Physical Systems in Practice

Ameerah-Muhsinah Jamil[1]([✉]), Lotfi Ben Othmane[1], and Altaz Valani[2]

[1] Iowa State University, Ames, IA, USA
amjamil@iastate.edu
[2] Security Compass, Toronto, Canada

Abstract. Traditional Cyber-physical Systems (CPSs) were not built with cybersecurity in mind. They operated on separate Operational Technology (OT) networks. As these systems now become more integrated with Information Technology (IT) networks based on IP, they expose vulnerabilities that can be exploited by the attackers through these IT networks. The attackers can control such systems and cause behavior that jeopardizes the performance and safety measures that were originally designed into the system. In this paper, we explore the approaches to identify threats to CPSs and ensure the quality of the created threat models. The study involves interviews with eleven security experts working in several different domains. We found through these interviews that the practitioners use a combination of various threat modeling methods, approaches, and standards together when they perform threat modeling of given CPSs. Key challenges practitioners face are: they cannot transfer the threat modeling knowledge that they acquire in a cyber-physical domain to other domains, threat models of modified systems are often not updated, and the reliance on mostly peer-evaluation and quality checklists to ensure the quality of threat models. The study warns about the difficulty to develop secure CPSs and calls for research on developing practical threat modeling methods for CPSs, techniques for continuous threat modeling, and techniques to ensure the quality of threat models.

1 Introduction

In the past, CPSs operated on their own networks, which were separated or air-gapped from the corporate IT networks. The OT and IT networks started converging in response to the need to provide data and insights to stakeholders on IT networks. The challenge with integrating these technologies is the velocity of change: IT technologies tend to change very frequently, and updates or patches can be readily done while OT technologies have a considerably longer shelf life. Legacy security concerns when OT technologies were initially deployed can be significantly different from the present security concerns. Trying to capture this disparity is done, in part, through threat modeling.

B. Luo et al. (Eds.): CRiSIS 2021, LNCS 13204, pp. 3–19, 2022.
https://doi.org/10.1007/978-3-031-02067-4_1

Until recently, attackers needed physical access to CPSs. The trend of integrating these systems to IP networks and the internet for services, such as remote car diagnostic and cooperative adaptive cruise control, has extended the attack surface. The goals of attacks on CPSs, such as Stuxnet and Triton, are often not to breach the confidentiality, integrity, or availability of the system's data but to make the target system perform activities other than the ones planned and expected by the original designers. Hence changing the actual process and unleashing damaging consequences.

Threat modeling is a "systematic exploration technique to expose any circumstance or event having the potential to cause harm to a system in the form of destruction, disclosure, modification of data, or denial of service" [1]. It is an approach for identifying threats to a system and suggesting mitigations. In this paper, we will not discuss mitigations and limit the scope to threats.

There are several methods for threat modeling, including threat tree, attack tree, STRIDE, and abuse cases [2]. Xiong and Lagerstrom surveyed threat modeling literature. The authors of many of the surveyed papers validated their proposed approaches (22 out of the 54 selected papers) using, for example, case studies, and simulation while only two papers used real-word applications [3]. Most of these methods have been designed for information systems where the assets are data at rest and in-transit. The focus on data within the IT network is an important one. Threat modeling of OT components can often be physically dangerous, expensive, or even identifying the data flow before it gets to the OT but may not be sufficient to identify misuses of CPSs.

Xiong and Lagerstrom's survey of threat model literature [3] discussed above shows that there is a gap between the academic research on and the practice of threat modeling of CPSs. This paper aims to address that by answering the question: *What are the practices of threat modeling of CPSs by cyber-security experts?* To address this question, we interviewed eleven security experts who perform threat modeling of CPSs in their respective organizations. Then, we transcribed the interviews, extracted the main information, and grouped them into themes, and analyzed the findings. We found that:

1. there is a lack of effective systematic threat modeling methods for CPSs; the practitioners use a combination of threat modeling methods, approaches, and standards, together, when performing threat modeling of CPSs;
2. organizations often do not update the threat models of their modified CPSs;
3. there is no effective method for ensuring the quality of threat models besides peer-evaluation and quality checklists;
4. the practitioners face several challenges when performing threat modeling of CPSs, including the difficulty to transfer the threat modeling knowledge they acquire in a cyber-physical domain to other domains.

The results of this work could be used by organizations when performing threat modeling of CPSs and by academia to develop solutions and techniques that help practitioners perform threat modeling efficiently.

This paper is organized as follows: Sect. 2 discusses related works, Sect. 3 describes the research approach, Sect. 4 presents the results of the study, Sect. 5 summarizes the study results and discusses the impacts and limitations of the study, and Sect. 6 concludes the paper.

2   Related Work

This section discusses related work on the security of CPSs and threat modeling methods and standards.

Security of CPSs. Security issues of CPSs has been studied for several years. For instance, Alguliyev et al. [4] analyzed the main types of attacks and threats of CPSs and proposed a tree of attacks that includes the attacks on sensing, actuation, computing, communication, and feedback loops; Lu et al. [5] proposed a framework of CPSs security, which includes the security objectives, approaches, and applications of CPSs; and Pakizeh [6] proposed a framework that aims to understand the cyber attacks and related risk of different elements of CPSs [6]. In addition, using the expert knowledge on security aspects, such as the forms of attacks, attacker positions, operating systems, and routing permissions Klaudel and Rataj [7] proposed an attack graph that describes the software and hardware of a CPS and their mutual mapping with security artifacts and a workflow that automates the construction of a vulnerability model of a CPS that is used to quantitatively analyze the threat models of the CPSs, and estimate their exploitation costs.

The concern in security in IT is the reduction of monetary losses and is the safety of people and controllability of the systems, besides the reduction of monetary losses, in the case of CPSs [8]. Sabaliauskaite and Mathur [9] proposed the integration of safety and security life-cycle processes and a model that unifies the attack tree and the fault tree and their countermeasures. Dong et al. [10] proposed security and safety framework, and security framework that focuses on the security of information and controllability of the CPSs.

The National Institute of Standards and Technology (NIST) developed a CPS framework to assist in developing secure and safe CPSs [11]. The security concern of the framework is to protect CPSs from unauthorized accesses, change damages, and destruction in addition to the CIA triad, and the safety concern is preventing negative consequences of cyber attacks on the stakeholders, including life, health, property, data, and damage to the physical environment.

Threat Modeling Methods and Standards. There exist several works on threat modeling for CPSs [3]. For instance, Martins et al. [12] proposed a tool for systematic analysis of threat models that includes sketching metamodel of the system using GME, defining the data-flow and its attribute, and identifying the vulnerabilities that may exist in the data-flow connections. Also, Khan et al. [13] adapted the STRIDE method for CPSs by focusing on the data-flow between the components of the system, which demonstrated promising results when applied to a case study as it identifies the vulnerabilities at cyber subsystems and their potential consequences on the physical components of the system. In addition, Casola et al. [14] developed a threat catalog that consists of known threats affecting different components of IoT and classified them based on asset types.

Several researchers acknowledged the impact of application domains on the threat modeling of CPSs. For instance, Meyer et al. [15] proposed an attack tree to threat model building and home automation systems in order to identify security faults either in implementation or deployment, and Suleiman et al. [16] developed a comprehensive threat modeling by integrating the results of smart grid system security threat analysis with the reference architecture of smart grid including the components and communication among them.

The International Standards Organization (ISO) and SAE International released standard ISO/SAE 21434 - Road vehicles cybersecurity engineering to address the need in cybersecurity engineering of electrical and electronic systems within road vehicles. The standard provides guidelines to integrate cybersecurity concerns in product development, and perform cybersecurity assessment and monitoring, and develop policies to handle cybersecurity incidents.

This paper addresses the gap between the development of threat modeling methods, techniques, and standards and the practice of threat modeling of CPSs.

3   Research Approach

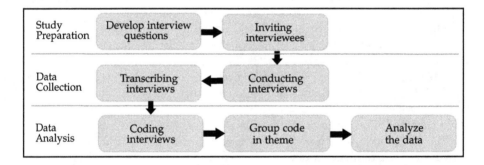

Fig. 1. Phases of the study.

This study aims to explore the practice of threat modeling of CPSs in the industry. The data source of the study comes from interviewing a set of security experts practicing threat modeling. Figure 1 illustrates the process of the study, which has three phases: study preparation, data collection, and data analysis. The descriptions of the phases follow.

3.1   Study Preparation

The description of the study preparation follows.

Table 1. Business of each participant.

Participant	Business
P1	Security consultation
P2	Software engineering
P3	Security consultation
P4	Areal vehicles integrator
P5	Software engineering
P6	Software engineering
P7	Security consultation
P8	Ground vehicles integrator
P9	Ground vehicles integrator
P10	Original Equipment Manufacturer (OEM)
P11	Ground vehicles integrator

Table 2. Threat modeling themes.

Theme	Description
Security aspects	It concerns confidentiality, integrity, and availability
Threat business impacts	The other aspects that the participant is concerned about when performing threat modeling including users' safety and company reputation
Threat modeling approaches	The approaches and methods that the participants use for threat modeling, e.g., asset-centric, attacker-centric, STRIDE etc.
Threat identification methods	The methods that the participants use to identify the threats which is part of the threat modeling process
Threat modeling steps	The activities or steps performed by the experts to identify the threat model of a given system
Continuous Threat modeling	The process used to update threat models to address system changes
Quality assurance of threat models	The methods used to assess and evaluate the quality of the threat models
Tools	The tools used in the threat modeling process
Involved people	People involved in the threat modeling process
Challenge	The challenge that experts face when performing threat modeling for CPSs
Suggestion	Suggestions to improve the threat modeling process for CPSs

Interview Protocol. We reviewed the literature on threat modeling of a CPS. We used the knowledge that we acquired to develop a questionnaire protocol. We specified the research goal with the project sponsor and formulated a set of open-ended interview questions. The questionnaire was tested by trial runs with team members and revised based on the feedback. The set of questions consists of eleven open-ended questions–Open-ended questions encourage the participants to provide detailed responses.

Participants Selection. We invited a set of security experts working in cyber-security companies. Eleven participants accepted our requests and participated in the study with the goal to contribute to science, not to represent their employers. Table 1 shows the experience of each participant on threat modeling and the business of their employers. Among the participants, three work for major software development companies and five work for major companies that develop CPSs.

3.2   Data Collection

The data collection consists of two sub-phases: conducting the interviews and transcribing the interviews. The descriptions of these sub-phases follow.

Conducting the Interview. We scheduled a one-hour meeting with each expert. The meetings were held through Zoom and Web-ex because the interviewers and participants are located in different places. The interviews were conducted by one of the authors. The interviewer explained to each of the interviewees at the beginning of each of the meetings the goal of the project, the interview process and requested the consent of the participant to record the interview.

Transcription of the Interviews. The interviews were transcribed using oTranscribe[1] and Otter.ai.[2]

3.3   Data Analysis

Interview Coding. We used the thematic analysis method for the interview coding [17]. Thematic analysis is "a method for identifying, analyzing and reporting patterns within data" [18]. It allows researchers to explore phenomena through interviews, stories, and observations [19].

Interview coding uses the interview transcripts as the input and outputs codes that identify the aspects mentioned during the interviews. A code is a word or short phrase identifying the essence of a portion of text. At the end of this step, we assigned codes to each of the eleven interview transcripts. For example, we assigned code *security properties/goal* to the text *"When it comes to the CPSs, the availability of the system matters a lot"*. Codes that were semantically similar across transcripts were consolidated. We used Atlas.ti[3] tool to code the interviews.

Data Extraction and Classification. Similar codes are grouped into themes. A theme generalizes a set of codes belonging to a given concept. The process of assigning themes to codes was done for each transcript. For example, the code

---

[1] oTranscribe: https://otranscribe.com/.
[2] Otter.ai: https://otter.ai/.
[3] ATLAS.ti: https://atlasti.com/.

other aspect and *safety aspect* is grouped together as *threat business impact* theme. Table 2 lists the themes and associated categories.

Analysis of the Results. From the code groups, we identified information on security properties, threat business impacts, threat modeling approaches, and method, threat modeling details activity, continuous threat modeling approach, threat identification methods, continuous threat modeling approaches, risk assessment approaches, quality assurance approaches, roles involved in threat modeling, tools, and challenges. We then modeled the relationships among these themes.

4   Data Analysis

This section describes the themes that we extracted from the eleven interviews.
    We used *Pi* to refer to participant *i* in the interview.

4.1   Security Properties

Security experts focus on protecting the confidentiality, integrity, and availability (CIA triad) of the data managed by their systems. Table 3 lists the number of participants that discussed each of the security properties. We observe that the participants are concerned about data integrity and availability but not about data confidentiality. They are also concerned about secure modification, availability, consistency, accuracy, and misuses of the data over their life-cycle in their system. For instance, P9 said: *"so things that are important to us are maybe not, as you said, the confidentiality of it if you're talking about a control system, but you're looking at the integrity of the messaging [...], the data is the control message."* The reason is: data is used to process the control commands of the physical components of CPSs. Modification and misuses of these data can cause damages or losses, and unavailability of data and system components could prevent real-time feedback behaviors of certain CPSs and cause losses and damages.

Table 3. No. of participants concerned with each of the security properties/goal.

Security properties	# Participants
Confidentiality	1
Integrity	6
Availability	6

Table 4. No. of participants who used known methods for threat modeling.

Method	Ref	# Participants
Attack tree	[20]	1
DREAD	[21]	1
EVITA or variant of	[22]	2
LINDDUN	[23]	1
PASTA	[24]	1
STRIDE	[13]	6

4.2   Threat Business Impacts

Many CPSs, including connected cars, involve human as users and are safety-critical systems. Security and safety are closely related in these systems [9]. The exploitation of systems' weaknesses and vulnerabilities could have a high impact on the safety of the users. For example, P3 said: *"..the cyber threats can actually impact the physical safety of workers, [...], cause an explosion within a plant or any number of potential outcomes"*. Besides safety, financial losses, and reputation damage are also important aspects that participants consider when performing threat modeling of CPSs. Security weaknesses in the supply chain is a typical example.

4.3   Threat Modeling Approaches

The participants in the study have either control systems or IT background. The participants with control systems background focus on the malicious controllability of the physical components of the studied system as P11 said *"All these methodologies started from this classic [Referring to ISO27005] as an approach with slight modifications. What was added by Evita is the notion of controllability"*. **P1**, for example, uses a field-tested custom engine derived from the ISA/IEC 62443 standard [25] to identify the physical/cyber threats that apply to each of the assets, zones (a group of assets), and conduits of the system under consideration, keeping in mind that a cyber threat can have a physical attack surface, and **P2** uses the STRIDE taxonomy [13] and analyze the failure scenarios that might apply to the components considering the behavior of the physical components and the safety of the system. In general, these participants combine the use of the known approaches such as STRIDE or PASTA with the analysis of failure modes and criticality of the physical systems.

Participants with IT background apply the classic threat modeling approaches such as STRIDE [13] and DREAD [21]. They identify the assets, the components, and the data managed by the studied system and focus mostly on threats to the integrity, availability, and confidentiality of the data. For example, **P5** approach is: understand the system, identify the weaknesses, identify potential attacks and mitigations, and prioritize the identified threats. They consider that each CPS operates in a specific environment, is associated with specific weaknesses and type of attacks, which justifies the use of threats on data rather than misbehavior of the components of the studied system.

Most of the participants decompose the system being analyzed into components and analyze the threats to each of the components. Participant **P7** deviates from this approach and analyze the studied system as a whole.[4] They look at the weaknesses related to the integration of the components of the given system.

---

[4] This approach is similar to the approach used to improve business processes [26].

4.4   Threat Identification Methods

Threat identification, a key process in threat modeling, allows identifying the weaknesses of a given system that could cause harm and damage when exploited by attackers. Table 4 provides the frequency of using the common individual threat modeling methods by the participants. The participants use (1) Known methods, such as attack-tree and STRIDE, (2) a combination of known methods, and (3) a combination of security standards and known approaches.

Known Method. Several participants reported that they use known methods such STRIDE, PASTA [24], LINDDUN [23], and attack-tree [20]. Most of the participants (6 out of 11) use STRIDE. One expert mentioned that they use the attack-tree method because of its ability to cover all entry points of the attacks. Hence, they can identify all possible threats to the system. Some participants start with a known method and then elaborate further on their threat model based on their experience and knowledge. For example, participant **P2** identify the data flow diagram and the physical locations of the components of the studied system and apply the STRIDE method to identify the initial list of threats.

Combination of Known Methods and Approaches. Some participants reported the use of multiple approaches, such as asset-centric and attacker-centric, in the same project because they believe that each of the approaches and methods gives a different perspective of the system weaknesses and using a set of methods, although time-consuming, helps to identify the "complete" list of threats to a given system.

Combination of Threat Modeling Standards and Known Approaches. One Participant, **P1**, uses real-world experience jointly with the ISA/IEC 62443 standard [25] to identify the physical/cyber threats that apply to each of the assets or zones (a group of assets).

4.5   Continuous Threat Modeling Approaches

Developers often modify parts of their CPSs [27] to introduce new features, fix existing defects, or improve the maintainability and the performance of these systems. The evolution of a system often involves changes to its components, which could invalidate the initial threat model since the changes could modify the attack surface and introduce new threats to the system.

Some participants do not have processes and/or experience with managing the evolution of the threat models of their systems. For instance, one participant reported that they do not need to have processes for revising threat models as they are not involved in the businesses of the systems that they perform threat modeling of and another participant reported that they do not review the threat models of their systems even if these systems change. In addition, Participant **P11** reported that the manufacturers of cars cannot do a correct continuous threat modeling. They said *"..you have two updates per year for the cars...the information flow concerning various threats is not so good today because car manufacturers are not aware about all the threats related to the parts coming from their suppliers."*

The rest of the participants (eight from eleven) have processes or approaches to manage continuous threat modeling. For example, Participant **P1** identifies the changes or triggers to a system under consideration and does a thorough threat and vulnerability assessment update, re-assessing the attack surfaces/sources and the related impacts, and adding new threats and vulnerabilities if necessary; Participant **P5** performs threat modeling as an activity of their adapted scrum [28] process; Participant **P6** uses version control on source code of the software to identify changes and periodically assess in collaboration with the architect the potential impacts of the changes on the threat model of the given system; Participant **P7** performs a full threat modeling of new systems and partial threat modeling when new components are added to existing systems (only the new components and impacted components are considered the partial threat modeling); Participant **P8** assesses the exploitability of the threats of changed systems and updates the priority of addressing the threats accordingly; and Participant **P9** uses a questionnaire to assess the impacts of the software changes on the previous ranking of the threats to the their system. We note that some participants report that they perform continuous threat modeling only for formality: to pass their systems to the next phase of the DevOps [29].

We observe that most of the participants practice continuous threat modeling, and there is no common continuous threat modeling approach. This mixed input shows the importance of continuous threat modeling of CPS for the industry and the lack of rigorous and efficient approaches to do so.

4.6   Risk Assessment Approaches

The participants reported the use of several risk analysis and scoring approaches, which we discuss in the following.

Using Risk Standard and/or Regulations. P1 uses risk assessment standards ISA/IEC 62443 [25], which provides guidelines to organize and facilitate a cyber security risk assessment for industrial automation and control systems (IACS) while considering the necessary regulations and sector's security/risk specifics, and Participant **P7** considers the impacts of the threats on the compliance with the regulations that their products must adherent to. For instance, **P7** said *Regulations play a major role in telling [..] the stakeholders what's more important to sustain the [business], right. I mean, basically, the products [could] fail [because of] the regulator, and you could be out of the business."*

Known Approach. Many of the participants use common risk assessment approaches, such as FAIR [30] and Bug Bar [31]. The bug bar method, for example, requires assessing the criticality and severity of the threats in collaboration with the customer (which allows considering their concerns) and prioritize the threats based on their severity levels. The FAIR method allows using FAIR data to analyze and highlight the threats of the threat model. For instance, Participant P9 said *" So we use the fair [...] threat modeling to highlight the threats and then run that in fair to actually turn that into a risk."*

In-House Risk Assessment Methods. Three participants have their own risk assessment methods. For instance, Participant **P2** uses a risk register to report the risks of a given system and continuously monitor these risks, and Participants **P8** uses a custom formula to compute the risks of a system using the revenue generated by the system and the criticality of the threats.

4.7 Quality Assurance Approaches

Most of the participants reported that the quality of threat modeling exercises depends on the experience and skills of the experts who perform the threat modeling and the thoroughness of the assessment, including the detailed level of the used architecture and profoundness of the interviews with the stakeholders of the given system. For instance, **P1** said *"the ISA/IEC 62443 standard provides the basic framework but most of the quality of the assessments is based on real-world experience, which also helps with the quality of the specific deviations for every different sector"* and **P11** said "the expert, nothing else."

Few participants use techniques to ensure the quality of their threat models. For instance, Participant **P2** uses peer-evaluation to assess the quality of the threat models that they create. They Said *" There were certain folks that we would do peer reviews [of their] threat models."*. Participant **P3** performs review at each project milestone to ensure the work done at the given milestone is of sufficient quality. They said *"at each of the gates or milestones, you do the proper review to make sure that the work that was done up until that point is of sufficient quality."* And, Participant **P6** uses a set of requirements to verify the coverage of the developed threat model of the important security aspects related to the domain of the given system.

Table 5. Roles in the threat modeling processes.

Role	Description
Security team	Initiate the threat modeling process and perform the threat modeling exercise
Architect	Provide the documentation and artifacts about the system. The security team may interview them to get more details about the system
Developer	The security team interviews the developers to get more details about the system
Stakeholder	The security team interviews the other stakeholders of a system as needed to get more details

4.8   Roles Involved in Threat Modeling

Table 5 lists the common roles that the participants work with when performing threat modeling. Some of the participants involve the CPS operators, the management staff, the subject matter experts, and the equipment suppliers in their threat modeling exercise as they need. These roles help to gain depth understanding of the system, including the different environments of running the given CPS, the operations of the system, the used equipment, and possibly other aspects. Interviewing different stockholders helps to develop a "complete" threat model.

4.9   Tool

Three participants use Microsoft Threat Modeling Tool [32] although the tool does not cover the physical components of CPSs and three participants use their own tools, including custom templates, for threat modeling. For instance, **P9** said *"Microsoft has a threat modeling tool [...], and there is actually an automotive template that we look at to plug into our system."*

4.10   Challenges

The participants reported few challenges that they face when performing threat modeling of CPSs, which we discuss in the following.

Variety of CPSs. Several of the participants had to work on threat models of CPSs for several applications domains (e.g., mining, transportation, smart grid) and use a variety of physical components that are often not familiar with at the beginning of the projects. They find it impossible to have broad knowledge about threats for CPSs and difficult to generalize expertise across CPSs's application domains.[5] Participants that have IT background find themselves with limited knowledge about the physical components: they are not familiar with the threats to the system that they analyze and to the mechanisms that could be utilized to mitigate the threats to these systems. Some participants proposed developing a repository of patterns and mitigation strategies since there are many threat vectors and attack agents to consider.

Limitation of Current Threat Modeling Approaches and Methods. The existing threat modeling approaches, such as STRIDE and PASTA, focus on computer security. The use of these methods to perform threat modeling for CPSs may produce incomplete threat models because these methods do not cover the physical aspects of CPSs. Some participants suggest the development of a framework that allows identifying common practical attack scenarios based on the application domains of CPSs.

---

[5] This different from IT systems that use known architecture styles and follow standard components definitions, e.g., web applications.

Limitation of Tools. Microsoft Threat Modeling Tool is commonly used to generate an initial list of threats to a given system based on a default template that uses the STRIDE taxonomy. It is known that STRIDE focuses on computer security threats; hence it would produce incomplete threat models for CPSs.

Challenge in Current Culture. Current business culture of "publish now and fix later" has been a challenge for some participants–sometimes only the threats that are related to publicly known attacks are considered. To address this problem, Participant **P4** proposes to have the security experts develop quality threat models that use publicly available threat patterns. They said: *"I think that would be very useful for the industry at large is a set of threat model patterns."*

5   Discussion

This section summarizes the results of the study and discusses the impacts of the study and its limitations.

5.1   Summary

Figure 2 shows the themes extracted from the study and the relationships among these themes. The figure shows that CPSs have security properties requirements and other associated requirements such as safety. The goal of the threat modeling processes and the continuous threat modeling sub-processes is to identify and rank system weaknesses that violate these requirements. The participants use several threat modeling methods and approaches and involve several stakeholders of the CPSs that they perform threat models of using the existing tools such as Microsoft Threat Modeling Tool.

According to the participants, integrity and availability are the security properties the most of concern for CPSs. In addition, many participants use threat modeling method STRIDE, which is unexpected since the method focuses on the threats to IT systems, not CPSs. Also, most of the participants use a combination of known approaches, known methods, and known standards when performing threat modeling of a CPS. We note that the participants associate the quality of threat models mainly to the skills and experience of the security experts who perform the threat modeling. The two techniques that some participants use to ensure the quality of threat models developed by their subordinates are peer-evaluation and the use of the quality checklist.

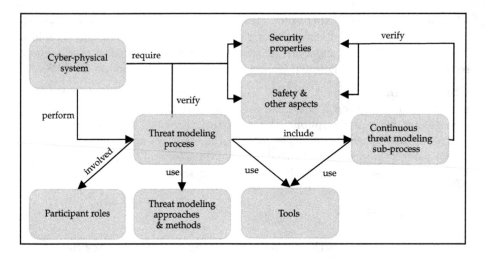

Fig. 2. Entity-relationship model of the threat modeling concepts.

5.2 Impact of the Study

Existing threat taxonomies, such as STRIDE, focus on either the CIA triad or the controllability of the physical components of a system. This study reveals that experts focus on the threats to the integrity, availability, controllability, and safety of the systems threat model a CPSs. The community should develop a knowledge base of practical threats to CPSs that consider the business impacts of failure of physical components, including safety besides the CIA triad.

We found that most of the participants use a combination of known threat modeling approaches, methods, and standards, which makes threat modeling time consuming–it is done two or more times. This calls for developing *practical* new threat modeling approaches that integrate both the IT and OT security needs of CPSs effectively. The method should be generic and flexible to fit the needs and requirements of every CPS domain, and consider the industry standards. Such methods should help security practitioners to produce quality threat models for CPS that could be trusted by the project managers.

We also observed that the participants use their own template to tie the risk to the threats of CPSs. Developing risk assessment methods for CPSs acceptable by the major actors in the industry will help the experts to communicate better and exchange information about risks of CPSs.

In addition, we found that most of the participants do not use quality assurance methods for the threat models that they produce. The managers sometimes request threat models for their CPSs from more than one experts, especially when the system gets hacked. The community should explore techniques and standards for assessing the quality of threat models.

5.3   Threats to Validity

Initially, we gave an open-source of a CPS to some of the selected participants and hoped that they provide us with their threat models, which we could use to study the practice of threat modeling in depth. The volunteer participants did not want that given, among others, the required important time commitment to do so. Therefore, we opted for exploitative interviews for our research.

The limitations of the study are classified into construct validity, internal validity, conclusion validity, and external validity are discussed as the following [33,34].

Construct Validity. To address the validity of the relations between the performed study and the goal of the study, we performed a literature review, designed an interview protocol, and tested it with some experts. We collected information from eleven participants who have different roles and are located in different cities. This gives confidence in the stability of the collected data.

Internal Validity. To address the validity of the relationship between the study and its results, we tell the participants at the beginning of the interviews the goals of the interview, which should help in ensuring that the participant and the interviewer share the same goal.

Conclusion Validity. To address the validity of the ability to make correct conclusions from the results of the study, the main author provided the second author their codes and the themes for each of the interview, who reviewed them, to reduce the subjectivity of the results.

External Validity. To address the validity of the generalization of the study, the eleven participants in the study are selected to be security experts from nine organizations in different businesses. We believe the diverse experience of the participants supports generalizing the results.

6   Conclusion

This paper reports about the practice of threat modeling of CPSs. We conclude that (1) ensuring the integrity and availability of data and system's components in addition to controllability and safety of CPSs is the concern of threat modeling of CPSs, (2) there are differences between experts with a background in control system and experts with a background in IT regarding the approaches to perform threat modeling, (3) the experts use a combination of known approaches, methods, and standards to perform threat modeling of a given CPS, (4) most of the threat modeling participants perform continuous threat modeling, (5) the experts often use custom risk scoring methods, (6) most of the participants do not use quality assurance techniques for the threat models that they produce and rely on the experience and skills of the expert who performs the threat model, and (7) four roles are commonly involved in threat modeling, namely security team, architect, developer, and stakeholder.

The studies highlights several future research directions to improve the practice of threat modeling of CPS. First, we need to develop a new threat modeling approach that flexible to fit the different CPSs domains, and supports for easy integration of industry standards. Second, we need to develop a threat knowledge-base that accounts for the different CPSs domains and links the threats to the target surfaces, attack means, countermeasures, and impacts. Lastly, we need to develop techniques for semi-automated threat modeling of CPSs will help experts to do incremental and effective threat models.

Acknowledgment. The author thank Simone Curzi from Microsoft, Zafar Ali from John Deere, Rohini Narasipur from Bosch, Arun Prabhakar from Security Compass, and Youssef Jad from PM SCADA Cyber Defense for participating in the study and reviewing this paper. The authors thank also the other anonymous participants in the study for their contributions. The participants were not representing their respective employers in the study.

References

1. Definition of threat modeling. https://pascal.computer.org/
2. Shostack, A.: Threat Modeling: Designing for Security. Wiley (2014)
3. Xiong, W., Lagerström, R.: Threat modeling - a systematic literature review. Comput. Secur. **84**, 53–69 (2019)
4. Alguliyev, R., Imamverdiyev, Y., Sukhostat, L.: Cyber-physical systems and their security issues. Comput. Ind. **100**, 212–223 (2018)
5. Lu, T., Zhao, J., Zhao, L., Li, Y., Zhang, X.: Towards a framework for assuring cyber physical system security. Int. J. Secur. Appl. **9**, 25–40 (2015)
6. Pakizeh, M.: Threat identifying cyber physical systems security. Int. J. Electric. Power Eng. **13**, 5–11 (2019)
7. Klaudel, W., Rataj, A.: Towards a formalisation of expert's knowledge for an automatic construction of a vulnerability model of a cyberphysical system. In: ICISSP 2021–7th International Conference on Information Systems Security and Privacy, Vienne, Austria, February 2021
8. ben Othmane, L., Al-Fuqaha, A., ben Hamida, E., van den Brand, M.: Towards extended safety in connected vehicles. In: 16th International IEEE Conference on Intelligent Transportation Systems (ITSC 2013), pp. 652–657 (2013)
9. Sabaliauskaite, G., Mathur, A.P.: Aligning cyber-physical system safety and security. In: Cardin, M.-A., Krob, D., Lui, P.C., Tan, Y.H., Wood, K. (eds.) Complex Systems Design & Management Asia, pp. 41–53. Springer, Cham (2015). https://doi.org/10.1007/978-3-319-12544-2_4
10. Dong, P., Han, Y., Guo, X., Xie, F.: A systematic review of studies on cyber physical system security. Int. J. Secur. Appl. **9**, 155–164 (2015)
11. Griffor, E.R., Greer, C., Wollman, D.A., Burns, M.J.: Framework for cyber-physical systems: volume 1, overview, November 2018. https://www.nist.gov/publications/framework-cyber-physical-systems-volume-1-overview
12. Martins, G., Bhatia, S., Koutsoukos, X., Stouffer, K., Tang, C., Candell, R.: Towards a systematic threat modeling approach for cyber-physical systems. In: 2015 Resilience Week (RWS), pp. 1–6 (2015)

13. Khan, R., McLaughlin, K., Laverty, D., Sezer, S.: Stride-based threat modeling for cyber-physical systems. In: 2017 IEEE PES Innovative Smart Grid Technologies Conference Europe (ISGT-Europe), pp. 1–6 (2017)
14. Casola, V., De Benedictis, A., Rak, M., Villano, U.: Toward the automation of threat modeling and risk assessment in IoT systems. Internet Things **7**, 100056 (2019)
15. Meyer, D., Haase, J., Eckert, M., Klauer, B.: A threat-model for building and home automation. In: 2016 IEEE 14th International Conference on Industrial Informatics (INDIN), pp. 860–866 (2016)
16. Suleiman, H., Alqassem, I., Diabat, A., Arnautovic, E., Svetinovic, D.: Integrated smart grid systems security threat model. Inf. Syst. **53**, 147–160 (2015)
17. Saldana, J.: The Coding Manual for Qualitative Researchers. Sage Publications, London (2015)
18. Braun, V., Clarke, V.: Using thematic analysis in psychology. Qual. Res. Psychol. **3**(2), 77–101 (2006)
19. Connelly, L.M.: What is phenomenology? Medsurg Nurs. **19**(2), 127–129 (2010)
20. Saini, V., Duan, Q., Paruchuri, V.: Threat modeling using attack trees. J. Comput. Sci. Coll. **23**, 04 (2008)
21. Marshall, D., Coulter, D.: Threat modeling for drivers, June 2018. https://docs.microsoft.com/en-us/windows-hardware/drivers/driversecurity/threat-modeling-for-drivers
22. Ruddle, A., et al.: Deliverable D2.3: security requirements for automotive on-board networks based on dark-side scenarios, December 2009. https://www.evita-project.org/deliverables.html
23. Home. https://www.linddun.org/
24. UcedaVelez, T., Marona, M.M.: Intro to PASTA. Wiley (2015)
25. Isa/iec 62443 cybersecurity certificate programs-isa. https://www.isa.org/training-and-certification/isa-certification/isa99iec-62443/isa99iec-62443-cybersecurity-certificate-programsjournal=isa.org
26. Goldratt, E.: The Goal: A Process of Ongoing Improvement. North River Press, Great Barrington (2004)
27. Ying, A.T.T., Murphy, G.C., Ng, R., Chu-Carroll, M.C.: Predicting source code changes by mining change history. IEEE Trans. Software Eng. **30**, 574–586 (2004)
28. Takeuchi, H., Nonaka, I.: The new new product development game. Harvard Bus. Rev. **64** (1986)
29. Mohan, V., ben Othmane, L.: SecDevOps: is it a marketing buzzword? - Mapping research on security in DevOps. In: 2016 11th International Conference on Availability, Reliability and Security (ARES), Salzburg, Austria, pp. 542–547 (2016)
30. Fair Institute: The importance and effectiveness of cyber risk quantification. https://www.fairinstitute.org/what-is-fair
31. Curzi, S.: Bug bars and stride-based calibration, February 2020. https://simoneonsecurity.com/2020/02/20/bug-bars-and-stride-based-calibration/
32. Jegeib: Microsoft threat modeling tool overview - Azure. https://docs.microsoft.com/en-us/azure/security/develop/threat-modeling-tool
33. Cruzes, D.S., ben Othmane, L.: Threats to validity in software security empirical research. In: Empirical Research for Software Security: Foundations and Experience, pp. 275–300. Taylor & Francis Group, LLC (2017)
34. Wohlin, C., Runeson, P., Höst, M., Ohlsson, M.C., Regnell, B., Wesslén, A.: Experimentation in Software Engineering: An Introduction. Kluwer Academic Publishers, Norwell (2000)

AVSDA: Autonomous Vehicle Security Decay Assessment

Lama Moukahal[1]([⊠]), Mohammad Zulkernine[1], and Martin Soukup[2]

[1] Queen's University, Kingston, Canada
{lama.moukahal,mz}@queensu.ca
[2] Irdeto, Ottawa, Canada
martin.soukup@irdeto.com

Abstract. Security practices become weaker over time as attackers' capabilities evolve. Security decay within vehicle software systems can have devastating consequences as it can pose a direct threat to people's lives. Thus, it is crucial to monitor the changing threat level on vehicles during their full lifespan. We present an Autonomous Vehicle Security Decay Assessment (AVSDA) framework that analyzes and predicts the system's security risk over vehicles' lifespan. The framework analyzes vulnerable software components periodically and estimates the security risk level to identify security decay. AVSDA employs several metrics specifically designed for autonomous vehicle systems to automatically identify potentially weak components and quantify security risk. We evaluate the framework on OpenPilot, an autonomous driving system. The case study demonstrates the effectiveness of the AVSDA framework in identifying security decay over time. The results show an accuracy rate of 94% and a recall rate of 78%, outperforming all other known metrics by at least 50%.

Keywords: Security vulnerability · Autonomous vehicle systems security · Decay assessment · Risk analysis

1 Introduction

Attackers' capabilities evolve with time. What was once secure can become an easy target for skilled attackers to take advantage of systems' weaknesses to initiate attacks. Hence, any software system should be carefully monitored to identify possible security decay that can expose it to malicious behavior. Software integration and internet connectivity expose vehicles to cybersecurity challenges that, if not handled, can lead to destructive results. It is essential to identify security decay in automobile systems.

Automotive manufacturers are striving to diminish the chances of attacks. Currently, many developed automotive standards provide software guidelines to enhance vehicle security [1,9,10,16]. Following security standards during Vehicle Software Engineering (VSE) helps create more resilient Connected Autonomous

Vehicles (CAVs) that defend against current attacks [28]. Nevertheless, attackers' techniques are advancing. The average age of cars and trucks is more than ten years, and future vehicles are expected to operate for even a longer period. With such a long lifespan, new software vulnerabilities will be discovered, new attacker tools will be developed, and adopted security practices will become weaker. Ensuring CAV security requires planning that does not bind security assurance and risk assessment to the development phase but spans to cover the vehicles' operation phase.

Security decay represents a drop in system resilience due to newly discovered vulnerabilities, more skilled attackers, or changes in the operating environment of vehicle software. This research aims to identify security decay across vehicle software systems' full lifespan. We achieve this by identifying vulnerabilities in the system and assessing the evolving risks. We propose an Autonomous Vehicle Security Decay Assessment (AVSDA) framework composed of two phases. The first phase, vulnerability analysis, automatically and efficiently identifies potentially weak or vulnerable components. The second phase, risk analysis, focuses on quantifying the risk of weak components by determining an attack's likelihood and assessing its impact.

Traditional threat and risk assessment methods (e.g., E-Safety Vehicle Intrusion Protected Applications (EVITA) threat and risk model [30]) determine security risks by identifying and classifying potential threats. In contrast, we identify security risks by targeting the source of issues. The AVSDA framework distinguishes the vulnerable components that are responsible for the vast majority of vehicle cyberattacks. Considering the operational environment of vehicles, quantifying various threat scenarios becomes a daunting task. Hence, vulnerability analysis is used to efficiently measure the weak components that make vehicle software systems unprotected against attacks (e.g., unauthorized access to data, acceptance of bogus information, and unauthorized control of vehicles).

Assessing autonomous system security decay at the software level can help prevent malicious behavior and maintain vehicle safety. The AVSDA framework offers security engineers the opportunity to strengthen vehicles' resilience against attacks. It also warns security specialists about severe security decay that might require immediate update or even vehicle recalls to prevent incidents. This framework is critical for the United Nations Economic Commission for Europe (UNECE) WP.29 cybersecurity compliance [8].

The rest of the paper is organized as follows: Sect. 2 reviews related work. Section 3 outlines the AVSDA framework. Section 4 presents results from applying the AVSDA framework. Finally, Sect. 5 concludes the paper.

2 Related Work

Evaluating security decay in software systems is a recent topic in the literature and standards. As we assess security decay based on risk analysis, we review the existing security risk estimation efforts.

SAE J3601 [16] recommends assessing security threats in the automotive industry to identify possible threats. However, it does not identify a specific

Threat Analysis and Risk Assessment (TARA) method that can best identify the automotive industry's security risks [22]. The EVITA threat and risk model [30] is considered one of the potent risk assessment models in the automotive industry. The model focuses on identifying all possible attacks against a specific target. However, the sets of attacks and targets within autonomous vehicle systems are practically large, making risk assessment a time-consuming and challenging job. ISO/SAE 21434 [4] proposes a generic risk assessment process that involves vulnerability analysis, which is estimated based on previously identified vulnerabilities. However, historical data is not sufficient to identify the evolving vulnerabilities of vehicles.

Burton et al. [14] stress the importance of identifying intentional third party hazards to enhance vehicle safety. The researchers suggest enhancing safety standards to include the categorization of malicious hazards that can affect safety. Similarly, Macher et al. [23] highlight the need for threat and risk assessment techniques for the automotive domain. The researchers propose an approach to classify cybersecurity threats and merge it with ISO 26262 safety HARA framework. However, it is not enough to address vehicle security from a safety perspective only. Security risks have several impacts other than safety, including operational and financial impacts.

Islam et al. [20] introduce a risk assessment framework that aims to identify security requirements for automotive systems. Though the researchers propose a solid framework, their approach operates based on the system's data flows that can be difficult to obtain in the automotive industry. Othmane et al. [13] propose including attacker's capabilities in threat likelihood estimation and follow a manual vulnerability identification approach. However, considering the size and complexity of automotive systems, manual validation may not always be feasible.

This paper offers a security decay assessment framework that quantitatively evaluates the system without any additional overhead. The framework is not bound to the development phase; it assesses security during the operation phase too.

3　Framework Design

This section introduces the Autonomous Vehicle Security Decay Assessment (AVSDA) framework and discusses its phases. We begin by providing an overview of AVSDA and then dive deeper into the framework phases.

3.1　Overview

The AVSDA framework aims to identify security decay of autonomous vehicle software systems. The proposed framework analyzes the security decay at the Software Component (SWC) level. We define SWC as *a structural element that provides an interface. It can utilize different automotive communication means and is connected to other parts to fulfill a function.* This includes all types of SWCs defined by Automotive Open System Architecture (AUTOSAR) [1], covering all kinds of embedded hardware and firmware in a vehicle system.

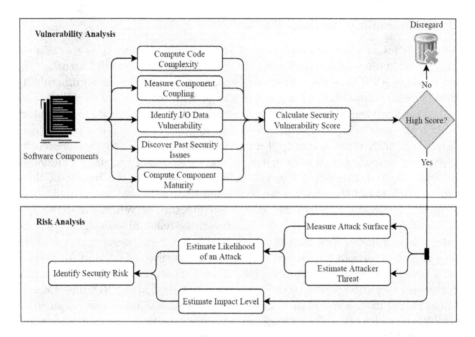

Fig. 1. Autonomous Vehicle Security Decay Assessment (AVSDA) framework.

Unauthorized access, acceptance of falsified information, interruption of service, and unauthorized control are all types of threats that an attacker can initiate to jeopardize vehicle software systems. Such threats violate vehicles' security and can threaten individuals' safety. The AVSDA framework utilizes a vulnerability analysis approach to estimate the vehicle software system's weak components that facilitate the existence of security threats.

As depicted in Fig. 1, AVSDA comprises two phases: vulnerability analysis and risk analysis. The first phase identifies potentially vulnerable components that can cause security failures. Attackers take advantage of existing software defects to initiate malicious behavior. Hence, to detect security decay, we first quantitatively identify the weak components based on the security metrics designed to target autonomous systems' vulnerabilities. The second phase thoroughly analyzes the system's vulnerable components to determine an attack's likelihood and impact. It also identifies security risk level for vulnerable components. Inspired by our previously proposed metrics [27], we define new and enhanced security metrics for this framework.

Estimating security risks before a product release is essential to prevent catastrophic results. AVSDA should be applied before moving a vehicle model to production and periodically during the operation phase to help security engineers measure vulnerabilities, estimate changing risk levels, and avoid unwanted security breaches. Comparing the results of subsequent runs can help security engineers in identifying system security decay. An increase in the security risk level can alert security engineers to apply the proper mitigation measures.

3.2 Vulnerability Analysis Phase

Vulnerabilities in autonomous systems are common. Hence, it is essential to identify weaknesses before they are exposed and lead to successful attacks. The first phase of AVSDA, vulnerability analysis, measures the security vulnerability score of every component. Components with a high security vulnerability score are further analyzed in the risk analysis phase. Measuring security vulnerability involves six steps: (1) Compute code complexity, (2) Measure component coupling, (3) Identify input and output data vulnerability, (4) Discover past security issues, (5) Compute component maturity, and (6) Calculate security vulnerability score. Steps 1 through 5 can run simultaneously, and the results of these steps are utilized in the final assessment (Step 6).

In this phase, we consider the unique architecture of vehicles and the specific development challenges of vehicle software systems. Since vehicle software systems have vulnerability factors similar to other software systems, some of the steps of this phase can be applied to other systems (Steps 1, 4, and 5). Steps 2 and 3 are specific to autonomous vehicles. Step 2 measures how reliant a component is on other subsystems by defining the set of reachable Electronic Control Units (ECUs) from a component ECU. Step 3 identifies input and output data risks. We consider the different communication means that transmit inputs and outputs within vehicle software systems and the various threat levels that each poses on a vehicle.

Compute Code Complexity. Autonomous systems are by far one of the largest pieces of software in terms of size. A modern vehicle features around 100 million code lines, and this number is expected to grow to 300 million shortly as we move toward code-driven vehicles [26]. Integrating millions of code lines in vehicles enabled them to become more aware of their environment. However, the code complexity of autonomous vehicle systems can increase the number of defects. Many researchers associated code complexity with the existence of vulnerabilities [15,17,32]. Complex code is challenging to understand, test, validate, and maintain. Attackers look for defects in the system that can be exploited. Hence, complex code increases attackers' chances and is a good indicator of a high number of vulnerabilities. Researchers propose different attributes to calculate code complexity, including Source Line of Code (SLOC), Nesting Count, Nesting Depth (ND), McCabe's Cyclomatic, and Number of Children (NOC).

Durisic et al. [17] in collaboration with Volvo Car Corporation show that code complexity and coupling can efficiently be used in the automotive industry. In general, developers consider Nesting Count, Nesting Depth (ND), and lack of structure to be the attributes that most reflect complexity in a system [12]. Moreover, ND and Number of Children (NOC) correlate to vulnerabilities the most [15,32]. Accordingly, we define Code Complexity (CX) as a combination of Source Line of Code (SLOC), ND, and NOC. The CX of component C can be calculated using Eq. (1). We use different weights ω_1, ω_2, and ω_3 to give security experts a chance to assign different importance to different attributes. The weight values should be defined at the beginning of the assessment to apply them consistently to all components.

$$CX(C) = \omega_1 SLOC + \omega_2 ND + \omega_3 NOC \tag{1}$$

Measure Component Coupling. Coupling between objects is the concept that two or more entities rely on each other to fulfill functionality. In the automotive industry, code coupling can support engineers in finding complex components that might require more attention and testing than other parts in the system [17]. Code coupling is not only used to recognize complexity but is also extensively used to identify vulnerabilities [15,25]. The dependability of entities in a system can help a malicious message propagate from one component to another, making an attack impact more severe.

In autonomous vehicle systems, coupling can be at two levels: components and functions. We covered function coupling in the code complexity. Component Coupling (CC) aims to measure how reliant a component is on other subsystems. Communication between autonomous systems components is needed to offer customers various functionalities. For example, the safety system in modern vehicles can communicate with the central locking system to lock the doors when the vehicle reaches a certain speed and unlock them when it stops. Such communication between components is essential to ensure the safety of passengers. However, components coupling permits the propagation of malicious messages [35].

We define CC as the set of ECUs reachable from a component's ECU, calculated using transitive closure. The transitive closure determines direct and indirect coupling. For example, consider component A which runs on ECU_A and connects through the gateway ECU to components B and C through ECU_B and ECU_C, respectively. Component A does not rely on component D, so no communication between ECU_A and ECU_D occurs. However, component B communicates with component D. Consequently, a malicious message can propagate indirectly from ECU_A to ECU_D through ECU_B. The CC of component C is calculated using Eq. (2), where R is the set of relationships between the ECUs of Component C.

$$CC(C) = \bigcup_{i=1}^{\infty} R^i \tag{2}$$

Identify Input and Output Data Vulnerability. Components of autonomous systems operate based on the collected data from sensors, radars, cameras, vehicles, infrastructure, users' mobile devices, and other sources. According to the inputs received and the embedded functionality, a component will transmit signals that control the vehicle's behavior. Inputs and outputs (I/O) offer an exceptional opportunity for attackers. Vehicles' diverse operating conditions make data validation a challenging job. Vehicles are always moving and sensing their surrounding environment. Hence, it is impossible to quantify all possible I/O.

Inputs and outputs are transmitted through different communication means. For example, autonomous systems depend on data received by the Global Positioning System (GPS) receiver to identify a vehicle position and navigate drivers to their destinations. Vehicle to Vehicle (V2V) communication is used to distribute traffic information. GPS and V2V channels each pose different risks on

CAVs. GPS is vulnerable to jamming and spoofing [29], while V2V communication exposes the vehicle to external attacks like eavesdropping, spoofing, Denial of Service (DoS), and spamming [34]. While both of these communication means put the vehicle at risk, the level of threat between one communication means and the other is different. V2V communication exposes the autonomous system to a broader range of attacks [34].

The Input and Output Data Vulnerability (DV) observes two elements: the type and the mean of communication used. Fixed I/O data types (e.g., data types with constant values) are easier to validate and considered less risky compared to fluctuating I/O data types (e.g., an integer value that has an extensive range) that are challenging to validate. Moreover, different communication technologies are subject to various security issues. Thus, each communication mean is assigned a weight according to its criticality. The DV of component C can be calculated using Eq. (3). K represents the total number of communication means, FI and FO represent fixed inputs and outputs, respectively, LI and LO represent fluctuating inputs and outputs respectively, ω_k is the weight of a specific communication mean, and α and β are weights of fluctuating I/O.

$$DV(C) = \sum_{k=1}^{K} \omega_k |FI(C)| + \alpha\omega_k|LI(C)| + \omega_k|FO(C)| + \beta w_k|LO(C)| \qquad (3)$$

Discover Past Security Issues. There have been many successful attacks against CAVs [35]. News of a security breach often gets the attention of malicious users who take advantage of an exposed vulnerability to conduct similar events. Hence, any bug, vulnerability, or attack on the vehicle software system must be carefully examined to prevent future malicious actions. Past Security Issue (PSI) gives higher importance to components that were subject to attacks.

PSI examines the frequency and age of an incident. A security incident that occurs regularly indicates a weakness in the system. Thus, attacks that happen many times are given higher importance. Attacks that arose from a long time ago and did not recur are more likely resolved. Hence, PSI introduces the forgetting factor to give more importance to recently discovered vulnerabilities. Equation (4) illustrates how the PSI of component C can be calculated. Y represents the total number of years since the first vehicle attack, α_y represents the number of attacks that occurred in year y, and λ is the forgetting factor.

$$PSI(C) = \sum_{y=1}^{Y} \alpha_y \lambda^{Y-y} \mid 0 \leq \lambda \leq 1 \qquad (4)$$

Compute Component Maturity. Component Maturity (CM) is essential for identifying vulnerabilities and security decay during vehicle operation. A component can witness many changes due to requirements changes, enhancements, security updates, and bug fixes. Researchers observe that continuous updates and code changes can weaken code robustness and make it more prone to vulnerabilities [18,32]. Code Churn (CCH) calculates the modifications made to a component over time and quantifies the changes' extent. We evaluate CCH by identifying the ratio of changes in a component, including deleted, added, and modified SLOC, as presented in Eq. (5).

As we are interested in evaluating a component's security decay, it is vital to exclude the changes that are meant to enhance the security of an element while calculating CCH. Reviewing the security practices developed within a component can enhance the security measures and improve the component's defense mechanism. We consider components that witness security improvements as more resilient against cyberattacks. We calculate the Security and Maintenance Intensity (SMI) by counting the security enhancement activities since a product release. The reverse percentage is used to determine a low risk for proper security-maintained components, as shown in Eq. (6). Therefore, CM covers extensively changed and low security-maintained code. The CM of component C can be calculated following Eq. (7).

$$CCH(C) = \frac{|Changed\ SLOC|}{|SLOC|} \tag{5}$$

$$SMI(C) = 1 - \frac{|Security\ Maintenance\ Activity|}{Age} \tag{6}$$

$$CM(C) = CCH(C) + SMI(C) \tag{7}$$

Calculate Security Vulnerability Score. The final assessment of a component's Security Vulnerability (SV) is calculated based on the values obtained from the previous five steps. As presented in Eq. (8), to have proportional values, the results obtained from each step for a component C are divided by the maximum (MAX) value that can be acquired by the corresponding step covering all components of the system. Different weights can be assigned to each step.

$$SV(C) = \alpha \left(\frac{CX(C)}{MAX(CX)} \right) + \beta \left(\frac{CC(C)}{MAX(CC)} \right) + \gamma \left(\frac{PSI(C)}{MAX(PSI)} \right)$$
$$+ \delta \left(\frac{DV(C)}{MAX(DV)} \right) + \theta \left(\frac{CM(C)}{MAX(CM)} \right) \tag{8}$$

3.3 Risk Analysis Phase

The vulnerability analysis phase and risk analysis complement each other in identifying system security decay. The second phase of the decay model examines the potentially weak entities closely and quantifies the system's overall risk level. The risk analysis phase involves five steps: (1) Measure attack surface, (2) Estimate attacker threat, (3) Estimate likelihood of an attack, (4) Estimate impact level, (5) and Identify security risk.

The risk analysis phase is tailored to accommodate the uniqueness of vehicle software systems. For example, Step 1 of the second phase starts by measuring vehicle software systems' attack surfaces. We consider all communication means used by vehicle software systems. Moreover, we describe the attacker threat and impact level parameters specifically for vehicle software systems.

Measure Attack Surface. The attack surface of a component is the subset of system resources that an attacker can use to initiate malicious behavior [31]. To conduct an attack, malicious users connect to one of the vehicle's networks and invoke certain functions to send or/and receive information. For example, in 2015, a simulated attack was initiated on Jeep Cherokee while operating on the highway. Using the telematics system's Wi-Fi connection, the attackers transmitted messages to disable the brakes and halt the engine functions [2]. Hence, an attacker usually connects to one of the system's channels, invokes some methods, and sends data items to establish an attack on the system.

The attack surface examines the sets of entry points, exit points, communication channels, and untrusted data of a system [24]. The entry point set holds the means through which data can enter into the autonomous software system from the vehicle's environment (e.g., user inputs, sensor inputs, and incoming signals). The exit point set carries the means that enable data to exit from the system (e.g., outgoing signals). There exist various communication channels that an attacker can use to connect to a vehicle. A remote attack in the vehicle software system may occur through long-distance communication mechanisms such as cellular and satellite radio. Access to the vehicle's on-board diagnostics (OBD) port permits physical attacks that enable attackers to connect to the internal vehicle network [33]. In between are close-range wireless communications such as Near Field Communication (NFC) and Bluetooth, which can be utilized to perform remote attacks with nearby relays and proxies. Finally, the untrusted data set contains persistent data items stored on the nonvolatile memory of ECUs to send or receive data indirectly.

The DV calculates the risk of I/O considering their type and the used mean of communication. Nevertheless, not all I/O can be used in an attack. The attack surface metric includes only the resources contributing to an attack. Hence, in this step, some manual validation is required. We closely look at the DV metric result to identify which elements can ease attacks.

The attack surface (AS) of each component is assigned one of the three levels[1]: large (value of 8), medium (value of 3), and small (value of 1). Large AS indicates that the component's attack surface sets expose the system to multiple attacks. Medium AS means that the attack surface of the component indicates the possibility of some attacks. Small AS suggests a very low probability of initiating an attack on this component. The AS of component C is then estimated using Eq. (9), where ω_a is a weight assigned by security experts to emphasize the importance of the attack surface, and L_a is the value assigned based on the level.

$$AS(C) = \omega_a L_a \qquad (9)$$

---

[1] We define specific level values to rate the risk. These values are identified to reflect the level of risk and enable quantitative measurement. Different risk values have comparable ranges to reflect various risk levels accurately. Consistently, the highest risk level between different parameters has a value of 8, and the lowest has 1. In between these two levels, values are assigned depending on the number of medium levels (e.g., one medium level assigned value 3, two medium levels assigned values 4 and 2). Security engineers can assign other values but have to follow the same approach assuring proportional ranges in the risk values of different levels.

Table 1. Attacker threat parameters. (see Footnote 1)

Parameter	Definition	Level	Value
Skill	Technical experience an agent should possess	Non-specialists: No experience is required to conduct an attack	8
		Skilled: Some experience is expected in the fundamentals of technology to initiate a successful attack	3
		Specialist: Profound knowledge in attacking techniques is required to break the system	1
Knowledge	Background knowledge an agent should acquire about the vehicle software system architecture	Public: Information needed to attack a system is publicly available (e.g., standards and protocols)	8
		Restricted: Data required to initiate an attack is shared with partners and protected by non-disclosure agreement	4
		Private: Sensitive data shared internally with specific members is needed to conduct an attack	2
		Critical: Information required to conduct an attack is strictly shared with few members (e.g., cryptography keys)	1
Equipment	Software tools and hardware tools needed to attack a vehicle	Standard: Tools needed are cheap and broadly available (e.g., RTL-SDR)	8
		Sophisticated: Obtaining the equipment is not easy and expensive	3
		Rare: Equipment required is not available and may entail designing or producing a sophisticated tool	1
Opportunity	The time and attack type (remote, physical) needed to break the system	Large: Attacking the system takes a short time and can be conducted remotely	8
		Medium: Attacking the system needs some time, and either physical or remote access is required	3
		Small: Attacking the system requires much time with physical and remote access to achieve the attack	1

Estimate Attacker Threat. We take a closer look at the agent that initiates a threat. This step of the framework is vitally important to identify security decay. As discussed earlier, attackers' experience and knowledge are always evolving, which affect the security of the system and make it weaker. To estimate the attacker threat (AT), we employ four parameters: Skill, Knowledge, Equipment, and Opportunity. Table 1 describes the parameters and assigns values (see Footnote 1) based on the defined levels. Similar parameters are utilized in the literature with slightly different definitions [3,11,20]. The AT of component C is estimated using Eq. (10), where P is the set of parameters, ω_p is the weight, and T_p is the value of the parameter.

$$AT(C) = \sum_{p=1}^{P} \omega_p T_p \tag{10}$$

Estimate Likelihood of an Attack. An attack takes place by an agent that targets vehicle system vulnerabilities. Hence, to estimate the likelihood of an attack (LA) Eq. (11) is used, multiplying the attack surface probability with the attacker threat probability.

$$LA(C) = AS(C) \times AT(C) \tag{11}$$

Estimate Impact Level. Attacks' impact may vary significantly; some may cause minor issues that do not necessitate a rapid response, while others can have devastating outcomes that require prompt resolution. We estimate the impact level (IL) with five parameters: Safety, Operational, Financial, Privacy, and Reputational. Vehicle attacks can affect different parties in the vehicle industry, including passengers, drivers, pedestrians, vehicle manufacturers, and associated companies. The five defined parameters estimate the impact considering all these parties. For example, the safety parameter evaluates the direct physical damage caused by an attack on the vehicle users, while the reputational parameter considers the indirect harm to manufacturers. The parameters are presented in detail in Table 2 with values(see Footnote 1) based on the impact level. We define the safety impact levels based on ISO 26262 [10], a well-established safety standard for vehicles. Similar parameters are utilized in the literature, but we tailor the parameters' level to fit the vehicle industry [4,19,21,30]. To estimate the IL of an attack on Component C, Eq. (12) is used. F is the set of attack impact parameters, ω_f is the weight of the parameter assigned by security specialists, and I_f is the value of this parameter.

$$IL(C) = \sum_{f=1}^{F} \omega_f I_f \qquad (12)$$

Identify Security Risk. The final security risk (SR) of a component is obtained using Eq. (13), which links the likelihood of an attack with the impact level. The security measures applied to protect the vehicle can lessen the threat. Thus, when estimating the SR, security specialists have to analyze and review the security controls adopted within a component to assess their ability to protect the attack surface and diminish attackers' capabilities. According to the analysis, a vehicle component's SR is classified into three levels: low, moderate, and severe. Low level means that the component is not under risk. This could be due to the security measures applied or because an attack probability is very low. Moderate level indicates that an attack risk exists. However, countermeasures can be used to lessen the risk. Severe level indicates that the component is facing very high risk, and the result of an attack may be critical. Applying security measures at this level might not be sufficient.

$$SR(C) = LA(C) \times IL(C) \qquad (13)$$

4   Case Study

This section demonstrates the use of the AVSDA framework. We utilize Open-Pilot (Version 0.7.9) [5], an open-source driver assistance system in our case study [6]. OpenPilot is an Autopilot system that can perform various functionalities, including Adaptive Cruise Control, Automated Lane Centering, Forward Collision Warning, and Lane Departure Warning (LDW). Hence, the Autopilot system offers SAE level three [7] driving features that can be integrated with different car models such as Honda and Toyota. OpenPilot has one component only,

Table 2. Impact level parameters. (see Footnote 1)

Parameter	Definition	Level	Value
Safety	Safety of vehicle passengers, pedestrians, and road users.	High: Life-threatening injuries with the possibility of casualties.	8
		Medium: Critical injuries with the possibility of survivals.	3
		Low: Moderate injuries with the assurance of survivals.	1
		None: No injuries.	0
Operational	Interruption of vehicular services.	High: Loss of significant subsystem in the vehicle that causes poor driving conditions.	8
		Medium: Some functionalities within the vehicle system may not be operating correctly without affecting passengers' safety and driving conditions.	3
		Low: Minor operations are interrupted that do not affect the vehicle performance (e.g., audio services, calling services).	1
		None: No interruption	0
Financial	Direct and indirect financial losses affecting the vehicle owner and manufacturer.	High: Enormous financial damages that leave the vehicle manufacturer with bankruptcy risk.	8
		Medium: Significant financial losses that slightly affect the financial situation of the manufacturer.	3
		Low: Minor financial losses that do not affect the manufacturer operation.	1
		None: No losses.	0
Privacy	Damages caused by data misusage, including users and manufacturer information.	High: Data leakage and privacy violations affecting a high number of users.	8
		Medium: Data leakage and privacy violations affecting a small number of users.	3
		Low: Minor privacy violation without any data leakages.	1
		None: No data misusage.	0
Reputational	Damages that affect the reputation of the manufacturer organization.	High: Loss of a large number of customers and shareholders with the inability to recover and restore a good reputation.	8
		Medium: Loss of some customers.	3
		Low: Some unsatisfied customers that can be compensated.	1
		None: No damages.	0

Autopilot. We apply the AVSDA phases on the Autopilot component, illustrating the usefulness of this framework. Such an examination can verify the metrics' effectiveness by comparing the files' vulnerability scores with the number of discovered vulnerabilities in every file. We finalize this section by demonstrating the importance of applying AVSDA periodically.

4.1 Vulnerability Analysis

We show that the vulnerability analysis phase of AVSDA can be automated efficiently to identify potentially weak components. We apply five steps of the vulnerability analysis phase to OpenPilot, and the results are summarized in Table 3. We assign the weights of the parameters based on the security criticality

Table 3. Vulnerability analysis of OpenPilot.

Steps	Value	Details
Compute Code Complexity (CX)	$CX(OpenPilot) = 52,608 + 2(6,298)$ $+3(6,148) = 83,648$	The system has a total of 52,608 SLOC, 6,298 ND, and 6,148 NOC. Since ND and NOC are associated with vulnerabilities, we give them weights of 2 and 3, respectively.
Measure Component Coupling (CC)	$CC(OpenPilot) = 9$	OpenPilot communicates with the Engine Control Module, Brake Control Module, Safety System, Seat Control Unit, Powertrain Control Module, Transmission Control, Telematics Control Unit, Active Front Steering, and Battery Junction Box.
Identify Input and Output Data Vulnerability (DV)	$DV(OpenPilot) = 242 + 2(407) +$ $3(397) + 5(1) + 5(1) + 15 + 2(73) +$ $5(211) + 5(1) = 3,478$	OpenPilot's defined I/O are all fluctuating. The system receives and sends data using serial (inputs: 242 and outputs: 15), Controller Area Network (CAN) (inputs: 407 and outputs: 73), Global Positioning System (GPS) (inputs: 397 and outputs: 0), Vehicle to Infrastructure (V2I) (inputs: 1 and outputs: 211), and User to Vehicle (U2V) (inputs: 1 and outputs: 1) communications. We assign different weights for these communication means as they pose different risks.
Discover Past Security Issues (PSI)	$PSI(OpenPilot) =$ $(0.5)^2 + 18(0.5^1) + 50(0.5^0) = 59.25$	There are 69 reported bugs in OpenPilot reported since 2018 (1 in 2018, 18 in 2019, and 50 in 2020). Higher weight is assigned to attacks that occurred in 2020.
Compute Component Maturity (CM)	$CM(OpenPilot) = 100(\dfrac{30,688}{52,608}) = 58$	Within OpenPilot, 30,688 SLOC is modified. None of the applied changes are labeled as security enhancement or maintenance.

with respect to the architecture of OpenPilot.[2] For example, since Nesting Depth (ND) and Number of Children (NOC) of Code Complexity (CX) are associated with vulnerabilities, we apply weights of 2 and 3, respectively. This assessment verifies the applicability of the designed steps.

We then quantitatively evaluate the vulnerability analysis phase's effectiveness in identifying vulnerabilities in OpenPilot files. Such an examination can verify AVSDA metrics' effectiveness by comparing the files' vulnerability scores with the number of discovered vulnerabilities in every file. In total, as of October 2020, OpenPilot has 425 files and 60 documented resolved bugs. We reviewed the reported bugs and linked 24 bugs to the system files. We compare the performance of the used metrics in the AVSDA vulnerability analysis phase with two other sets of metrics. One set is code complexity and churn metrics [32], and the other set is code complexity, code coupling, and cohesion metrics [15]. We identify true-negative, true-positive, false-positive, and false-negative cases. Then, we measure accuracy, precision, and recall rates.

The results are summarized in Table 4. The AVSDA metrics outperform the other approaches in accuracy, precision, and recall. Our metrics achieve a 78% recall ratio indicating that they can identify vulnerable files efficiently. AVSDA

---

[2] Security experts can change these values if needed.

Table 4. Comparison of AVSDA metrics with other metrics.

	AVSDA metrics	Complexity, and code churn metrics [32]	Complexity, coupling, and cohesion metrics [15]
True-negative	390	395	344
True-positive	11	7	10
False-negative	3	7	4
False-positive	21	16	10
Accuracy	94%	94%	83%
Precision	34%	30%	12%
Recall	78%	50%	71%

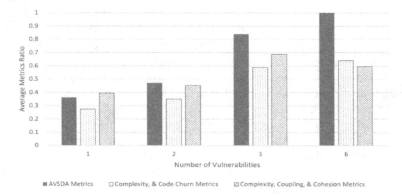

Fig. 2. Relationship between average metrics ratio and number of vulnerabilities.

had a notably high ratio of 94% for accuracy, indicating that the overall vulnerability identification is correct. Though the precision ratio of AVSDA is better than the other approaches, it is relatively low. This means that the number of files recognized as vulnerable and do not possess any vulnerability is high. While this causes extra unneeded work, having more false-positive cases to enhance the true-positive results is better in vulnerability identification.

We further analyze the performance of AVSDA by examining the relationship between the average metrics ratio and the number of bugs reported in a file as shown in Fig. 2. The highest number of reported bugs in a file is 6, which AVSDA identifies as the most vulnerable with a ratio of 1. As shown in Fig. 2, the Security Vulnerability (SV) assigned by the AVSDA metrics is proportional to the files' number of vulnerabilities. The higher the number of vulnerabilities, the higher is the SV value. In contrast, the other two sets of metrics [15,32] show more arbitrary behavior where files with three reported bugs are assigned a higher vulnerability value than files with six bugs.

4.2   Risk Analysis

To validate the risk analysis phase's applicability, we apply the steps to Open-Pilot and show their usefulness. We measure the attack surface (AS) of OpenPilot by reviewing the system's inputs, outputs, channels, and methods. All the system inputs are fluctuating and OpenPilot utilizes multiple communication means, increasing the attack surface. For example, users can connect their smartphones to OpenPilot, exposing the vehicle to different remote attacks [33]. OpenPilot uses nonvolatile memory, allowing untrusted data to be stored. Accordingly, AS's level is considered as large (value of 8), and we assign a weight of 3 to emphasize the criticality of the attack surface. According to Eq. (9), the estimated value of AS is 24.

Next, we estimate attacker threat (AT) using the parameters of Table 1. Attacking the Autopilot system requires outstanding experience in different domains, including networking and security. Hence, specialist skill (value of 1) is required to pose a risk on the system. Some background knowledge about the system is required to initiate an attack. Since OpenPilot is open source, we assign the knowledge parameter a value of 8. Moreover, the equipment needed to conduct an attack is standard (value of 8), like a computer and ports. Finally, performing an attack on the Autopilot system requires preplanning, and either physical or remote access is needed (value of 3). With these level values, AT is 20. The likelihood of an attack (LA) can now be estimated 480 based on Eq. (11).

Next, we determine the impact level of an attack (IL). Establishing an attack on an autopilot system might not have severe direct consequences but can lead to drastic indirect results. The vehicle can operate without autopilot functionality. However, such functionality communicates with critical components (e.g., engine and brake ECUs). If a malicious attack successfully propagates, the vehicle's safety and operational status are left in critical condition. Hence, the safety and operational parameters are both at a high level (value of 8). The manufacturing company might face significant financial losses (value of 3) when all the models affected by such an attack are recalled. Moreover, OpenPilot collects data, including locations, Controller Area Network (CAN) messages, and road conditions. The leakage of such data can violate the privacy of affected users *only* (value of 3). Finally, such attacks have a moderate reputational impact, with some possible customer loss (value of 3). After estimating all the parameters of Table 2, the impact level (IL) can be determined using Eq. (12). We assign a weight of 4 for the safety and operational parameters to emphasize their importance, and the final value of IL is 73.

The last step is determining the security risk (SR) based on the likelihood of an attack, impact level, and practiced security measures. First, we evaluate SR using Eq. (13), which results in 35,040. Then we review OpenPilot's security practices to identify the SR level. OpenPilot follows MISRA c2012 [9] software development guidelines, preventing common coding errors. However, this is not enough to mitigate all security issues. Accordingly, we assign a moderate SR level, which indicates that an attack risk exists.

4.3 Framework Application Frequency

The AVSDA framework should be applied periodically to identify security decay. For example, consider a vehicle attack technique becomes publicly available with a video explaining how to accomplish the attack. The effect of such an incident on the vehicle system's security can be detected by the AVSDA framework. Attacker threat skill parameter is changed from a specialist to a non-specialist with a value of 8. Accordingly, AT rises to 27, increasing the likelihood of an attack to 648. The system's security risk extends from 35,040 to 47,304, indicating a security decay and the need for applying robust security measures to defend the vehicle.

5 Conclusion

We propose an Autonomous Vehicle Security Decay Assessment (AVSDA) framework that estimates the security decay of vehicle software systems by quantitatively measuring systems' vulnerabilities and risks. The AVSDA framework is composed of two phases. The vulnerability analysis phase uses security metrics to identify vulnerable components. The risk analysis phase carefully evaluates attack likelihood by identifying the attack surface and estimating attackers' threats. The framework further analyzes attacks' severity by assessing their impact. The final step of the risk analysis phase defines security risk based on the applied security measures. The AVSDA framework should be applied periodically to recognize changes in the security risk and possible decay.

Though AVSDA is highly effective at identifying likely locations of software defects that lead to vulnerabilities, a software focus risk analysis cannot address certain classes of vehicle attacks that do not target vulnerabilities. For example, sensor spoofing attacks, sybil attacks, and replay attacks are not software defects related attacks and cannot be estimated by the AVSDA framework.

We evaluated AVSDA vulnerability analysis phase metrics' performance by experimenting with their usefulness in identifying vulnerabilities of OpenPilot, an Autopilot system. The results show that the framework is capable of identifying vulnerabilities with an accuracy rate of 94%. The case study shows the efficiency of AVSDA in systematically estimating security risks and discovering security decay.

Acknowledgment. This work is partially supported by Irdeto, the Natural Sciences and Engineering Research Council of Canada (NSERC), and the Canada Research Chairs (CRC) program.

References

1. AUTOSAR enabling continuous innovations. https://www.autosar.org/
2. Black hat USA 2015: The full story of how that jeep was hacked. https://www.kaspersky.com/blog/blackhat-jeep-cherokee-hack-explained/9493/
3. ISO/IEC 18045:2005 information technology - security techniques - methodology for it security evaluation. https://www.iso.org/standard/30830.html

4. ISO/SAE 21434 road vehicles cybersecurity engineering. https://www.iso.org/standard/70918.html
5. Openpilot. https://comma.ai/
6. Openpilot source code. https://github.com/commaai/openpilot
7. Society of automotive engineers. https://www.sae.org/
8. UNECE WP.29-Introduction. https://unece.org/wp29-introduction
9. What is MISRA? https://www.misra.org.uk/MISRAHome/WhatisMISRA/tabid/66/Default.aspx
10. What is the ISO 26262 functional safety standard? https://www.ni.com/en-ca/innovations/white-papers/11/what-is-the-iso-26262-functional-safety-standard-.html
11. Alberts, C.J., Dorofee, A.J.: Managing Information Security Risks: The OCTAVE Approach. Addison-Wesley Professional, Boston (2003)
12. Antinyan, V., Staron, M., Sandberg, A.: Evaluating code complexity triggers, use of complexity measures and the influence of code complexity on maintenance time. Empir. Softw. Eng. **22**(6), 3057–3087 (2017). https://doi.org/10.1007/s10664-017-9508-2
13. Ben Othmane, L., Ranchal, R., Fernando, R., Bhargava, B., Bodden, E.: Incorporating attacker capabilities in risk estimation and mitigation. Comput. Secur. **51**, 41–61 (2015)
14. Burton, S., Likkei, J., Vembar, P., Wolf, M.: Automotive functional safety = safety + security. In: Proceedings of the First International Conference on Security of Internet of Things, pp. 150–159 (2012)
15. Chowdhury, I., Zulkernine, M.: Using complexity, coupling, and cohesion metrics as early indicators of vulnerabilities. J. Syst. Architect. **57**(3), 294–313 (2011)
16. SAE Vehicle Electrical System Security Committee: SAE j3061-cybersecurity guidebook for cyber-physical automotive systems. SAE-Society of Automotive Engineers (2016)
17. Durisic, D., Nilsson, M., Staron, M., Hansson, J.: Measuring the impact of changes to the complexity and coupling properties of automotive software systems. J. Syst. Softw. **86**(5), 1275–1293 (2013)
18. Giger, E., Pinzger, M., Gall, H.C.: Comparing fine-grained source code changes and code churn for bug prediction. In: Proceedings of the 8th Working Conference on Mining Software Repositories, pp. 83–92 (2011)
19. Henniger, O., Apvrille, L., Fuchs, A., Roudier, Y., Ruddle, A., Weyl, B.: Security requirements for automotive on-board networks. In: 2009 9th International Conference on Intelligent Transport Systems Telecommunications, (ITST), pp. 641–646 (2009)
20. Islam, M.M., Lautenbach, A., Sandberg, C., Olovsson, T.: A risk assessment framework for automotive embedded systems. In: Proceedings of the 2nd ACM International Workshop on Cyber-Physical System Security, pp. 3–14 (2016)
21. Kotenko, I., Chechulin, A.: A cyber attack modeling and impact assessment framework. In: 2013 5th International Conference on Cyber Conflict (CYCON 2013), pp. 1–24. IEEE (2013)
22. Macher, G., Armengaud, E., Brenner, E., Kreiner, C.: A review of threat analysis and risk assessment methods in the automotive context. In: Skavhaug, A., Guiochet, J., Bitsch, F. (eds.) SAFECOMP 2016. LNCS, vol. 9922, pp. 130–141. Springer, Cham (2016). https://doi.org/10.1007/978-3-319-45477-1_11
23. Macher, G., Armengaud, E., Brenner, E., Kreiner, C.: Threat and risk assessment methodologies in the automotive domain. Procedia Comput. Sci. **83**, 1288–1294 (2016)

24. Manadhata, P.K., Wing, J.M.: An attack surface metric. IEEE Trans. Software Eng. **37**(3), 371–386 (2010)
25. Medeiros, N., Ivaki, N., Costa, P., Vieira, M.: Software metrics as indicators of security vulnerabilities. In: 2017 IEEE 28th International Symposium on Software Reliability Engineering (ISSRE), pp. 216–227. IEEE (2017)
26. Mössinger, J.: Software in automotive systems. IEEE Softw. **27**(2), 92–94 (2010)
27. Moukahal, L., Zulkernine, M.: Security vulnerability metrics for connected vehicles. In: 2019 IEEE 19th International Conference on Software Quality, Reliability and Security Companion (QRS-C), pp. 17–23 (2019)
28. Moukahal, L.J., Elsayed, M.A., Zulkernine, M.: Vehicle software engineering (VSE): research and practice. IEEE Internet Things J. **7**(10), 10137–10149 (2020)
29. Nighswander, T., Ledvina, B., Diamond, J., Brumley, R., Brumley, D.: GPS software attacks. In: Proceedings of the 2012 ACM Conference on Computer and Communications Security, pp. 450–461 (2012)
30. Ruddle, A., et al.: Deliverable D2.3: security requirements for automotive on-board networks based on dark-side scenarios. EVITA Project (2009)
31. Salfer, M., Eckert, C.: Attack surface and vulnerability assessment of automotive electronic control units. In: 2015 12th International Joint Conference on E-Business and Telecommunications (ICETE), vol. 4, pp. 317–326. IEEE (2015)
32. Shin, Y., Meneely, A., Williams, L., Osborne, J.A.: Evaluating complexity, code churn, and developer activity metrics as indicators of software vulnerabilities. IEEE Trans. Software Eng. **37**(6), 772–787 (2010)
33. Sommer, F., Dürrwang, J., Kriesten, R.: Survey and classification of automotive security attacks. Information **10**(4), 148 (2019)
34. Tangade, S.S., Manvi, S.S.: A survey on attacks, security and trust management solutions in VANETs. In: 2013 Fourth International Conference on Computing, Communications and Networking Technologies (ICCCNT), pp. 1–6. IEEE (2013)
35. Thing, V.L., Wu, J.: Autonomous vehicle security: a taxonomy of attacks and defences. In: 2016 IEEE International Conference on Internet of Things (iThings) and IEEE Green Computing and Communications (GreenCom) and IEEE Cyber, Physical and Social Computing (CPSCom) and IEEE Smart Data (SmartData), pp. 164–170. IEEE (2016)

A TSX-Based KASLR Break: Bypassing UMIP and Descriptor-Table Exiting

Mohammad Sina Karvandi[1], Saleh Khalaj Monfared[1],
Mohammad Sina Kiarostami[2], Dara Rahmati[3(✉)], and Saeid Gorgin[4]

[1] School of Computer Science, Institute for Research in Fundamental Sciences (IPM),
Tehran, Iran
{karvandi,monfared}@ipm.ir
[2] Center for Ubiquitous Computing, Faculty of ITEE, University of Oulu,
Oulu, Finland
mohammad.kiarostami@oulu.fi
[3] Computer Science and engineering Department, Shahid Beheshti University,
Tehran, Iran
d_rahmati@sbu.ac.ir
[4] Iranian Research Organization for Science and Technology (IROST), Tehran, Iran
gorgin@ipm.ir

Abstract. In this paper, we introduce a reliable method based on Transactional Synchronization Extensions (TSX) side-channel leakage to break the KASLR and reveal the address of the Global Descriptor Table (GDT) and Interrupt Descriptor Table (IDT). We indicate that by detecting these addresses, one could execute instructions to sidestep Intel's User-Mode Instruction Prevention (UMIP) and the Hypervisor-based mitigation and, consequently, neutralized them. The introduced method is successfully performed after the most recent patches for *Meltdown* and *Spectre*. Moreover, we demonstrate that a combination of this method with a call-gate mechanism (available in modern processors) in a chain of events will eventually lead to a system compromise despite the restrictions of a super-secure sandbox in the presence of Windows's proprietary Virtualization Based Security (VBS). Finally, we suggest software-based mitigation to avoid these issues with an acceptable overhead cost.

Keywords: Cache side-channel · TSX · Meltdown · KASLR

1 Introduction

As signs of progress in computer science, from Artificial Intelligence [15] to High-Performance Computing [9,26] continues, the role of computer security research in both hardware and software is drawing more attention to the community. Recently discovered microarchitectural attacks in modern CPUs, are known to be devastating. They are easily implemented, practical, and often independent from the operating system making them an imminent threat to computer privacy.

© The Author(s), under exclusive license to Springer Nature Switzerland AG 2022
B. Luo et al. (Eds.): CRiSIS 2021, LNCS 13204, pp. 38–54, 2022.
https://doi.org/10.1007/978-3-031-02067-4_3

Among them, speculative-execution based side-channel attacks are more ubiquitous as new disclosures continue to showcase the increasing failure of secured design in the computer hardware [2]. These attacks are capable of circumventing all existing protective measures, such as CPU microcode patches, kernel address space isolation (Kernel Virtual Address (KVA), shadowing, and Kernel Page-Table Isolation (KPTI)). While side-channel attacks have been well-known for a relatively long time, speculative-execution based attacks are contemporary, known facts indicate that they will persist for some time in the future.

Pioneered by Meltdown [22] and Spectre [18] attacks, numerous variations, and extension of microarchitecture vulnerabilities have been found, and their corresponding exploitation has proposed latterly. ForeShadow [35], MDS [24], and ZombieLoad [29] should be alluded as the most famous ones. Moreover, new works have shown the extensiveness of these attacks. As an example, NetCAT [20] presents a practical network-based side-channel attack.

After Meltdown, more strict KASLRs such as KAISER [5] have been employed in today's operating systems to prevent similar attacks since short-term hardware mitigation is not effortlessly attainable. KAISER completely isolates the user-mode and kernel-mode memory layout by creating a *Shadow* representation of the mapped memory. However, there are still some unprotected addresses and parts by KALSR that required by the architecture. Hence, knowing these structure's addresses could lead to severe problems. In addition, discovered hardware-based vulnerabilities on Memory (DRAM) such as RowHammer [17] allow attackers to execute more destructive and offensive malicious code, to trespass or gain access to restricted and private information [32].

Furthermore, it is possible and suitable to take advantage of some hardware-specific structures that are implemented across operating systems. In the same way, once can gather masked and hidden internal information of the operating system which could be used for malicious purposes. To be more precise, the structures of Global Descriptor Table (GDT) and Interrupt Descriptor Table (IDT) are one of the essential parts of protected mode, which are not heavily isolated in the user-mode and kernel-mode address layout. By overwriting these structures in certain conditions, one can perform a privilege escalation attack. Also, by the use of the same variations of timing side-channel attacks as in Meltdown, (e.g., TSX-based attacks), the virtual addresses of these structures in the kernel memory could be revealed.

In this work, we demonstrate that GDT and IDT addresses could be discovered by TSX side-channel to perform privilege escalation attacks, even after Meltdown mitigation, bypassing the mitigations in modern Intel processors, particularly User-Mode Instruction Prevention (UMIP). Furthermore, it is illustrated that the proposed attacks can be executed in virtualized environments, such as the latest Microsoft Hypervisor release (Hyper-v) and Virtualization Based Security (VBS). In summary, the contributions of this paper are as follow:

- A concrete TSX side-channel attack is performed to discover *GDT* and *IDT* addresses in the kernel mode in a system with *KAISER* isolated memory layout bypassing UMIP.

- We show that a full system compromise could be achieved by revealing *GDT*
  and *IDT* virtual addresses in the memory, incorporated with *call-gate* mechanism along with a conventional *Write What Where*.
- The possible mitigation investigated for this vulnerability and low-cost
  software-based mitigation for the operating systems to avert these attacks
  is suggested.

2   Preliminaries and Background

In this section, required preliminaries and background knowledge for the
software-based side-channel attacks, along with some concepts KAISER, TSX
side channels, UIMP and Descriptor-Table Exiting are reviewed.

2.1   KASLR, Meltdown and KAISER

The security of computers highly relies on memory isolation, meaning that the
kernel address ranges are not meant to be accessible from user prospective. The
most conventional method to address such requirement is the Kernel Address
Space Layout Randomization (KASLR) which include the random assignment of
kernel objects rather than constant addressing. Discovered Meltdown [22] attack
was able to exploit side effects of out-of-order execution on modern processors to
read arbitrary kernel memory locations, including crucial personal information
and passwords. By exploiting the out-of-order execution as an indispensable
performance feature, the attack is independent of the operating system, and it
does not rely on any software vulnerabilities. Meltdown was able to break all
the security considerations provided by address space isolation as well as the
virtualized isolation developed by the same infrastructure. The affected systems
by Meltdown include a wide range of personal computers, smart phones, and
even the enterprise cloud servers. Moreover, available TSX technology in Intel
CPUs enables Meltdown to read the protected kernel memory addresses with
the high-performance speed of 500 Kbps. [22].

Generally, Meltdown mitigation relies on isolating kernel and user memory
pages with different methods. The widely used approach to address this issue is
the employment of KAISER [5], which is implemented as Kernel Virtual Address
Shadow (KVAS) (a term coined by Microsoft) [23] in Microsoft Windows and
KPTI in Linux [4]. In KAISER, placing a small portion of information in the
user-mode is inevitable since operating systems are required to implement functions necessary to handle system calls and interrupts, which are directed to kernel
space.

As will be discussed, leaving the tables which hold the addresses of interrupt
handler (e.g., Interrupt Descriptor Table) or other tables managing the segmentation (e.g., GDT) visible to user mode, and ignoring to protect their addresses,
allow the attacker to endanger the system. However, to adversely take advantage
of the information left unprotected in the user-mode, essential internal mechanisms should be known which will be explored later.

2.2   TSX Cache Attack

Intel TSX refers to a product name for two x86 instruction set extensions, called Hardware Lock Elision (HLE) and Restricted Transactional Memory (RTM) [33]. HLE is a set of prefixes that could be added to specific instructions. These prefixes are backward-compatible. Hence, the code including them, also works on older hardware platforms. On the other hand, RTM is an extension adding several instructions to the instruction set that are used to declare regions of code that should execute as part of a hardware transaction. A RTM transaction comprises the region of the code that is encapsulated between a pair of *xbegin* and *xend* instructions. Instruction xbegin also provides a mechanism to define a fall-back handler that is called if the transaction is aborted. *xabort* can be used by the executing code to abort the transaction explicitly. By employment of the TSX, generating an exception or an interrupt which is handled in the kernel could be avoided, resulting in side-channel attacks to be more resistant to noise with a more reliable outcomes [22]. As will be explored later on, We employ TSX to trigger the initialization of our proposed attack.

2.3   Descriptor-Table Exiting

Descriptor-Table Exiting is a hardware mechanism to restrict guest machines in VMX Non-Root from executing instructions such as LGDT, LIDT, LLDT, LTR, SGDT, SIDT, SLDT, and STR [6]. This mechanism has been used in Microsoft Virtualization Based Security as an exploit mitigation, which avoids memory address leakage and provides an absurd situation for the attacker to find the base address of GDT or IDT, among other details such as Control Registers. Microsoft uses hypervisor as a hardware security mechanism, and in VM Control Structure. In order to configuring this hardware feature, an special field is presented which is referred as the *Descriptor-Table Exiting*. Descriptor-Table Exiting is declared in Intel Manual [6]. This control field determines whether executions of LGDT, LIDT, LLDT, LTR, SGDT, SIDT, SLDT, and STR cause VM exits. This declaration would be critical to the attack model we intend to describe.

2.4   User-Mode Instruction Prevention (UMIP)

UMIP is a security feature present in new Intel Processors. If enabled, it prevents the execution of particular instructions if the Current Privilege Level (CPL) is greater than 0. If these instructions were executed when CPL > 0, user space applications could have access to system-wide settings such as the global and local descriptor tables, the task register and the interrupt descriptor table. These are the instructions covered by UMIP in accordance to the Intel [6]:

- SGDT: Store Global Descriptor Table, SIDT: Store Interrupt Descriptor Table
- SLDT: Store Local Descriptor Table, SMSW: Store Machine Status Word
- STR: Store Task Register

If any of these instructions are executed with CPL > 0, a general protection exception (GP) is issued when UMIP is enabled. In order to enable this feature, operating systems can set the 11th bit of the CR4 [6].

3   Attack Primitives: GDT and Call-Gate Mechanism

Our proposed attack is fundamentally based on the existing hardware features in the processors. As an indispensable part of the suggested attack, GDT and its properties are described in detail in the this section. Moreover, here we discuss how the improper configuration might create vulnerabilities caused by the existing and possibly disabled hardware features.

3.1   Global Descriptor Table

GDT is an important data structure available in Intel x86-family CPUs providing the characteristics of the memory areas used during program execution. It includes the base address, the size, and access privileges which is fundamental in terms of the security prospective. GDT is a main table in x86 and protected-mode that still exists in AMD64 [1] and Intel IA-32e. The GDT structure in the x86 system is shown in Fig. 1.

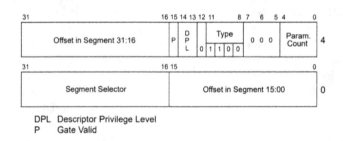

Fig. 1. GDT structure in a 32-bit machine

While the proposed attack here works on both x86 and x64 architectures, we have used the x64 version of GDT since it is more widespread rather than the other version.

3.2   GDT in 64-Bit

Although the segmentation is omitted in the modern systems in protected-mode with paging enabled, the GDT still presents in 64-bit mode. A GDT must be defined but is generally never changed or used for segmentation. The size of the register has been extended from 48 to 80 bits, and 64-bit selectors are always *Flat* (thus, from 0000000000000000 to FFFFFFFFFFFFFFFF) which should also be taken into account when the attack chain is designed.

On the other hand, 64-bit versions of Microsoft Windows forbid hooking of the GDT. Attempting to do so would cause the machine to *bug check*. In our circumstances, it is not a problem for our case as long as some mechanisms for preventing these hooks called Kernel Patch Protection exists. This mechanism is known as *PatchGuard*, which checks the system in random intervals of between 3 to 10 min. So it is possible to patch GDT in a glance then revert everything to the previous normal state again to avoid such errors. In this context, we use GDT as a descriptor for call-gate to complete the attack chain instead of a descriptor for segmentation.

3.3   Call-Gate Mechanism

Call-gates are used to transfer the execution to other rings e.g., ring 0, 1, 2, 3. Instructions like *SYSENTER* and *SYSCALL* are used in modern operating systems for transitioning between every rings to ring 0. But for the transition between other rings (e.g., ring 3 to 2 or 2 to 1), the call-gates would be used. The *type* field located in the GDT structure as indicated in Fig. 1 represents a 4-bit field that could get various values and completely change the GDT entry behavior and definition [13].

After finding the target entry, the type value should be changed to one *Gate* accordingly. For example, we use *0xc* (1100 - 32-bit call-gate) in the final payload. There are specific terms in call-gate used to build the final payload. In order to exploit the features that call-gate provides, the suitable privilege level should be set in the data segmentation used in the GDT. Here are the privilege levels defined in this context:

- **Current Privilege Level (CPL).** CPL is stored in the selector of currently executing the CS register. It represents the privilege level (PL) of the currently executing task and also PL in the descriptor of the code segment and designated as Task Privilege Level (TPL) [13].
- **Descriptor Privilege Level (DPL).** It is PL of the object which is being attempted to be accessed by the current task or put differently, the least privilege level for the caller to use this gate [13].
- **Requester Privilege Level (RPL).** It is the lowest two bits of any selector. It can be used to weaken the CPL if craved [13].
- **Effective Privilege Level (EPL).** It is maximum of CPL and RPL thus the task becomes less privileged [13].

Fundamentally, any task in an arbitrary code needs to fetch the data from the data segment. Therefore, the privilege levels are checked at the time a selector for the target segment is loaded into the data segment register. Three privilege levels are invoked into the privilege checking mechanism. Ultimately, the payload must meet the following conditions in the fields:

- RPL of the selector of the target segment.
- DPL of the descriptor of the target segment

Note that the access is allowed only if *DPL* is greater than or equal to the maximum of CPL and RPL, and a procedure can only access the data that is at the same or less privilege level.

3.4   From Call-Gate to Code Execution in Ring-0

Call-Gate in x86. In order to use x86, fields of a unique set of call-gate should be filled as described in Table 1.

Selector field should be *0x8* to point to KGDT_R0_CODE entry of GDT, which describes the kernel-mode in Windows. The type of it should be set to *0xc*, and the minimum ring that can invoke this call-gate is *0x3* (DPL = 0x3 (user-mode)), and also, it should be present in memory (*pFlag = 0x1*) [13].

Table 1. Organization of the fields in the GDT

Selector	0x8
Type	0xc
dpl	0x3
pFlag	0x1
Offset 0_15	0x0000ffff & address
Offset 16_31	0x0000ffff & (address >>16)

Call-Gate in Long Mode. Call-gate are unavoidable parts of Intel structure, and even in 64-bit long mode. In addition to GDT, LDT is also present but special cases like segmentation using the FS/GS segment are replaced by the new MSR-based mechanism using *IA32_GS_BASE* and *IA32_KERNEL_GS_BASE* MSRs [7]. The fact that LDT and GDT are still presented in long mode is used in Windows when the kernel utilizes the UMS (User-Mode Scheduling). So Windows creates a Local Descriptor Table if a thread tends to use UMS [11].

3.5   Disabled UIMP

As described previously UIMP protection could be employed as an external privilege check. However, in our observations Linux and Windows do not use UIMP features for some compatibility issues. Thus, this opens a kernel memory address leak to user-mode applications, and valid addresses can be used for exploiting the Operating System Kernel or as a valid address for other side-channel measurements. In the following section, we demonstrate how these addresses could lead to a full system compromise. Nevertheless, Microsoft decided to remove the support for GDT, SIDT, SLDT, SMSW, and STR instructions in hypervisor as explained. Our observation shows that even if operating systems use UMIP or DESCRIPTOR-TABLE EXITING separately or both of them simultaneously, it is still vulnerable to side-channel attacks based on TSX.

3.6 Far Calls and Far JMPs

The far forms of JMP and CALL refer to other segments and require privilege checking. The far JMP and CALL can be performed in two methods:

- Without call-gate Descriptor: The processor permits a JMP or CALL directly to another segment only if:
  1. DPL of the target segment = CPL of the calling segment
  2. Confirming bit of the target code is set and DPL of the target segment ≤ CPL

  Note that Confirming Segment may be called from various privilege levels, but is executed at the privilege level of the calling procedure.
- With call-gate Descriptor: The far pointer of the control transfer instruction uses the selector part of the pointer and selects a gate. The selector and offset fields of a gate form a pointer to the entry of a procedure.

4 The Proposed Attack

In this section, we describe how the explored mechanism are used to create the attack. Then, we show the results obtained from the Intel processor and show how the valid base address of IDT and GDT could be obtained without using SIDT and SGDT. Next, we show how to build a valid call-gate entry and use it in combination with a write-what-where to execute an adversary code. Then attacker crafts the shellcode in *ring 0* in order to elevate privilege or hide the malware in the kernel. Figure 2 illustrates the high level overview of the proposed attack.

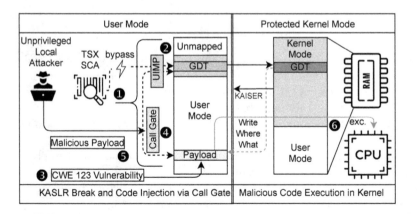

Fig. 2. A high-level overview of the proposed attack.

According to Fig. 2, in ❶ the local unprivileged adversary carries out a conventional TSX timing side channel in order to disclose GDT address, bypassing UMIP ❷. The details is explained in Sect. 4.3. In ❸, the attacker arms the procedure with an existing Write Where What vulnerability explained in Sect. 4.7.

Then in ❹, the adversary configures The GDT descriptions to point out his own malicious payload via the Call Gate features in accordance to the descriptions in Sect. 4.5. Finally the malicious data is loaded in the desired address in ❺ and wrongly executed by the processor with the proper permissions in ❻.

4.1   Threat Model

As a basic assumption for the attack model, the attacker can execute code in the victim's computer in a limited level of privilege, including a highly limited user-mode or in a sandboxed application with all the common defenses (e.g., SMEP, SMAP, DEP) enabled and configured suitably. In order to fully compromise the system an attacker has a prior *write-what-where* (CWE-123) [25] vulnerability in operating system kernel. Furthermore, as an extension to the proposed attack mechanism, the adversary might also execute code in a vitalized environment as well in the shared-computing platform (e.g. cloud computing) scenario.

4.2   Experimental Setup

The experiment to showcase the effectiveness of the attack chain has been executed on a system equipped with 9th generation of Intel processor (i9-9880H), running on a Windows 19H1 (also known as 1903) with 16 GB of DDR4 RAM. Moreover, the same attack procedure is carried out on a system with a 6th generation CPU (6820HQ), to ensure the generalization of the method. The test has also been successfully experimented on 19H2 and the latest 20H1 Microsoft Windows, Ubuntu Debian 7, and Mac OSX Mojave as well.

4.3   Finding GDT Address

In order to locate the GDT address, a timing measurement is required to discover the elapsed time in accessing a *mapped* and an *unmapped* address in the kernel space memory. Experimentally, a valid address gives the response time about 190–197 clock-cycles (different based on architecture) and an invalid address access returns after about 220–234 clock-cycles based on our results in 6th Gen Intel (6820HQ).

To implement such a measurement, a combination of the kernel memory address and access time (RDTSCP) + TSX (XBEGIN, XEND) is employed. Then the response time difference in accessing a mapped and unmapped addresses could lead to the identification of mapped addresses.

Furthermore, if a particular processor does not support the RDTSCP instruction, then one could get similar results by the serialization process. More precisely, it is required to serialize instructions to execute all of the instructions fetched before the targeted instruction. So a combination of CPUID + RDTSC is adequately employed.

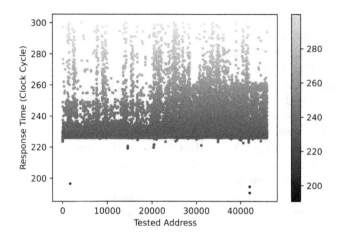

Fig. 3. The results of timing TSX-based measurements on a uni-core system

Note that the first implementation indeed gives more precise results compared to executing RDTSC. Our experiments show that it is not suitable to use CPUID for the second RDTSC as it takes several clocks-cycles. Also, it would be possible to use the timing thread, if a operating system prohibits the usage of RDTSC or RDTCSP [8], or intercepts the execution of CPUID using Intel VMX [14] or Intel FlexMigration [10]. Timing threads could even have a higher resolution rather than RDTSC/RDTCSP on many processors [30,31]. By deploying these instructions, an automatic process is triggered to find valid targeted addresses.

```
1   rdtscp    ; get the current time clock of processor
2   ...            ; save the rdtscp results somewhere (e.g registers)
3
4   mov rax,[Kernel Address]  ; Move a kernel address into tax
5   xbegin $+xxx    ; Use Intel TSX in order to suppress any error
        in user-mode
6   ; The error always happens because we are trying to read
        kernel address
7   mov byte ptr [rax], 0    ; Try to write into kernel address
8   ...            ; Error occurs here (program never reaches here)
9
10  xend    ; End of TSX
11  rdtscp    ; Compute the core clock timing again in order to see
        how many
12            ; clocks CPU spends when trying too write into our
        address
```

Listing 1.1. The timing measurement code deployed by the use of TSX technology (RDTSCP)

The result consists of four valid elements. The first one is the addresses that are valid for IDT. Second is the address of GDT, and third is the address of SYSCALL MSR_LSTAR (0xC0000082) - (The kernel's RIP SYSCALL entry for

64-bit software) [36]. Finally, the fourth is where the page tables are mapped. The timing results of the deployed measuring method is depicted in Fig. 3.

Our observation in the latest 20H1 (and other versions of Windows) shows that GDT and IDT are mapped in a particular order, even though there is no limitation to assign different addresses. By way of example, Windows maps IDT in a unique address. IDTR is fffff80021eeb000, and GDTR fffff80021eedfb0 (GDTR = GDT Base + GDT size) and this sequence is the same each time Windows is restarted when the KASLR addresses changed. The difference is 0x2000 bytes or two pages. Thus, the address of IDT could first be determined, leading to revealing the address of GDT where another page of 0x2000 bytes is mapped following the first valid page address.

While there are other pages mapped into memory addresses (e.g., shadow functions for system-calls and interrupts), the addresses are far from the target addresses (e.g., fffff8001d34e500). Therefore, the address among IDT, GDT, Interrupt Shadows, and System Call Shadows could be identified. A payload for call-gate could build later finding the GDT base address. The following commands in Listing 1.2 shows the process of identification of valid addresses on all the cores by realizing the distance between GDT and IDT addresses.

```
 2  ; Accessing First Core's IDT and GDT
 3  0: kd> r idtr
 4  idtr=fffff8077925b000
 5  0: kd> r gdtr
 6  gdtr=fffff8077925dfb0
 7  ; Accessing Second Core's IDT and GDT
 8  0: kd> ~1
 9  1: kd> r idtr
10  idtr=ffff8401bc053000
11  1: kd> r gdtr
12  gdtr=ffff8401bc055fb0
13  ; Accessing Third Core's IDT and GDT
14  1: kd> ~2
15  2: kd> r idtr
16  idtr=ffff8401bc0f5000
17  2: kd> r gdtr
18  gdtr=ffff8401bc0f7fb0
19  ; Accessing Forth Core's IDT and GDT
20  2: kd> ~3
21  3: kd> r idtr
22  idtr=ffff8401bc1a4000
23  3: kd> r gdtr
24  gdtr=ffff8401bc1a6fb0
```

Listing 1.2. The procedure of employing IDTR and GDTR

We observed that allocated addresses for IDT and GDT have a special pattern for each core. For instance, here are several addresses that Windows allocated for IDT of its first core:

- `fffff8036385b000, fffff8027ca5b000`
- `fffff80053a5b000, fffff8076525b000`

Our experiments indicate that these addresses tend to follow a specific pattern. As the pseudo-code illustrated in Listing 1.2, the GDT has the same pattern As IDT as well. Our experiments show that, regardless of the system in hand, for the first core, the pattern of `fffff80XXXX5b000` is spotted, where `XXXX` can be changed due to the prevention mechanism of KASLR. The first bytes in the pattern address is to create a canonical address, and the least significant byte has a constant value of `5b000` pattern. This brings 0xffff = 65535 possibilities to find the address of IDT and GDT in the first core of Windows. The same pattern can be applied to other cores as well. In a uni-core system, one can test up to 10 addresses per second with excellent precision, using the explained timing side-channel. Moreover, one could also hasten this measurement up to 20 addresses per second, in compromise to the loss of accuracy. Approximately, it takes 109 min to find the address of the GDT for the first core. Of course, the patterns for other cores could be discovered as well. As an example, in the 8-core system, there are eight possibilities for IDT and GDT addresses, which could speed up the search 8x faster. Also, it is possible to use other cores simultaneously for accelerating the search process.

4.4   Build Call-Gate Entry

We have built our payload based on the description discussed in Sect. 3.4.

4.5   Using FAR JMPs, FAR CALLs

As explored in Sect. 3.6, the near forms of JMP and CALL transfer within the current code segment requires only limited checking. However, the far forms of JMP and CALL are referred to as other segments and require privilege checking. Hence, when the CPU fetches a far-call instruction, it will use that instruction's 'selector' value to look up a descriptor in the GDT (or in the current LDT).

If the call-gate descriptor is fetched, and if access is allowed (i.e., if CPL $\leq$ DPL), then the CPU will perform a complex sequence of actions which will accomplish the requested ring-transition. CPL is based on the least significant 2-bits in register CS (also in SS). The new value for SS:SP comes from a special system-segment, known as the TSS (Task State Segment). The CPU locates its TSS by referring to the value in register TR (Task Register).

4.6   Returning Back to the User-Mode

After the call-gate is executed in kernel-mode, and we run shellcode in kernel-mode, it is time to return to the user-mode in order to avoid a crash in kernel-mode like BSOD in Windows or Kernel Panic in Linux.

In order to return to user-mode or any other outer ring that is used as the source of FAR CALL or FAR JMP, one should execute *lret* instruction in the inner ring. It is analogous to the procedure when an interrupt is returned to the previous state.

1. Use the far-return instruction: 'lret'
   – Restores CS:IP from the current stack, Restores SS:SP from the current stack
2. Use the far-return instruction: 'lret $n'
   – Restores CS:IP from the current stack
   – Discards n parameter-bytes from that stack, Restores SS:SP from that current stack

4.7   Combining Attack with CWE-123

CWE-123 stands for write-what-where bugs. We have employed CVE-2016-7255 to modify our specific GDT entries. Consequently, the kernel-mode code execution of the shell-code using a FAR CALL is achieved. Also, another effect of this attack is to change the supervisor bit of page table so that page tables are readable and writable in user-mode (or *self-ref of death attack*).

5   Discussion: The Possible Mitigation

The simple approach of complete isolation of the kernel is not able to fully unmap GDT from the user-mode since, in all modes of execution, the GDT descriptors should be available. Every segment register has a *visible* part and a *hidden* part. The hidden part sometimes referred to a *descriptor cache* or a *shadow register*. When a segment selector is loaded into the visible part of a segment register, the processor also loads the hidden part of the segment register with the base address, segment limit, and access control information from the segment descriptor pointed to by the segment selector. The information cached in the segment register (visible and hidden) allows the processor to translate addresses without taking extra bus cycles to read the base address and limit from the segment descriptor. In systems in which multiple processors have access to the same descriptor tables, it is the responsibility of software to reload the segment registers when the descriptor tables are modified. Otherwise, an old segment descriptor cached in a segment register might be used after its memory-resident version has been modified [6].

In our mitigation setup we used a custom hypervisor to monitor and detect any *SYSCALL*, *SYSRET*, and interrupt execution. We deploy the proposed mitigation to switch GDT/IDT entries between user mode and kernel mode. Our hypervisor simulation shows a 2.7% delay overhead due to the additional execution introduced by the mitigation. However, the same methodology could be deployed within the operating system reducing the overhead significantly.

It is worthy of mentioning that, complete mitigation to this attack would be the employment of separate GDT base in kernel and user layout. The kernel GDT should not be mapped into the user-mode, and Operating System Kernel has to change the address of GDTR each time a ring modification occurs. For example, it shall use SGDT to change the GDTR after every user-mode to kernel-mode switch caused by *SYSENTER* and *SYSCALL* or every interrupts handler routines. The mapped GDT in the user-mode should also be modifiable only by the kernel (not user-mode). Hence, the user-mode application cannot access a valid address for GDT, and the discovered GDT address by the attacker is only valid when it is on user-mode. So, if a bug such as Write-What-Where occurs in the kernel or any system-level driver or kernel module, it cannot modify the user-mode GDT; thus, if the user-mode application tries to use call-gate in ring 3, the corresponding GDT entry is invalid, and the attack fails.

6   Related Efforts

Micro-architectural software attacks have been widely investigated in the context of revealing or damaging private and sensitive data. Recent works such as [3,34,37] aim to discover data on the victim system secretly. Recent works have demonstrated that the state of the art mitigation for such attack are still insufficient. Authors in [16], present a novel memory-sharing-based attack that breaks the KASLR on KPTI-enabled Linux virtual machines. Similarly, TagBleed [19], abuses tagged TLBs and residual translation information to break KASLR. Furthermore, adversary techniques for exploitation on shared Virtual Environments like [27] have shown to be promising in practice.

With regards to much older timing side-channel attacks, Osvik et al. [28] introduced the PRIME+PROBE on the L1 cache, to attack the AES implementations, discovering secret keys. Consequently, more promising and sophisticated methods like [37] were proposed.

Moreover, other software-based attacks take advantage of on DRAM pioneered by [17] have also shown to be very practical, jeopardizing the private data stored in memory in various circumstances. In terms of exploiting the abandoned, but existing technologies in modern CPU designs, which is the primary concern of this paper, the possible vulnerabilities regarding the structure of GDT and IDT, were previously studied by [12]. Researchers in [12] proposed a technique to gain a more stable kernel-level exploitation. These techniques were shown to be applicable in Windows-NT systems. Moreover, interestingly, several utilized mechanisms in this article, such as call-gate has also been used for securing the systems. For instance, [21] present an approach to prevent sandbox leakage based on call-gate.

7   Conclusion

The impact of the hardware vulnerability exploited by software techniques has been proved to be dreadful. In this paper, we presented a TSX based side-channel attack, revealing the addresses of GDT and IDT in the kernel space, which could be exploited by an arbitrary user-mode application. We demonstrated that a single *Write-What-Where* vulnerability in the operating system could lead to a full system compromise through call-gate feature available in today's CPUs, irrespective of the version of the operating system. We have successfully evaluated our method by implementing an attack on the 9th Generation *Intel* processors.

The attack presented here is based on the descriptor structures available on the modern processors (e.g., Intel as well as AMD [1]) although have hidden address by ASLR but are mapped into the user-mode address layout. The exploitation perfectly works with common *Write What Where* bugs. For instance, any bug in a *JavaScript* application on an isolated web-browser in the kernel address or graphic functions of the operating system (e.g., Win32k bugs in Windows) will be enough to be exploited. Moreover, we suggested software mitigation for this vulnerability since the presented attack bypasses the recent mitigation to Meltdown Attack (e.g., KAISER).

References

1. Devices, A.M.: AMD64 architecture programmer's manual volume 2: system programming (2006)
2. Ge, Q., Yarom, Y., Cock, D., Heiser, G.: A survey of microarchitectural timing attacks and countermeasures on contemporary hardware. J. Cryptogr. Eng. **8**(1), 1–27 (2018)
3. Gras, B., Razavi, K., Bos, H., Giuffrida, C.: Translation leak-aside buffer: defeating cache side-channel protections with TLB attacks. In: 27th USENIX Security Symposium (USENIX Security 18), pp. 955–972 (2018)
4. Gruss, D., Hansen, D., Gregg, B.: Kernel isolation: from an academic idea to an efficient patch for every computer. login: USENIX Mag. **43**(4), 10–14 (2018)
5. Gruss, D., Lipp, M., Schwarz, M., Fellner, R., Maurice, C., Mangard, S.: KASLR is dead: long live KASLR. In: Bodden, E., Payer, M., Athanasopoulos, E. (eds.) ESSoS 2017. LNCS, vol. 10379, pp. 161–176. Springer, Cham (2017). https://doi.org/10.1007/978-3-319-62105-0_11
6. Guide, P.: Intel® 64 and IA-32 architectures software developer's manual. Volume 3C: Chapter 24, Virtual Machine Control Structures (Table 24–6. Definitions of Primary Processor-Based VM-Execution Controls) 3C (2019)
7. Guide, P.: Intel® 64 and IA-32 architectures software developer's manual. Volume 4: Chapter 2, Model-Specific Registers (MSRS) (Table 2–2. IA-32 Architectural MSRs) 4 (2019)
8. Guide, P.: Intel® 64 and IA-32 architectures software developer's manual. Volume 3A: Chapter 1, System Architecture Overview, Time Stamp Disable, 3A (2019)
9. Hajihassani, O., Monfared, S.K., Khasteh, S.H., Gorgin, S.: Fast AES implementation: a high-throughput bitsliced approach. IEEE Trans. Parallel Distrib. Syst. **30**(10), 2211–2222 (2019)
10. Intel: Intel virtualization technology flexmigration application note (2012). https://www.intel.com/content/dam/www/public/us/en/documents/application-notes/virtualization-technology-flexmigration-application-note.pdf
11. Ionescu, A.: Blog post (2018). http://www.alex-ionescu.com/?p=340
12. Jurczyk, M., Coldwind, G.: GDT and LDT in windows kernel vulnerability exploitation (2010)

13. Karvandi, S.: Call gates' ring transitioning in IA-32 mode (2019). https://rayanfam.com/topics/call-gates-ring-transitioning-in-ia-32-mode/
14. Karvandi, S.: Hypervisor from scratch - part 6: virtualizing an already running system (2019). https://rayanfam.com/topics/hypervisor-from-scratch-part-6/
15. Kiarostami, M.S., Reza Daneshvaramoli, M., Monfared, S.K., Rahmati, D., Gorgin, S.: Multi-agent non-overlapping pathfinding with Monte-Carlo Tree search. In: 2019 IEEE Conference on Games (CoG), pp. 1–4 (2019)
16. Kim, T., Kim, T., Shin, Y.: Breaking KASLR using memory deduplication in virtualized environments. Electronics 10(17), 2174 (2021)
17. Kim, Y., et al.: Flipping bits in memory without accessing them: an experimental study of dram disturbance errors. In: ACM SIGARCH Computer Architecture News, vol. 42, pp. 361–372. IEEE Press (2014)
18. Kocher, P., et al.: Spectre attacks: exploiting speculative execution. arXiv preprint arXiv:1801.01203 (2018)
19. Koschel, J., Giuffrida, C., Bos, H., Razavi, K.: TagBleed: breaking Kaslr on the isolated kernel address space using tagged TLBs. In: 2020 IEEE European Symposium on Security and Privacy (EuroS&P), pp. 309–321. IEEE (2020)
20. Kurth, M., Gras, B., Andriesse, D., Giuffrida, C., Bos, H., Razavi, K.: NetCAT: practical cache attacks from the network. In: S&P, May 2020. https://www.vusec.net/download/?t=papers/netcat_sp20.pdf. Intel Bounty Reward
21. Lewis, P.: Using a call gate to prevent secure sandbox leakage, uS Patent 8,528,083, 3 September 2013
22. Lipp, M., et al.: Meltdown: reading kernel memory from user space. In: 27th USENIX Security Symposium (USENIX Security 18), pp. 973–990 (2018)
23. Microsoft Security Response Center: Kva shadow: mitigating meltdown on windows (2018). https://msrc-blog.microsoft.com/2018/03/23/kva-shadow-mitigating-meltdown-on-windows/
24. Minkin, M., et al.: Fallout: reading Kernel writes from user space. arXiv preprint arXiv:1905.12701 (2019)
25. MITRE: Cwe-123: Write-what-where condition (2019). https://cwe.mitre.org/data/definitions/123.html
26. Monfared, S.K., Hajihassani, O., Kiarostami, M.S., Zanjani, S.M., Rahmati, D., Gorgin, S.: BSRNG: a high throughput parallel bitsliced approach for random number generators. In: 49th International Conference on Parallel Processing-ICPP: Workshops, pp. 1–10 (2020)
27. Oliverio, M., Razavi, K., Bos, H., Giuffrida, C.: Secure page fusion with VUsion. In: Proceedings of the 26th Symposium on Operating Systems Principles, pp. 531-545 (2017). https://www.vusec.net/projects/vusion
28. Osvik, D.A., Shamir, A., Tromer, E.: Cache attacks and countermeasures: the case of AES. In: Pointcheval, D. (ed.) CT-RSA 2006. LNCS, vol. 3860, pp. 1–20. Springer, Heidelberg (2006). https://doi.org/10.1007/11605805_1
29. Schwarz, M., et al.: ZombieLoad: cross-privilege-boundary data sampling. arXiv preprint arXiv:1905.05726 (2019)
30. Schwarz, M., Maurice, C., Gruss, D., Mangard, S.: Fantastic timers and where to find them: high-resolution microarchitectural attacks in JavaScript. In: Kiayias, A. (ed.) FC 2017. LNCS, vol. 10322, pp. 247–267. Springer, Cham (2017). https://doi.org/10.1007/978-3-319-70972-7_13
31. Schwarz, M., Weiser, S., Gruss, D., Maurice, C., Mangard, S.: Malware guard extension: using SGX to conceal cache attacks. In: Polychronakis, M., Meier, M. (eds.) DIMVA 2017. LNCS, vol. 10327, pp. 3–24. Springer, Cham (2017). https://doi.org/10.1007/978-3-319-60876-1_1

32. Seaborn, M., Dullien, T.: Exploiting the DRAM rowhammer bug to gain kernel privileges. Black Hat 15 (2015)
33. Stecklina, J., Prescher, T.: LazyFP: leaking FPU register state using microarchitectural side-channels. arXiv preprint arXiv:1806.07480 (2018)
34. Van Schaik, S., Giuffrida, C., Bos, H., Razavi, K.: Malicious management unit: Why stopping cache attacks in software is harder than you think. In: 27th USENIX Security Symposium (USENIX Security 18), pp. 937–954 (2018)
35. Weisse, O., et al.: Foreshadow-NG: breaking the virtual memory abstraction with transient out-of-order execution (2018)
36. Wiki, O.D.: Sysenter (2017). https://wiki.osdev.org/SYSENTER
37. Yarom, Y., Falkner, K.: Flush + reload: a high resolution, low noise, L3 cache side-channel attack. In: 23rd USENIX Security Symposium (USENIX Security 14), pp. 719–732 (2014)

Attacks, Responses, and Security Management

A Stakeholder-Centric Approach for Defining Metrics for Information Security Management Systems

Anirban Sengupta$^{(\boxtimes)}$ (iD)

Centre for Distributed Computing, Jadavpur University, Kolkata 700032, India
anirban.sg@gmail.com

Abstract. An enterprise comprises of information processing systems that help realize its business processes. Automation of these systems is achieved with the help of IT assets like hardware, software and network devices. Assets and their interconnections may contain vulnerabilities, which can be exploited by threats, leading to breach of security of information and business processes. Such probable security risks are managed by implementing an Information Security Management System (ISMS). An important aspect of ISMS is the measurement of information security posture of the enterprise; this enables the comparison of information security status over time, and provides assurance to stakeholders about the *amount* of security that exists within the information processing systems. Different stakeholders have separate concerns regarding the security of an Enterprise IT System. This paper attempts to identify all such stakeholders and analyze their security concerns. A set of metrics has been defined that covers all facets of ISMS and addresses security concerns of all categories of stakeholders. This would help in the design of an effective and efficient ISMS.

Keywords: Enterprise information security · Enterprise stakeholders · ISMS · Security concern · Security metrics · Security risk

1 Introduction

An enterprise comprises of information processing systems that help realize its business processes. Automation of these systems is achieved with the help of assets like hardware, software and network devices. Assets and their interconnections may contain weaknesses, or *vulnerabilities* [1, 2], which can be exploited by *threats* [1], leading to breach of security and privacy of information and business processes. Such probable *risks* need to be controlled [1] and *all* stakeholders need to be assured that information is being processed securely by the enterprise. This is usually achieved by implementing an Information Security Management System (ISMS) [3]. An important aspect of ISMS is the measurement of information security and privacy posture of the enterprise; this enables the comparison of information security and privacy status over time, and provides assurance to stakeholders about the *amount* of security and privacy that exists within the information processing systems. Standards like ISO/IEC 27004 [4] and NIST

© The Author(s), under exclusive license to Springer Nature Switzerland AG 2022
B. Luo et al. (Eds.): CRiSIS 2021, LNCS 13204, pp. 57–73, 2022.
https://doi.org/10.1007/978-3-031-02067-4_4

SP 800-55 [5] describe the components of an enterprise security metrics programme to comply with ISMS standards ISO/IEC 27001 [3] and NIST SP 800-53 [6], respectively. However, they do not state specific metrics that may be used to measure assurance and improvement in enterprise security and privacy posture. Implementers of enterprise security usually limit themselves to finding gross measures like count of virus outbreaks, count of security-aware personnel etc. These can, at the most, provide sketchy ideas about some aspects of security metrics programme implementation; they do not pinpoint the ground-level effectiveness of ISMS. Moreover, researchers have mostly concentrated on finding ways of measuring specific characteristics of security devices. Such values can prove the efficacy of individual devices like firewalls, IDS/IPS etc. [7, 8]; they cannot provide stakeholders with composite figures that prove the effectiveness of complete ISMS. Thus, the definition, modelling and implementation of security and privacy metrics continue to intrigue researchers and it has remained a *hard problem* in information security research [9].

From an enterprise information security perspective, the need is to develop a comprehensive set of metrics that can i) address the security and privacy concerns of *all* types of stakeholders, and ii) help in the continual improvement of enterprise ISMS [4]. This paper tries to deal with this issue by defining metrics that i) cover all facets of ISMS, and ii) address security and privacy concerns of all categories of stakeholders of enterprise information systems. The paper is organized as follows. A survey of related work is given in Sect. 2. Section 3 categorizes the stakeholders of an enterprise and describes their concerns. Mapping between these concerns and security/privacy parameters is given in Sect. 4. Section 5 presents a set of ISMS metrics, while the relation between stakeholder concerns and ISMS metrics is detailed in Sect. 6. Finally, Sect. 7 concludes the paper.

2 Related Work

There has been some significant research on specific areas, and techniques, of information security measurement. Marcus Pendleton et al. have published a detailed survey on systems security metrics [10]. The authors have investigated the relationships among *metrics of system vulnerabilities, metrics of defense power, metrics of attack or threat severity* and *metrics of situations*, using a hierarchical ontology. Tupper and Zincir-Heywood defined VEA-bility (vulnerability, exploitability, attackability) as a security metric [11]. Victor-Valeriu Patriciu et al. proposed metrics to evaluate security vulnerabilities and controls [12]. Besides, several researchers have presented research on risk assessment and risk metrics [13, 14].

As is evident, most of the published works have drawn inspiration from software quality metrics. Though this can be a good starting point, and may give some idea about security aspects of software and hardware, such metrics cannot be used to comprehend the complete security posture of an enterprise information system. Now let us discuss some studies that have been performed specifically on ISMS metrics. ISO/IEC 27004 [4] and NIST SP 800-55 [5] describe how to implement information security metrics programmes in compliance with the requirements of ISMS. Gaffri Johnson has suggested that five core processes, namely *IT and business alignment, information security risk management process*, *compliance process*, *awareness process* and *audit process*, should be measured in order to maintain an effective ISMS [15]. The paper provides some examples illustrating the measurement of these processes. A. P. Aldya et al. [16] proposed a methodology for identifying the objects, measurement parameters and metrics based on the provisions of ISO/IEC 27004. Veselin Monev proposed a methodology [17] for evaluating the maturity level of the security controls and clauses of ISO/IEC 27001 [3]. In his master's thesis, Matthias Mödinger has proposed a set of metrics and key performance indicators for ISMS [18]. The work is based on the principles of ISO/IEC 27004 [4] and caters specifically to the requirements of universities.

Thus, it is obvious that the published papers and reports do not state specific metrics that may be used to measure assurance and improvement in enterprise ISMS. They either suggest some gross methodologies for implementing ISMS metrics programme, or cater to the needs of specific industries/domains. This paper tries to fill this research gap by defining ISMS metrics that will help stakeholders to understand the amount of security/privacy that exists within an enterprise. The metrics are domain-independent, and have been defined keeping in mind the security and privacy concerns of different categories of stakeholders.

3 Stakeholders of an Enterprise and Their Concerns

An enterprise comprises of different stakeholders who are directly, or indirectly, associated with its business processes and information assets. In fact, the existence and business of an enterprise are governed by its stakeholders. Analyses of standards like ISO/IEC 27001 [3] and ISO/IEC 27002 [19] reveal that stakeholders can be broadly categorized as Employees, Clients, Third Parties and Authorities. In this section, specific security and privacy concerns of different stakeholders are discussed; this is the outcome of interactions of the author with stakeholders during several instances of ISMS implementation. It may be noted that in case of some stakeholders, only a subset of the listed concerns (for that stakeholder category) may be applicable.

Employees - Employees are usually under the direct supervision of an enterprise. They can be further categorized as "management" or "operational" personnel. While, management establishes the objectives and business strategies of an enterprise, these are implemented and maintained by operational staff. Since, the nature of their contributions to enterprise functions are different, their concerns also vary. Specifically, managers own the business processes and critical information assets of an enterprise, and establish ISMS for protecting the same. This leads to the following security and privacy concerns: (i) Security of enterprise Business Processes and critical information assets – these are the primary assets of an enterprise, and are directly owned by senior management; (ii) Safety of client data – management of an enterprise are accountable for the protection of data of all its clients (individuals and other enterprises) with whom business relations exist; (iii) Safety of personal data – it is the concern of managers to ensure security of personal data of all employees (including their own data); (iv) Reputation of enterprise – if the reputation of an enterprise is sullied, the senior management is usually held accountable; and (v) Efficacy of the implemented ISMS – it is important to ensure that the implemented ISMS complies with the information security requirements of the enterprise, and effectively addresses the security concerns of all stakeholders; moreover, greater the efficacy of ISMS, higher is the Return on Investment (RoI) of security processes and controls.

As is obvious, management personnel have concerns pertaining to information security and privacy requirements of the entire enterprise. However, the concerns of operational staff would be more of a personal nature; they would be worried about issues that are directly related to their roles. Specifically, operational personnel are concerned about: (i) Safety of *their* personal data; and (ii) Whether they will be accountable for others' misdeeds – sometimes, owing to lack of proper audit trails and monitoring, innocent members of staff may be held accountable for misdeeds which have been actually perpetrated by others; this is a major area of concern for operational personnel.

Clients - Clients of an enterprise are bothered about the safety of their personal data or assets (e.g. money, devices etc.), and the legal protection of their consumer rights. They are usually *not* concerned about the security of the enterprise, unless it affects them directly, or indirectly.

Third Parties - Third parties refer to all such external organizations or individuals who help an enterprise to realize its business objectives. Some examples of third parties are: Internet Service Providers (ISPs), third party data centres, organizations to which software development is outsourced, materials suppliers, third party employees, and courier companies and delivery personnel. Third parties are concerned about the security and privacy of those business processes and information which may have a bearing on their own business interests. Specifically, they are interested in the following: (i) Security of third party enterprise data and Business Processes; (ii) Safety of *their* personal data; (iii) Protection of *their* reputation – third parties are usually concerned whether loss of reputation of an enterprise, with which they are doing business, will also tarnish their own image; (iv) Protection of legal and contractual obligations – this includes all statutory requirements and service-level agreements between organizations; and (v) Whether they will be accountable for others' misdeeds.

Authorities - Authorities refer to all such entities that define and enforce legal and regulatory frameworks for enterprises. It is mandatory for enterprises to conduct their businesses within the ambit of these frameworks and to comply with relevant requirements. Examples of authorities are Reserve Bank of India (for Indian banks), Office of the Comptroller of the Currency (for US banks), ARCEP (for France's Electronic Communications, Postal and Print media distribution), certifying authorities (ISO/IEC, ISACA etc.) and judiciary. Security and privacy concerns of authorities usually comprise of the following: (i) Safety of data and assets of clients of an enterprise; (ii) Safety of data and assets of third party enterprises; (iii) Security of nation – this is applicable for critical-sector enterprises like defense organizations, space research organizations, banks etc.; (iv) Reputation of nation; and (v) Compliance.

4 Security/Privacy Concerns and Parameters

The security and privacy concerns of stakeholders are addressed by implementing controls (like policies, procedures, laws, security tools etc.) within the ambit of ISMS. Controls, in essence, help to protect security and privacy parameters of enterprise assets [19]. Hence, in order to select appropriate controls, it is important to identify the parameters that relate to the existing concerns of stakeholders. Analysis of the concerns described in the previous section reveal that they can be decomposed into requirements for the protection of specific *security* and *privacy parameters* of Business Processes and information assets. The analysis is presented in this section.

The relevant parameters that have been considered are as follows [3, 20]: *confidentiality* (C); *integrity* (I); *availability* (A); *authenticity*; *non-repudiation* - ability to prove the occurrence of a claimed event or action and its originating entities; *anonymity* - inability to identify the owner of personally identifiable information; *unlinkability* - inability to establish a link between two or more pieces of data items; *undetectability* - inability to determine the existence of a data item; *accountability* - responsibility for actions; *legal & contractual requirements*; and *image/reputation*. Let us now identify the parameters corresponding to stakeholder concerns.

Security of Business Processes and Information Assets – Traditionally, security is interpreted as the ability to protect C, I, A of assets. Another parameter that is of significance is authenticity. It is important to ensure that a business process or information asset is authentic; that is, it is indeed that asset which it claims to be.

Safety of Client Data – Similar to the case for information assets, safety of client data items, which is in the possession of an enterprise, would entail the protection of their C, I and A. Additionally, safety would also require ensuring the *privacy* of those data items that comprise of personally identifiable information [19]. Privacy has been defined as the protection of anonymity, unlinkability and undetectability parameters, in addition to C, I and A [20]. Thus, this concern can be addressed by ensuring the protection of six parameters – C, I, A, anonymity, unlinkability and undetectability. It may be noted that another privacy parameter, unobservability, has not been explicitly considered in this work as it is a combination of unlinkability and undetectability.

Safety of Personal Data and Assets – This is similar to the above case. It can be addressed by ensuring the protection of C, I, A, anonymity, unlinkability and undetectability.

Reputation of enterprise – This concern can be directly mapped to the parameter image/reputation. This is an intangible parameter and depends on the perception of customers and users.

Efficacy of Implemented ISMS – This concern is not related to any parameter explicitly. However, effective and efficient ISMS would imply that *all* required security and privacy parameters have been adequately protected.

Accountability for Others' Misdeeds – It is important to implement controls (monitoring mechanisms, audit trails etc.) so that innocent operational personnel and third parties are not held responsible for misdeeds perpetrated by others. These controls help to protect the image/reputation of innocent personnel as miscreants are not able to repudiate, and can be held accountable for, their misdeeds. Hence, the parameters that are significant for this security concern are accountability, non-repudiation and image/reputation.

Legal Protection of Consumer Rights – The rights of consumers should be protected as per applicable legal and contractual requirements. This ensures that the image/reputation of consumers is not sullied due to mishap at the enterprise end. This also ensures that consumers are not held accountable for misdeeds perpetrated by others. Hence, the parameters accountability, legal & contractual requirements and image/reputation of consumers are important here.

Protection of Legal and Contractual Obligations – Third parties are concerned about the protection of legal and contractual obligations as specified in service level agreements and statutory requirements. This will ensure that their image/reputation is not sullied and they are not unnecessarily held accountable for others' misdeeds. Hence, the parameters accountability, legal & contractual requirements and image/reputation of third parties should be addressed here.

Security of Nation – Authorities are concerned about the protection of national security. Security and privacy breaches in critical-sector enterprises may jeopardize the integrity and/or availability of national assets (like power grids, networks etc.). This may, in turn, cause breaches of legal and contractual obligations with other countries, organizations etc., thus making the nation accountable for the same. Hence, this security concern should be addressed to protect integrity and availability of national assets, and accountability and legal and contractual obligations of the nation.

Reputation of Nation – It is essential to prevent security and privacy breaches in critical-sector enterprises so that the image/reputation of the nation is not tarnished.

Compliance – An enterprise has to comply with all relevant legal and contractual obligations. Failure to do so may lead to litigations, loss of business, blacklisting etc.

The above analyses show that each security and privacy concern pertains to the protection of a set of relevant *security* and/or *privacy parameters*. The results have been summarized in Table 1 (columns 2 and 3).

Table 1. Security and privacy concerns, corresponding parameters and ISMS metrics.

Sl. No	Security concern	Security/Privacy parameter	ISMS metric
1	Security of business processes and information assets	Confidentiality, integrity, availability, authenticity	Risk metric
2	Safety of client data	Confidentiality, integrity, availability, anonymity, unlinkability, undetectability	Risk metric, policy compliance metric
3	Safety of personal data and assets	Confidentiality, integrity, availability, anonymity, unlinkability, undetectability	Risk metric, policy compliance metric
4	Reputation of enterprise	Image/Reputation	Risk metric, legal/regulatory compliance metric, contractual compliance metric, controlled incident metric, uncontrolled incident metric

(continued)

Table 1. (*continued*)

Sl. No	Security concern	Security/Privacy parameter	ISMS metric
5	Efficacy of implemented ISMS	All parameters	Risk mitigation metric, controlled incident metric, uncontrolled incident metric, process effectiveness metric, efficiency metric
6	Accountability for others' misdeeds	Accountability, non-repudiation, image/reputation	Risk metric, non-repudiation metric, policy compliance metric, legal/regulatory compliance metric, contractual compliance metric, composite compliance metric
7	Legal protection of consumer rights	Accountability, legal & contractual requirements, image/reputation	Legal/Regulatory compliance metric, contractual compliance metric
8	Protection of legal and contractual obligations	Accountability, legal & contractual requirements, image/reputation	Legal/Regulatory compliance metric, contractual compliance metric
9	Security of nation	Integrity, availability, accountability, legal & contractual requirements	Risk metric, legal/regulatory compliance metric, contractual compliance metric, controlled incident metric, uncontrolled incident metric
10	Reputation of nation	Image/Reputation	Risk metric, legal/regulatory compliance metric, contractual compliance metric, controlled incident metric, uncontrolled incident metric
11	Compliance	Legal & contractual requirements	Policy compliance metric, legal/regulatory compliance metric, contractual compliance metric, composite compliance metric

Security/privacy requirements of an enterprise can be derived as a union of the security/privacy concerns of *all* its stakeholders, as described above. An enterprise implements ISMS, including controls and specific techniques, to address its security and privacy requirements. The next section proposes a set of metrics that can be used to comprehensively measure the effectiveness of implemented ISMS, along with the amount of security and privacy that exists in the enterprise.

5 ISMS Metrics

Establishment of ISMS requires the implementation of controls that can address stake-holder concerns. It is important for stakeholders to assess the efficacy of the ISMS in meeting their security and privacy requirements. This can be achieved by defining and generating relevant metrics that correctly convey the status of the ISMS. In this section, a set of ISMS metrics is defined. These metrics cover the ISMS processes and activities as required by ISO/IEC 27001 standard [3].

Risk Metric - Risk values are measures of insecurity in an enterprise. *Risk* is defined as the probability that threats will exploit vulnerabilities to breach security parameters and cause harm to assets [1]. Lower the risk value corresponding to a parameter, greater is the assurance that the parameter is difficult to breach. The process of computing risk values is referred to as *risk assessment*. There are several well-known risk assessment methodologies [1]; hence, this paper does not propose any new methodology or risk metric.

Authenticity Metric - Authenticity metrics provide assurance that the information assets, along with related processing systems/applications, and users of assets are gen-uine. These metrics can be derived from data generated by mechanisms that verify the claimed identities of the source and destination of information. Thus, authenticity metric for application ap_i, $\mu_{auth}(ap_i)$, can be computed as:

$$\mu_{auth}(ap_i) = \left(count_{auth}(ap_i) / count(ap_i)\right) + \left(count_{auth}(inp(ap_i)) / count(inp(ap_i))\right)$$
$$+ \left(count_{auth}(usr(ap_i)) / count(usr(ap_i))\right)$$

$$(1)$$

where, $count_{auth}(ap_i)$ denotes the no. of authentic instances of application ap_i that were executed in the enterprise during the period of measurement; $count(ap_i)$ is the total no. of instances (authentic and unauthentic) of application ap_i for the same period; $count_{auth}(inp(ap_i))$ denotes the no. of authentic inputs received by ap_i, while $count(inp(ap_i))$ gives the total no. of authentic and unauthentic inputs received; $count_{auth}(usr(ap_i))$ denotes the no. of authentic users and systems that have accessed application ap_i during the period of measurement; $count(usr(ap_i))$ gives the total no. of users and systems that have accessed ap_i.

Thus, it may be seen that:

i. $\mu_{auth}(ap_i) = 0$ when $count_{auth}(ap_i) = count_{auth}(inp(ap_i)) = count_{auth}(usr(ap_i)) = 0$ for a measurement period;

ii. $\mu_{auth}(ap_i) = 3$ when all instances of application api, along with its inputs and users, have been authentic during a period of measurement.

Hence, $0 \le \mu_{auth}(ap_i) \le 3$.

Non-repudiation Metric - This metric signifies the denial of actions of users per-taining to the access and use of an application or system and/or receipt of output from the application or system. Thus, non-repudiation metric for application ap_i, $\mu_{nrep}(ap_i)$, can be computed as:

$$\mu_{nrep}(ap_i) = \left(1 - count_{rep}(acc(ap_i)) / count(acc(ap_i))\right)$$
$$+ \left(1 - count_{rep}(out(ap_i)) / count(out(ap_i))\right) \tag{2}$$

where, $count_{rep}(acc(ap_i))$ denotes the no. of instances, during the period of measurement, when users have falsely denied accessing/using application ap_i, while $count(acc(ap_i))$ gives the total no. of accesses of application ap_i by users during that measurement period; $count_{rep}(out(ap_i))$ denotes the no. of cases, during the period of measurement, when users have falsely denied receiving output from application ap_i, while $count(out(ap_i))$ gives the total no. of instances when users have received output from application ap_i during that measurement period.

Thus, it may be seen that:

i. $\mu_{nrep}(ap_i) = 0$ when $count_{rep}(acc(ap_i)) = count(acc(ap_i))$ and
     $count_{rep}(out(ap_i)) = count(out(ap_i))$ for a measurement period;
ii. $\mu_{auth}(ap_i) = 2$ when $count_{rep}(acc(ap_i)) = count_{rep}(out(ap_i)) = 0$.

Hence, $0 \leq \mu_{auth}(ap_i) \leq 2$.

Compliance Metrics - These metrics depict the level of compliance of implemented security processes with enterprise's objectives and policies, laws, regulations and contracts. Compliance objects (policies, laws, contracts etc.) comprise of sets of *to-do activities*. These activities can be mapped to implemented security controls, processes and techniques. Gap Analysis may be performed to identify compliance gaps. Weighted averages of gaps (with policies, laws, contracts etc.) generate different types of compliance metrics, namely Policy-compliance, Legal/Regulatory compliance and Contractual-compliance metrics.

Policy Compliance Metric - Information security policies state the objectives of an enterprise with respect to establishment of security practices and techniques. Examples of policies are Acceptable Use Policy, Access Control Policy, Anti-Virus Policy, Backup Policy, E-Mail Policy, Incident Management Policy etc. Evidence of implementation and enforcement of a policy is demonstrated with the help of records, which can be maintained either as physical documents or soft copies. Successful implementation of a security policy signifies execution of the statements specified in the policy document.

sAn enterprise should assign relative weights (w_i) to policy statements in [0, 1] based on their priorities ("1" signifies highest priority). Implementation scores (s_i) of policy statements can be obtained in [0, 1] by analyzing corresponding records ("1" means "completely implemented"). The policy compliance metric $^{comp}\mu_{py}(py_i)$ for policy py_i can be computed as follows:

$$^{comp}\mu_{py}(py_i) = \Sigma \ w_i s_i | 0 \leq w_i, \ s_i \leq 1 \text{ and } \Sigma \ w_i = 1 \tag{3}$$

Table 2 lists some statements of Backup Policy, along with a sample assignment of relative weights. It also shows the implementation scores of policy statements for a particular measurement period. Hence, the compliance metric for backup policy is:

$$^{comp}\mu_{py}(\text{Backup Policy}) = (0.30 * 1) + (0.25 * 0.8) + (0.20 * 0.5) + (0.25 * 0.9)$$
$$= 0.825 \approx 0.8$$

Table 2. Sample statements of backup policy, their relative weights, implementation scores.

Policy statement	Rel. Wt. (w_i)	Imp. score (s_i)
All critical information shall be backed up periodically	0.30	1
The backup media shall be stored with sufficient protection	0.25	0.8
Backup copies of critical information system software shall not be stored in the same location as the operational software	0.20	0.5
Backup information shall be tested at some specified frequency	0.25	0.9

It may be seen that $0 \leq {}^{comp}\mu_{py}(py_i) \leq 1$; ${}^{comp}\mu_{py}(py_i)$ has a value 0 when *none* of the statements of policy p_i has been implemented, while it has max. value 1 when the policy has been completely implemented. Compliance metrics for individual policies can be combined to obtain the overall Policy Compliance Metric for the enterprise:

$$^{comp}\mu_{py} = \Sigma \left(w_i * {}^{comp}\mu_{py}\left(py_i\right)\right)|0 \leq w_i \leq 1 \text{ and } \Sigma w_i = 1 \qquad (4)$$

Here, w_i denote the weights that can be assigned to individual policy compliance metrics as per their relative importance. The weights may vary depending on the specific requirements and priorities of the enterprise. ${}^{comp}\mu_{py}$ signifies the status of compliance of the entire enterprise with respect to applicable security policies.

Legal/Regulatory Compliance Metric - Laws and Regulations that are applicable to an enterprise need to be identified and implemented. Examples include IT Act, Privacy Laws, Cryptographic Laws, Reserve Bank of India (RBI) regulations for Indian banks and financial institutions etc. Like policy statements, applicable provisions and sections of laws and regulations should be listed, and relative weights (w_i) should be assigned as per their priorities. Records of implementation should be maintained as evidence of legal and regulatory compliance. There is a difference between implementation of policies and laws/regulations; the latter are either implemented in totality, or not implemented at all. Partial implementation of laws and regulations is not acceptable to authorities. Hence, in case of legal/regulatory compliance metrics, implementation scores (s_i) assume binary values. If a section or provision has been implemented completely, the value of s_i is 1; else it is 0.

Legal/regulatory compliance metric ${}^{comp}\mu_{lg}(lg_i)$ for law/regulation lr_i can be computed as follows:

$$^{comp}\mu_{lr}(lr_i) = \Sigma w_is_i|0 \leq w_i \leq 1, \Sigma w_i = 1, s_i \varepsilon \{0, 1\} \qquad (5)$$

Like policy compliance metric, $0 \leq {}^{comp}\mu_{lr}(lr_i) \leq 1$.

Compliance metrics for individual laws and regulations can be combined to derive the overall Legal/Regulatory Compliance Metric for the enterprise as follows:

$$^{lr}\mu_{comp} = \Sigma \left(w_i * {}^{comp}\mu_{lr}(lr_i)\right)|0 \leq w_i \leq 1, \Sigma w_i = 1 \qquad (6)$$

Here, w_i denote the weights that can be assigned to individual legal/regulatory compliance metrics as per their significance. ${}^{comp}\mu_{lr}$ gives the status of compliance of the entire enterprise with respect to applicable laws and regulations.

Contractual Compliance Metric - An enterprise may enter into contracts with third parties for supply of goods, software, services, personnel etc. Such contracts define terms and conditions to be followed by the participating enterprises, including service levels. It is important to periodically check for compliance with the terms of contracts so that deviations can be detected and corrected early.

The executable items of a contract need to be identified and prioritized by an enterprise. Based on the priorities, relative weights have to be assigned to each item. As in case of legal and regulatory compliance, partial fulfillment of a feature, or contract item, does not hold any significance. A feature is either implemented fully, or not implemented at all. Hence, using notations similar to the ones for legal/regulatory compliance metric, contractual compliance metric $^{comp}\mu_{ct}(ct_i)$ for contract ct_i is given by:

$$^{comp}\mu_{ct}(ct_i) \;=\; \Sigma\; w_i s_i | 0 \leq w_i \leq 1,\; \Sigma\; w_i = 1,\; s_i \,\varepsilon\, \{0, 1\} \tag{7}$$

As is obvious, $0 \leq {}^{comp}\mu_{ct}(ct_i) \leq 1$. The composite Contractual Compliance Metric for all applicable contracts of an enterprise is obtained as:

$$^{comp}\mu_{ct} \;=\; \Sigma\; \left(w_i * {}^{comp}\mu_{ct}(ct_i)\right) | 0 \leq w_i \leq 1,\; \Sigma\; w_i = 1 \tag{8}$$

Here, w_i denote the relative weights of individual contractual compliance metrics.

Composite Compliance Metric - It may be important for senior management of an enterprise to obtain an overall idea about the status of compliance of its business and management functions with applicable policies, laws, regulations and contracts. The composite compliance metric would serve this purpose and is computed by combining the values of individual compliance metrics in a specified proportion. Thus,

$$\begin{aligned}
^{comp}\mu \;=\; & \left(w_1 * {}^{comp}\mu_{py}\right) + \left(w_2 * {}^{comp}\mu_{lr}\right) \\
& + \left(w_3 * {}^{comp}\mu_{ct}\right) | 0 \leq w_i \leq 1,\; \Sigma\; w_i = 1
\end{aligned} \tag{9}$$

Here, w_1, w_2 and w_3 represent relative weights of individual compliance metrics. It is obvious from Eqs. (4), (6) and (8) that $0 \leq {}^{comp}\mu \leq 1$. Legal/regulatory compliance of an enterprise is more critical than others; also, compliance to policies may be, in general, least significant in the overall compliance wheel. Hence, the following values of relative weights are suggested for computing $^{comp}\mu$: $w_2 = 0.5$, $w_3 = 0.3$, $w_1 = 0.2$. Thus, following this scheme,

$$^{comp}\mu \;=\; \left(0.2 * {}^{comp}\mu_{py}\right) + \left(0.4 * {}^{comp}\mu_{lr}\right) + \left(0.3 * {}^{comp}\mu_{rg}\right) + \left(0.1 * {}^{comp}\mu_{ct}\right) \tag{10}$$

However, an enterprise may choose the values of relative weights based on its specific requirements.

Effectiveness Metrics - These metrics measure the effectiveness of implemented ISMS processes and controls; this includes all security management activities like business continuity management, threat management, incident management, asset management, awareness, education and training programmes etc. As stated above, ISMS processes and controls address stakeholder concerns, enterprise objectives, risks, and legal/regulatory issues. It is important to check the effectiveness and performance of the processes and controls vis-à-vis the security needs.

While *compliance metrics* help measure the conformance of implemented processes to various compliance objects, *effectiveness metrics* produce measures that indicate whether the processes have been actually successful in securing the enterprise. There are different ways in which such effectiveness can be measured.

Risk Mitigation Metric - The amount of risk that is mitigated by implementation of a process produces risk mitigation metric. This can be measured at an asset-, business process-, or enterprise-level, whose criticality is considered while computing the metric. A process that is able to reduce risk to a critical asset (or business process, or enterprise) is considered to be more effective than one that reduces risk to a non-critical asset. Also, this metric can assume different values at different points of time. For example, it may be the case that a control (say, a firewall) is able to mitigate risk (say, unauthorized access to a bank's online portal) at a particular time of day (when network traffic is low), but it is not able to do so during other times (when network traffic is high).

Considering the above factors, the value of risk mitigation metric, $^{rmit}\mu_{tc}(pr_j)$, at time t_c, for a process (or control) pr_j, can be computed as follows:

$$^{rmit}\mu_{tc}\left(pr_j\right) = (\Sigma\ cr(a_i) * rf_r(a_i))\ /\ n$$

$$\text{where, } rf_r(a_i) = \begin{cases} (rf_o(a_i) - rf_c(a_i))\ /\ rf_o(a_i), & \text{if } rf_o(a_i) \geq rf_c(a_i) \\ (rf_o(a_i) - rf_c(a_i))\ /\ rf_c(a_i), & \text{if } rf_o(a_i) < rf_c(a_i) \end{cases} \tag{11}$$

Here, $a_1, \ldots, a_n$ denote the assets whose risks are supposed to be addressed by pr_j; $cr(a_i) \in \{1, 2, 3\}$ represents criticality of asset a_i (or business process, or enterprise); $rf_o(a_i)$ denotes original risk factor (that is, before implementation of process or control) of asset a_i (or business process, or enterprise); and $rf_c(a_i)$ denotes current risk factor (at time t_c) of asset a_i (or business process, or enterprise). Values of criticality are assigned as follows: $cr(a_i) = 1$ if loss of asset a_i has limited adverse impact on the business of an enterprise; $cr(a_i) = 2$ if loss of a_i has serious adverse impact on enterprise business; and $cr(a_i) = 3$ if loss of a_i causes severe or catastrophic adverse impact on the business of an enterprise. The value of $^{rmit}\mu_{tc}(pr_j)$ for a process (or control) pr_j is computed by considering all assets (or business processes, or the entire enterprise) whose risks are supposed to be addressed by pr_j; this is obvious from the summation (Σ) used in Eq. (11).

It may be observed that the value of $rf_r(a_i)$ can be positive or negative depending on the relative values of $rf_o(a_i)$ and $rf_c(a_i)$. $rf_o(a_i)$ will be greater than $rf_c(a_i)$ if the implemented process (or control) is successful in mitigating the risk, leading to $rf_r(a_i)$ having positive value. $rf_r(a_i)$ will be zero if the process has failed to mitigate the corresponding risk. On the other hand, negative value of $rf_r(a_i)$ indicates that the implemented process (or control) has actually *increased* the risk; this is a cause for serious concern and should be corrected without delay.

Since, $cr(a_i) \in \{1, 2, 3\}$ and $-1 \leq rf_r(a_i) \leq 1$, the value of each product $cr(a_i) * rf_r(a_i)$ belongs to $[-3, 3]$. Hence, $-3 \leq {}^{rmit}\mu_{tc}(pr_j) \leq 3$.

Incident Metric - This measures the incidents that occur despite implementation of security processes. The reason could be either, a) improper/incomplete implementation, or b) non-implementation of relevant processes owing to lack of correct identification of security needs. Hence, these metrics can be classified as i) *Controlled* incident metrics, and ii) *Uncontrolled* incident metrics. An incident may cause breach of security and/or privacy parameters, physical loss of IT assets, financial loss, loss of image or reputation, or destruction of lives. Examples include buffer overflows, malware attacks, theft of assets etc. An incident may be classified as low-impact (causing limited adverse effect on enterprise business), medium-impact (serious adverse effect), or high-impact (severe or catastrophic adverse effect) [6]. Different enterprises may perceive criticality of impacts differently, depending on the significance of those impacts on their business processes. For example, while defense-sector organizations may consider loss of confidentiality to be of serious concern, the entire business of an e-commerce organization may revolve around maximizing information dissemination. In case of the latter, loss of availability of product information may have serious consequences.

Controlled Incident Metric - An enterprise should detect and record all information security-related incidents and quantify their impacts to business processes. All such incidents, which have occurred during a period of measurement, are grouped according to the corresponding security processes or controls (that had been implemented to prevent these incidents). The value of controlled incident metric, $^{cinc}\mu_{tp}(pr_j)$, for period of measurement t_p, for a process (or control) pr_j, can be computed as follows:

$$^{cinc}\mu_{tp}\left(pr_j\right) = \begin{cases} 3 - (\Sigma \, Imp(In_i) \, / \, n), & \text{if } n > 0 \\ 3, & \text{otherwise} \end{cases} \tag{12}$$

where, $Imp(In_i)$ denotes the impact of incident In_i

Here, $In_1, \ldots, In_n$ denote the relevant incidents that have occurred during measurement period t_p.

Values of impact of incidents are assigned as follows: $Imp(In_i) = 1$ for low-impact incidents; $Imp(In_i) = 2$ for medium-impact incidents; and $Imp(In_i) = 3$ if impact is high. Since, $Imp(In_i) \, \varepsilon \, \{1, 2, 3\}$, $0 \leq ^{cinc}\mu_{tp}(pr_j) \leq 3$. It may be noted from Eq. (12) that the value of the metric is obtained after subtracting it from 3. This has been done in order to maintain uniformity in interpretation of metrics; higher value of a metric indicates positive result, that is proper ISMS implementation, while lower value means the security processes and controls have not been implemented correctly.

Uncontrolled Incident Metric - This metric provides the impact value of all information security-related incidents for which no relevant processes or controls have been implemented. The value of uncontrolled incident metric, $^{uinc}\mu_{tp}$, for period of measurement t_p can be computed as follows:

$$^{uinc}\mu_{tp} = \begin{cases} \Sigma \, Imp(In_i) \, / \, n, & \text{if } n > 0 \\ 0, & \text{otherwise} \end{cases} \tag{13}$$

where, $Imp(In_i)$ denotes the impact of incident In_i

Here, $In_1, \ldots, In_n$ denote the *uncontrolled* incidents that have occurred during measurement period t_p. As in the case of controlled incident metric, $0 \leq ^{uinc}\mu_{tp} \leq 3$.

Process Effectiveness Metric - Risk mitigation metric and controlled incident metric can be combined to derive the effectiveness metric for an ISMS process or security control. For a measurement period t_p, the value of process effectiveness metric, $^{efct}\mu_{tp}(pr_j)$, for a process or control, pr_j, can be obtained as follows:

$$^{efct}\mu_{tp}\left(pr_j\right) = floor\left(\left(^{rmit}\mu_{tc}\left(pr_j\right) + {}^{cinc}\mu_{tp}\left(pr_j\right)\right)/2\right) \tag{14}$$

The *floor* function has been used in order to derive a conservative estimate of process effectiveness in case of floating point values. An enterprise should always strive to achieve greater security by continually improving its ISMS implementation. Hence, a conservative estimate will help to put things in perspective and spur the enterprise towards better security implementation.

From Eqs. (11), (12), and (14), it may be seen that $^{efct}\mu_{tp}(pr_j) \varepsilon \{-2, -1, 0, 1, 2, 3\}$.

Efficiency Metrics - This measures the ability of implemented security processes and controls to address security concerns efficiently. Each security concern can be assigned a weight based on its priority. Priority of a concern usually considers business objectives of an enterprise, along with security issues. A process or control is judged for efficiency based on the *amount* of security concerns it addresses. *Amount* means no. of security needs along with their relative weights. *Time* and *cost* are also factored in to consider the amount of time and resources (money, manpower and infrastructure) needed to address the corresponding concern, and implement the process or control, respectively. The value of efficiency metric, $^{effy}\mu_{tc}(pr_j)$, at time t_c, for a process (or control) pr_j, can be computed as follows:

$$^{effy}\mu_{tc}\left(pr_j\right) = floor\left(\left(\Sigma \ p(a_i) \ / \ \left(t_i\left(pr_j\right) * c_i\left(pr_j\right)\right)\right) / n\right) \qquad (15)$$

Here, $p(a_i)$ = priority of the security concern of asset a_i being addressed by pr_j; $t_i(pr_j)$ = time needed by pr_j to address the security concern of asset a_i; $c_i(pr_j)$ = cost of implementation of pr_j; and $a_1, \ldots, a_n$ denote the assets whose security concerns are supposed to be addressed by pr_j.

Priority of a concern $p(a_i)$ can be assigned on a 3-point scale $\{1, 2, 3\}$ based on its relative importance, with 3 signifying highest priority. In order to estimate cost of implementation and time elapsed to address the concern, thresholds can be defined. For example, an enterprise may define a time threshold and a cost threshold, t_o and c_o, for each security concern. $t_i(pr_j)$ can be determined as follows: $t_i(pr_j) = 3$ if the time that was needed to address the concern was greater than the threshold $(t_i(pr_j) > t_o)$; $t_i(pr_j) = 2$ if the time needed was equal to or just less than the threshold $(t_i(pr_j) \leq t_o)$; and $t_i(pr_j) = 1$ if the time needed to address the concern was very less as compared to the threshold $(t_i(pr_j) \ll t_o)$. It may be noted that at any point in time only those cases are considered in computing $^{effy}\mu_{tc}(pr_j)$ where either the security concern has been addressed, or the threshold t_o has already been exceeded. The value of $c_i(pr_j)$ can be assigned similarly on a 3-point scale.

From the above discussion, it can be seen that $^{effy}\mu_{tc}(pr_j) \varepsilon \{0, 1, 2, 3\}$.

6   Mapping ISMS Metrics to Stakeholder Concerns

In this section, the proposed ISMS metrics are mapped to the security and privacy concerns of stakeholders.

Security of Business Processes and Information Assets – Since risk is the measure of insecurity with respect to the security and privacy parameters of assets, the value of *risk metric* can be used to provide appropriate information regarding this concern.

Safety of Client Data – Since this concern is addressed by ensuring the protection of C, I, A, anonymity, unlinkability and undetectability, the value of *risk metric* can provide proper idea regarding the safety of client data. Besides, enterprise policies ensure protection of assets. Hence, *policy compliance metric* will serve to provide assurance regarding relevant policies for the protection of client data.

Safety of Personal Data and Assets – This is similar to the previous case. Here, too, *risk metric* and *policy compliance metric* provide appropriate information.

Reputation of Enterprise – Since this is related to the image/reputation of an enterprise, the values of compliance metrics can be used to judge the same. Specifically, *legal/regulatory compliance metric* and *contractual compliance metric* will reflect on the reputation of the enterprise. The enterprise will also be judged on the presence/absence of incidents. Hence, *controlled incident metric* and *uncontrolled incident metric* are also important for this concern. Finally, the absence of risk within enterprise assets can serve to enhance its reputation; thus, *risk metric* is also significant here.

Efficacy of the Implemented ISMS – The efficacy of implemented ISMS can be understood by computing its efficiency and ascertaining the amount of risk that has been mitigated, and the reduction in the number of security/privacy incidents. Hence, the metrics that are important are *risk mitigation metric, controlled incident metric, uncontrolled incident metric, process effectiveness metric,* and *efficiency metric*. Uncontrolled incident metric has been considered here as absence of controls, either deliberately or due to oversight, is an inherent feature of the implemented ISMS.

Accountability for Others' Misdeeds – This pertains to operational personnel and third parties and concerns the parameters accountability, non-repudiation and image/reputation. Hence, the metrics that can provide useful insight are *risk metric* (to understand the protection mechanisms implemented), *non-repudiation metric, policy compliance metric* (to understand relevant enterprise policies), *legal/regulatory compliance metric* (to understand the legal protection angle for this concern), *contractual compliance metric* (in case of third parties) and *composite compliance metric*.

Legal Protection of Consumer Rights – Since this concerns legal protection, *legal/regulatory compliance metric* and *contractual compliance metric* are relevant here.

Protection of Legal and Contractual Obligations – Since these concern the legal and contractual obligations pertaining to third parties, *legal/regulatory compliance metric* and *contractual compliance metric* are relevant here.

Security of Nation – As discussed earlier, this addresses the protection of integrity and availability of national assets, and accountability and legal and contractual obligations of the nation. Hence, the metrics that can shed light here are *risk metric* (to know the status of integrity and availability of national assets); *controlled incident metric* and *uncontrolled incident metric* (to know whether incidents pertaining to national security have occurred); *legal/regulatory compliance metric* and *contractual compliance metric*.

Reputation of Nation – This concern needs metrics like in the previous case, that is *risk metric, controlled incident metric, uncontrolled incident metric, legal/regulatory compliance metric* and *contractual compliance metric*.

Compliance – All compliance metrics are relevant for this security concern, that is *policy compliance metric, legal/regulatory compliance metric, contractual compliance metric* and *composite compliance metric*.

Thus, the proposed metrics have been mapped to the identified security and privacy concerns of stakeholders. This is summarized in Table 1 (columns 2 and 4). This will provide assurance to the stakeholders of an enterprise regarding their specific concerns, and allow them to make informed decisions pertaining to their future course of actions.

7 Conclusion and Future Work

In this paper, the different categories of stakeholders of an enterprise have been identified. It has been shown that the stakeholders have separate security and privacy concerns as their job functions, responsibilities and expectations are different. The concerns, in essence, translate to requirements for the protection of specific security and privacy parameters of assets. These requirements are addressed by establishing ISMS within the enterprise. The paper has described how the identified concerns can be translated to such protection requirements; this will help an enterprise to design and implement an ISMS that caters to the requirements of all its stakeholders.

In order to assure stakeholders regarding the efficacy of the established ISMS, and status of protection of the security and privacy of their assets, it is essential to continually generate and convey relevant metrics. The paper has defined a set of comprehensive metrics for ISMS that address the requirements of ISO/IEC 27001 standard [3]. The metrics have been designed so that they correspond to the concerns of stakeholders and they can obtain assurance regarding their protection needs.

Future work is geared towards the design of algorithms corresponding to the metrics defined in this paper. A tool can be developed that generates attacks (for example, using attack graph methodology) and utilizes these algorithms to generate corresponding metrics for an enterprise ISMS.

References

1. The International Organization for Standardization, The International Electrotechnical Commission: ISO/IEC 27005, Information technology – Security techniques – Information security risk management. 3rd edn. ISO/IEC, Switzerland (2018)
2. Santos, J.C.S., Tarrit, K., Mirakhorli, M.: A catalog of security architecture weaknesses. In: Proceedings of 2017 IEEE International Conference on Software Architecture Workshops (ICSAW), pp. 220–223. IEEE (2017)
3. The International Organization for Standardization, The International Electrotechnical Commission: ISO/IEC 27001, Information technology – Security techniques – Information security management systems - Requirements. 2nd edn. ISO/IEC, Switzerland (2013)
4. The International Organization for Standardization, The International Electrotechnical Commission: ISO/IEC 27004, Information technology – Security techniques - Information security management - Monitoring, measurement, analysis and evaluation. 2nd edn. ISO/IEC, Switzerland (2016)
5. National Institute of Standards and Technology: NIST SP 800-55, Performance Measurement Guide for Information Security. 1st rev. NIST, USA (2008)
6. National Institute of Standards and Technology: NIST SP 800-53, Security and Privacy Controls for Federal Information Systems and Organizations. 4th rev. NIST, USA (2013)
7. Chen, H., Cho, J-H., Xu, S.: Quantifying the security effectiveness of firewalls and DMZs. In: Proceedings of Fifth Annual Symposium and Bootcamp on Hot Topics in the Science of Security (HoTSoS), pp. 1–11. ACM (2018)

8. Ulvila, J.W., GaffneyJr., J.E.: Evaluation of intrusion detection systems. J. Res. Nat. Inst. Stan. Technol. **108**(6), 453–473 (2003)
9. Scala, N., Reilly, A., Goethals, P., Cukier, M.: Risk and the five hard problems of cybersecurity. Risk Anal. **39**(10), 2119–2126 (2019)
10. Pendleton, M., Garcia-Lebron, R., Cho, J-H., Xu, S.: A survey on systems security metrics. ACM Comput. Surv. **49**(4), 62:1–35:1 (2017)
11. Tupper, M., Zincir-Heywood, A.N.: VEA-bility security metric: a network security analysis tool. In: Proceedings of Third International Conference on Availability, Reliability and Security (ARES 2008), pp. 950–957. IEEE (2008)
12. Patriciu, V.-V., Priescu, I., Nicolaescu, S.: Security metrics for enterprise information systems. J. Appl. Quant. Methods **1**(2), 151–159 (2006)
13. Foroughi, F.: Information security risk assessment by using Bayesian learning technique. In: Lecture Notes in Engineering and Computer Science, vol. 2170, no. (1), pp. 91–95 (2008)
14. Gao, G., Li, X.-Y., Zhang, B.-J., Xiao, W.: Information security risk assessment based on information measure and fuzzy clustering. J. Softw. **6**(11), 2159–2166 (2011)
15. Johnson, G.: Measuring ISO 27001 ISMS Processes. Neupart Information Security Management (2014). https://cdn2.hubspot.net/hubfs/163742/pdf_files/iso27001isms-kpi.pdf?t=1438891985360. Accessed 12 June 2021
16. Aldya, A.P., Sutikno, S., Rosmansyah, Y.: Measuring effectiveness of control of information security management system based on SNI ISO/IEC 27004: 2013 standard. IOP Conf. Ser. Mater. Sci. Eng. **550**, 1–11 (2019)
17. Monev, V.: Organisational information security maturity assessment based on ISO 27001 and ISO 27002. In: Proceedings of 2020 International Conference on Information Technologies (InfoTech), pp. 1–5. IEEE (2020)
18. Mödinger, M.: Metrics and key performance indicators for information security reports of universities. Master's thesis, Hochschule Augsburg University of Applied Sciences, Welden (2019)
19. The International Organization for Standardization, The International Electrotechnical Commission: ISO/IEC 27002:2013, Information technology – Security techniques - Code of practice for information security controls. 2nd edn. ISO/IEC, Switzerland (2013)
20. Pfitzmann, A., Hansen, M.: A terminology for talking about privacy by data minimization: anonymity, unlinkability, undetectability, unobservability, pseudonymity, and identity management (2010). https://dud.inf.tu-dresden.de/literatur/Anon_Terminology_v0.34.pdf. Accessed 10 Oct 2021

A Novel Approach for Attack Tree to Attack Graph Transformation

Nathan Daniel Schiele$^{(\boxtimes)}$ and Olga Gadyatskaya

Leiden Institute of Advanced Computer Science, Leiden University,
Leiden, The Netherlands
{n.d.schiele,o.gadyatskaya}@liacs.liedenuniv.nl

Abstract. Attack trees and attack graphs are both common graphical threat models used by organizations to better understand possible cyber-security threats. These models have been primarily seen as separate entities, to be used and researched in entirely different contexts, but recently there has emerged a new interest in combining the strengths of these models and in transforming models from one notation into the other. The existing works in this area focus on transforming attack graphs into attack trees. In this paper, we propose an approach to transform attack trees into attack graphs based on the fundamental understanding of how actions are represented in both structures. From this, we hope to enable more versatility in both structures.

Keywords: Graphical attack models · Attack trees · Attack graphs

1   Introduction

Attack trees are a common and useful tool for threat modeling. They allow us to present attack components in a graphical structure that is relatively easily explained and understood. Each node in an attack tree represents a action, and its children represent actions in service to their parent action. The relationship between the children of a node describe the relationship between the components, OR, AND and SAND, describing if all components or only one component need to be completed, and in which order. The major advantage of this model is its compactness, allowing for even complex threats to be modeled concisely. Attack trees are also usually more general: they model attacks applicable not to one specific system, but to a category of systems. However, attack trees have several downsides, particularly when understanding how the attacker interacts with the system. For instance, it is not immediately evident from an attack tree what is a possible plan of a successful attack.

An alternative modeling structure, which addresses these downsides, are *attack graphs* [21]. Attack graphs represent all possible states a system may hold, and the security-relevant transitions between those states. The major disadvantage of attack graphs is their size, with even small system models resulting in excessively large attack graphs [22].

B. Luo et al. (Eds.): CRiSIS 2021, LNCS 13204, pp. 74–90, 2022.
https://doi.org/10.1007/978-3-031-02067-4_5

Attack graphs are not as common in the security industry as the succinct nature of attack trees makes them more appealing to human experts. Additionally, attack graphs are arguably less intuitive, inhibiting their adoption and use by non-technical security experts [6].

However, attack graphs and attack trees represent similar information, and both are valid approaches for modeling potential attack vectors. Additionally, for both attack graphs and attack trees, there is a major consideration of how these models are to be generated, with automated generation at the forefront of current threat model research [1,10,23].

These two threat models each have their disadvantages, and these disadvantages are seemingly are easier to offset by using the other model. It would be useful to have a way to transform one model into the other, and thus be able to combine their perspectives. However, to the best of our knowledge, there is currently no well-defined transformation between these two models. There have been works proposing converting an attack graph into an attack tree [5,8,17]. Yet, to date, there has been little work into transforming an attack tree into an attack graph. This is the problem that we address in the present paper.

2 Related Work

Attack trees (ATs) have been fairly widely studied to date. First introduced by Schneier in 1999 as an efficient and effective means of conveying attack information [20]; several researchers have worked to develop the threat model further. Mauw and Oostdijk developed propositional and multiset semantics for attack trees [14]. Jhawar *et al.* developed a refinement of the sibling relationships, adding a Sequential AND or "SAND" relation, alongside discussing the utility and semantic implications (the SP graph semantics) of such a refinement [9]. Many works have attempted to generate attack trees automatically, given that many attack trees in industry are generated manually, and effective automatic attack tree generation would be a valuable contribution to this space [8,23].

Attack graphs (AGs) similarly have been widely studied. Sheyner *et al.* laid out a formal, syntactic structure of a state-based attack graph and proposed a model checking method to generate attack graphs [21]. Noel and Jajodia focused on using topological aggregation to manage the complexity of attack graphs [15]. Ou *et al.* described a more scalable methodology for generating attack graphs from a logical model [16]. In a broad review of previous works on attack graphs, Lippmann and Ingols found that scalability was the biggest limiting factor in the overall use of attack graphs, with attack graphs quickly becoming too large to be useful [13]. Other problems with attack graphs according to [13] include prescribing meaning to the states within the attack graph structure and the usability of attack graphs as a communication tool; given their size and complexity, attack graphs can be hard to use in industry, as developing recommendations from attack graphs is often too difficult. The primary recommendation in [13] was that future work on attack graphs would need to pay special attention to scalability.

An important topic in the attack graph literature is the meaning behind attack graph nodes. They most frequently represent the states of the associated system after some actions are taken. However, as Lallie *et al.* points out, attack graphs in literature suffer from inconsistency, and state definitions and labelling schema are not above these inconsistencies [12]. In our review of the literature, we have found much of the literature can be broadly classified into two categories in the context of the meaning or labeling of attack graph states, those that use logical conditions roughly based on state as in [16], or those that derive state meaning from some underlying system as in [17]. We take our cues from the literature in that final group, our states will be defined based on a set of actions defined from a system model. We note that other types of attach graphs assign different meaning to states, e.g., vulnerabilities or system hosts [10].

There have been some works on conversion between AGs and ATs, with the research largely focused on the conversion from attack graphs to attack trees.

$AG \rightarrow AT$. Pinchinat *et al.*, focused on generating attack trees from attack graphs using the ATSyRA approach [17,18]. We are attempting the reverse transformation, and a similar designed library based methodology also from Pinchinat *et al.* of these transformation give us insight into how such transformations can function [17].

Dawkins and Hale, focused on an analysis of network models, and in that analysis described a method of creating attack chains representing complete or near complete attack vectors [2]. These attack chains could then be used to construct attack trees. The primary purpose of the work was not to develop a transformation between attack graphs and attack trees, and thus the transition is not fully developed [2]. Most recently, Haque and Atkinson have overviewed existing approaches to generate attack graphs and attack trees, and to convert attack graphs into attack trees, and have found that those works have suffered from inefficiency or inaccuracy [6].

Hong *et al.* report that previous attempts to define a transformation from attack graphs to attack trees have failed due to the exponential size increases of attack graphs [8]. The state explosion problem broadly affects any state based modeling system, of which attack graphs are one; or better put by Valmari, "the number of states of almost any system of interest is huge". The biggest issue with the state explosion problem is the computational complexity, as the number of states in a system increases exponentially, the difficulty of handling this information becomes far more complex, as well as time and space inefficient. A major concern for any attack graph generation scheme will be handling the exponential number of states [16], and given a transformation from attack trees to attack graphs is a form of attack graph generation in itself, addressing the state explosion problem will be a major concern for us as well.

$AT \rightarrow AG$. To the best of our knowledge, there have been no works on transforming attack trees into attack graphs. The reason for this gap could be that attack trees are more succinct threat models, not suffering from the state explosion problem, and are thus more handy for security analysis with human experts [2].

However, creating a transformation into attack trees opens up new interesting research directions, for example, new approaches to automatically generate attack graphs starting from automatically generated attack trees, or using existing, human-designed attack trees to capture security issues in relevant systems with application of the attack graph-based security monitoring.

Finally, attack trees and attack graphs have been very popular graphical security notations in the last 20 years, being featured in many research papers. We refer the interested reader to several surveys for more details about these notations and their applications: on attack trees [23] and on attack graphs [1,3,24], and on both attack trees and attack graphs, possibly among other graphical security models [7,11,12].

3   Definitions

While many formal definitions of both attack trees (ATs) and attack graphs (AGs) exist, we will start from the following definitions. These definitions were selected because they share common properties with many modifications of both attack trees and attack graphs, and thus should enable modification of the algorithms described below to enable further development of this methodology. Specifically, we use a recursive attack tree definition à la Gadyatskaya *et al.* [4], and a basic state-based attack graph definition from Sheyner *et al.* [21].

Definition 1 (Attack Tree). *Let $\mathbb{B}$ denote a set of actions, OR and AND be two unranked associate and commutative operators that are disjunctive and conjunctive respectively, and SAND be an unranked associate but non-commutative conjunctive operator. An attack tree t is an expression over $\mathbb{B} \cup \{OR, AND, SAND\}$ generated by the following formal grammar (for $b \in \mathbb{B}$):*

$$t ::= b \mid b \lhd OR(t, \ldots, t) \mid b \lhd AND(t, \ldots, t) \mid b \lhd SAND(t, \ldots, t)$$

This definition is recursive, as each subtree is a complete attack tree in and of itself. A single action b by itself is an attack tree, and this fact will later be used to help develop our mapping schema in Sect. 5.

Definition 2 (Attack Graph). *An attack graph or AG is a tuple (S, f, S_0, S_s), where S is a set of states, $f : S \times \mathbb{B} \to S$ is a partial function that defines the transition relation for S by the set of actions $\mathbb{B}$, $S_0 \subseteq S$ is a set of initial states and $S_s \subseteq S$ is a set of success states.*

This definition of attack graphs is the same proposed by Pinchinat *et al.* [17], who defined an attack graph to attack tree transformation, the inverse of what we propose. The $\mathbb{B}$ is a set of actions based in the system model the attack graph is built around. Ultimately, the contents of $\mathbb{B}$ will be wholly defined by such a system model. By convention, we define partial function with a set of mappings, given in the set F. Expanding upon Definition 1, we can define two further functions that will be useful in the transformation algorithm. Both of these functions are inspired by the work of Gadyatskaya *et al.* [4] and focus on isolating specific elements of attack trees.

Definition 3 (Top Function). *This function obtains the action of the root node as follows (for $\Delta \in \{OR, AND, SAND\}$):*

$$top(b) = top(b \lhd \Delta(t_1, \ldots, t_n)) = b$$

We call an attack tree of depth one a *radical*. The auxiliary function *rad* defined below obtains a single transition (radical) from one level of an attack tree to another.

Definition 4 (Rad Function).

The rad function finds the uppermost radical of a provided tree as input as follows (for $\Delta \in \{OR, AND, SAND\}$):

$$rad(t) = rad(b \lhd \Delta(t_1, \ldots, t_n)) = b \lhd \Delta(top(t_1), \ldots, top(t_n))$$

The previous definition introduces the idea of radical elements of attack trees. The intuition behind these radicals is that a *radical* in an attack tree is the smallest possible subtree. It is a component consisting solely of a root node, an operator and a set of children that are singular nodes themselves. Our attack graph transformation will use radicals as base components. As outlined in the definition above, a radical is found by using the *rad* function. The child nodes in a radical can themselves be root nodes of different radicals, and these radicals are likewise found by using the *rad* function on those child nodes.

Definition 5 (Kid Function).

The kid function returns the set of children of a radical:

$$kid(t) = kid(b \lhd \Delta(t_1, \ldots, t_n)) = \{top(t_1), \ldots, top(t_n)\}$$

Fundamentally, our transformation approach will take the form of defining the separate radicals, creating a mapped transformation of those radicals from an attack tree to attack graph, and then combining the radicals that are in the attack graph in a manner that retains the attack component information expressed in attack trees.

Zero and Single Element Radicals. The radicals described thus far are of size n; they are dynamically defined such that any number of children in the radical can be directly mapped from attack trees to attack graphs. The implication is that $n \geqslant 2$, however this is not necessary. There are two edge cases that are worth mentioning, when $n = 0$ and when $n = 1$. When $n = 0$, we have the case of a radical without children; this is the case of $rad(b) = b$. Additionally, we have a graphical example of this single action mapping in Fig. 3.

When $n = 1$, this would fit our definition of a radical, as there would be a defined root, operator and set of children with cardinality 1. However, our three defined radicals all converge when $n = 1$. This follows from our understanding of these operators. The difference between AND and SAND being that SAND is an ordered AND; when $n = 1$, there is only one possible order, thus AND and SAND are equivalent. For similar reasons, OR is also the same as both AND and SAND.

We introduce these edge cases for the sake of completeness of our approach. However, single element radicals are rare in real-world attack trees as their children nodes are often considered redundant and removed from the tree.

4   Transformation Example

We begin with a simple example of an attack tree as seen in Fig. 1. The overall
goal is to get root access of a system. Directly below the overall root, we see
two sub goals in an OR relationship; if any sub-goal, either exploiting a buffer
overflow or exploiting an administrator, is accomplished, then the overall goal
of getting root access will be accomplished. With exploiting the buffer overflow,
we can see that there are two attack components, again in an OR relationship.
Once again, if either component is completed, then the sub-goal is accomplished
and by extension the overall goal is accomplished. With exploiting the administrator, we see two attack components in an AND relationship, meaning that both
components will need to be accomplished to accomplish the sub-goal. One of
these components has subcomponents in a SAND relationship, which need to be
accomplished in a particular order before the parent action can be completed.

In the provided example, the order of subcomponents for exploiting the
administrator is not important. There are AND relationships where the order
of components is important or where the components specifically need to occur
in parallel [9]; however, we are limiting our understanding of AND relationships
to be unordered AND relationships, i.e., the attacker can execute actions in any
order to successfully achieve the goal. The SAND component of the attack tree
is an ordered AND, where a defined order is provided. The elements in the SAND
relationship occur in the same order (first the administrator phone number needs
to be obtained, then the administrator can be invited somewhere).

In Fig. 2, we see an attack graph representation of the same information. First,
we see that the nodes of the AT have now become the state transitions in the AG.
We start from an initial state, with the only description of this state being that
no attack component has been applied yet. The initial attack vectors (transitions
outgoing from the initial state) are the basic components in the AT (the leaf nodes).
We see some basic structures that will enable us to generalize the transformation
procedure. Namely, we see that the components in an OR relationship ("Remote
login" and "Deploy .rhhost file") create fairly parallel paths through the attack
graph. Additionally, for the AND relationship ("Invent need for root access" and
"Befriend Administrator"), we see a type of a lattice structure, where transitions
between states occur internally within the AND components before returning to an
overall path. The generalization of these rules is introduced in the following section.

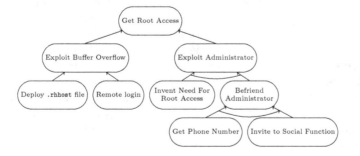

Fig. 1. A simple attack tree

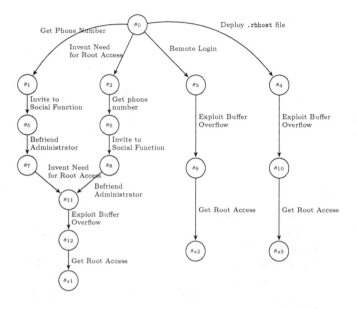

Fig. 2. An attack graph representation of the model in Fig. 1

5   Mapping

Fundamentally, nodes in attack trees represent actions, while nodes in attack graphs represent system states. The edges in an attack tree represent the relationships between actions, while the edges in attack graphs represent state transitions. Our intuition is that state transitions and actions are equivalent concepts, and as such, we will base our transformation on this equivalence. We now present our transformation approach for radicals.

We create a distinction of P and Q states, where P states are already in the attack graph due to the previous transformation steps, while Q states are generated by a specific transformation of a single radical.

5.1   Edge Cases

Single Node. To begin, let us consider an AT with a single action or node, and see what this extreme case would be in the form of an attack graph.

From Fig. 3, we can see that the attack tree of a single action is very simple, it is merely a single node named after the action. In the attack graph, we represent this in the form of a state transition, otherwise referred to as an edge. Let us now define the transformation as a complete attack graph.

In the case of the single node AT in Fig. 3, the defined state transition goes between two P states. These P are assumed to already exist in the AG. Following from Definition 2, the complete form of this attack graph is given in Eq. 1:

(a) Attack Tree   (b) Attack Graph

Fig. 3. Single action attack tree and attack graph

$$P = \{s_0, s_s\}$$
$$Q = \varnothing$$
$$F = \{(s_0, \text{Action}) \mapsto s_s\} \tag{1}$$
$$AG = (P \cup Q, f : F, \{s_0\}, \{s_s\})$$

Where the only two states, s_0 and s_s are the initial and final states respectively, and the action is the defined state transition between them.

Radical with One Child. From Fig. 4, we see a similar structure in the attack graph as in Fig. 3. Both actions in the attack tree are directly mapped to state transitions in the attack graph. However, unlike in Fig. 3, we now have two edges, and thus we will require a third node in the attack graph. These two edges necessitate the creation of an intermediate state. The meaning behind this state is it is the resulting state after the completion of "Action 2" but before the completion of "Action 1". This is our first encounter with Q states. As in Eq. 1, we have the same starting P states, but a Q state is also added as the generated intermediate state for this mapping. The Q state was not already in the attack graph. The resulting attack graph would be of the form:

$$P = \{s_0, s_s\}$$
$$Q = \{s_1\}$$
$$F = \{(s_0, \text{Action 2}) \mapsto s_1, (s_1, \text{Action 1}) \mapsto s_s\} \tag{2}$$
$$AG = (P \cup Q, f : F, \{s_0\}, \{s_s\})$$

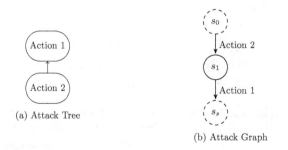

(a) Attack Tree

(b) Attack Graph

Fig. 4. Single child attack tree and attack graph

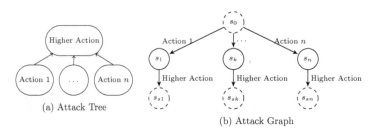

Fig. 5. OR radical

We can begin to develop an intuition regarding how our transformation will be structured. Namely, nodes in attack trees will be directly mapped to edges (the state transitions) in attack graphs, and states will be created to enable such state transitions to exist. The states are given meaning by where they fall in the transition relation partial function. The only remaining concept that requires mapping is the operators (AND, SAND, and OR) in attack trees. Once the operator mapping is defined, we will have the means to create a transformation algorithm from attack trees to attack graphs.

5.2   OR Radical

Our understanding of the OR radical in attack trees is that only a single component (child action) of an OR radical needs to be completed for the goal, or root, of the OR to also be accomplished. In an attack graph where individual attack vectors are expressed more explicitly, we would expect that each individual OR component would contribute to a separate attack vector. These separate attack vectors will introduce separate states in the attack graph, as each attack component is a different state transition, and different state transitions result in different states.

By convention, we organize separate the transition of different levels of the attack graph into separate F sets and combine them for the final definition of the partial function transition relation f. Transforming the OR radical as an attack graph, we will generate the following graph:

$$
\begin{aligned}
P &= \{s_0, s_{s1}, \ldots, s_{sn}\} \\
Q &= \{s_1, \ldots, s_n\} \\
F_1 &= \{(s_0, \text{Action } 1) \mapsto s_1, \ldots, (s_0, \text{Action } n) \mapsto s_n\} \\
F_2 &= \{(s_1, \text{Higher Action}) \mapsto s_{s1}, \ldots, (s_0, \text{Higher Action}) \mapsto s_{sn}\} \\
AG &= (P \cup Q, f : F_1 \cup F_2, \{s_0\}, \{s_{s1}, \ldots, s_{sn}\})
\end{aligned}
\tag{3}
$$

As we can see in Figs. 5a and 5b, and subsequently in Eq. 3, the OR radical in an attack graph is a series of disjoint "legs" with a state transition culminating in a state for each attack component represented in the attack tree. As each attack component is unique, the system states that are a result of the application of those attack components must also be unique. This does not rule out the possibility of the application of unique attack components resulting in the same state; that would be a possible expansion of the radical mapping we have laid out here. Given that the "Higher Action" in this radical could itself be a component in another radical, we see that the "Higher Action" in the attack tree radical is again represented as a state transition in the attack graph.

Given that the Actions 1 through n in Fig. 5b are distinct state transitions, we expect that the resulting states are different. The subgraph below the OR radical is thus duplicated for each element in the OR radical. If the only remainder of the graph below the OR radical was a final state then there would be a separate final state for each element in the OR radical. If we consider the transition relation f and the example of Fig. 5b, we operate under the expectation $f(s_1, \text{Action } 1) \neq f(s_n, \text{Action } 1)$; our expectation is the output of these functions are entirely different states in AG. This does not preclude the possibility of the output of different f inputs resulting in the same state, merely that we expect that with different state inputs, the output states would thus be different. Intuitively, if the same action is applied to two different states, the resulting state would be different.

5.3   AND Radical

In contrast to the OR operator, the AND operator represents that all actions in the AND needing to be performed for the AND to be completed. However, unlike the SAND operator, there is no defined order to the actions in an AND. Thus, the attack graph must represent all possible combinations of action orders for the actions within a single AND operator.

Consider the AND radical in Fig. 6a. Transforming it into an attack graph, we would obtain the following graph (we continue with the F convention presented in Eq. 3):

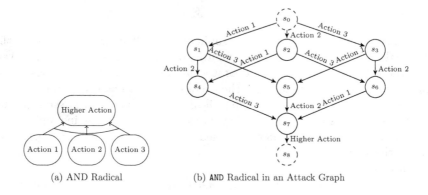

(a) AND Radical   (b) AND Radical in an Attack Graph

Fig. 6. AND radical

$$P = \{s_0, s_n\}$$
$$Q = \{s_1, \ldots, s_7\}$$
$$F_1 = \{(s_0, \text{Action 1}) \mapsto s_1, (s_0, \text{Action 2}) \mapsto s_2, (s_0, \text{Action 3}) \mapsto s_3\}$$
$$F_2 = \{(s_1, \text{Action 2}) \mapsto s_4, (s_1, \text{Action 3}) \mapsto s_5, (s_2, \text{Action 1}) \mapsto s_4,$$
$$(s_2, \text{Action 3}) \mapsto s_6, (s_3, \text{Action 1}) \mapsto s_5, (s_3, \text{Action 2}) \mapsto s_6\} \quad (4)$$
$$F_3 = \{(s_4, \text{Action 3}) \mapsto s_7, (s_5, \text{Action 2}) \mapsto s_7, (s_6, \text{Action 1}) \mapsto s_7\}$$
$$F_4 = \{(s_7, \text{Higher Action}) \mapsto s_s\}$$
$$AG = (P \cup Q, f : F_1 \cup F_2 \cup F_3 \cup F_4, \{s_0\}, \{s_s\})$$

As we can see in Fig. 6b and subsequently in Eq. 4, the AND radical in an attack graph creates a lattice structure such that intermediate states represent the application of some combination of different elements in an AND operator.

Generally speaking, on the ith row of the lattice, we see the application of i distinct state transitions. In the first row, every state is the result of a single state transition. On the second, every state is the result of two state transitions. On the nth row, every state is the application of n state transitions. We can find the number of states in a row k by calculating the number of unique unordered grouping of k state transitions with n possible state transitions, this is simply $\binom{n}{k}$. In the final row of the lattice, we have $\binom{n}{n}$ states, and thus we only have a single state. This follows from our understanding of the meaning of these states, as this state is the application of all the different actions in the AND radical. There is only one possible, unordered, way to apply all the actions in the AND radical, and this is the final resulting state. From this state, we apply the "Higher Action", but as this is only applied to a single state at the end of the lattice, we only have a single final state from this radical.

In Fig. 6b, we see an AND radical with $n = 3$, a so-called 3−AND. For the lack of space, generalization of the AND is provided in an extended version of this paper [19]. It is worthwhile to note that an n−AND will have $2^n - 1$ unique states.

5.4   SAND Radical

The SAND, or Sequential AND, radical is similar to the AND in that all actions in the SAND need to be completed for the operator to evaluate as successful. However, unlike the AND operator, the SAND operator has a specified order. Actions in the SAND need to occur sequentially for the overall radical to be successful.

As we can see in Fig. 7b, the SAND radical is by far the simplest structure we have developed thus far. Like the other radicals, the overall starting and ending states are P states. As the order is defined, the actions are chained together in order, with the intermediate states representing the state of the system after the application of some of the actions.

In the SAND radical, actions are applied sequentially. As such, in the attack graph state transitions are also applied sequentially. This results in n overall states (one state for each of n actions). For the tree shown in Fig. 7a we thus define the following AG:

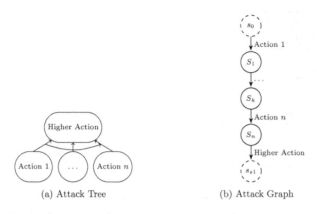

(a) Attack Tree   (b) Attack Graph

Fig. 7. SAND radical

$$P = \{s_0, s_s\}$$
$$Q = \{s_1, \ldots, s_n\}$$
$$F_1 = \{(s_0, \text{Action 1}) \mapsto s_1\}$$

   (5)

$$F_n = \{(s_{n-1}, \text{Action n}) \mapsto s_n\}$$
$$F_{n+1} = \{(s_n, \text{Higher Action}) \mapsto s_s\}$$
$$AG = (P \cup Q, f : F_1 \cup \ldots \cup F_{n+1}, \{s_0\}, \{s_s\})$$

6 Algorithm

The algorithm is effectively divided in two parts: analysis of the attack tree, and sequential construction of the attack graph. In the first portion of the algorithm, we find all the radicals present in the attack tree and store them in a radical dictionary. This radical dictionary, denoted as *RD* represents a deconstructed attack tree, where all elements of the original attack tree are stored separately as radicals. Once all the radicals in the attack tree are found and stored into the radical dictionary, the attack graph can be systematically constructed. This part is presented in Algorithm 1.

The algorithm starts with an attack graph containing two states, s_0 and s_s, the single starting and success states respectively. These two states are our initial *P* states. There is a single edge between these two states, which is defined as equivalent to the overall root of the attack tree. Intuitively, the meaning behind this simple 2-state attack graph is that accomplishing the overall goal represented by an attack tree (the root), we move from an initial state to a success state. Now, by expanding the edge between s_0 and s_s in the initial attack graph, we can add the detailed information of the subcomponents of the overall goal to the attack

---

Algorithm 1. AT → AG Transformation

Require: Attack Tree, AT
Require: Radical Dictionary, RD
  for $b \in \mathbb{B}$ **do**
    $r \leftarrow rad(b)$
    if $|kid(r)| \geqslant 0$ **then**
      Add $top(r) : r$ to RD
  Create Attack Graph, $AG = (\{s_0, s_s\}, f : \{(s_0, top(AT)) \mapsto s_s)\}, \{s_0\}, \{s_s\})$
  while $|RD| > 0$ **do**
    for $e \in AG.F$ **do**
      if e in Key Set of RD **then**
        $r \leftarrow RD(e)$
        Add Radical to Attack Graph(r, AG)
        Remove r from AG
  Assign values to states in attack graph
  return Attack Graph

Procedure 2. Add Radical to Attack Graph

Require: Attack Tree Radical: $t = b \lhd \Delta(c_1, \ldots, c_n), rad(t) = t$
Require: Attack Graph: $AG = (S, f : F, S_0, S_s)$
  Remove $(s_j, b) \mapsto s_k$ from F
  $AG_k \leftarrow$ the subgraph where $s_k \in AG_k.S_0$
  if $\Delta = $ OR **then**
    Remove AG_k from AG
    for c_i in $kid(t)$ **do**
      $AG_{k+i} \leftarrow AG_k$
      Add s_{j+i} to Q and $(s_j, c_i) \mapsto s_{j+i}$ to F
      Add s_{j+n+i} to Q and $(s_j, c_i) \mapsto s_{j+n+i}$ to F
      Add $AG_{k+i}.S$ to Q and $AG_{k+i}.F$ to F
      Add $(s_{j+n+i}, c_k) \mapsto s_{k+i}$, where $s_{k+i} \in AG_{k+i}.S_0$ to F
  else if $\Delta = $ AND **then**
    Create subgraph $AG_k = (Q, f : F_k, \varnothing, \varnothing)$
    $Q \leftarrow \{s_1, \ldots, s_n, s_{n+1}, \ldots, s_{2^n-1}\}$
    $F_1 \leftarrow \{(s_1, c_2) \mapsto s_{n+1}, \ldots, (s_n, c_{n-1}) \mapsto s_{\binom{n}{2}}, (s_2, c_1) \mapsto s_{n+1} \ldots, (s_n, c_n) \mapsto s_{\binom{n}{2}-1}\}$
    $\ldots$
    $F_{n-1} \leftarrow \{(s_{2^n-(n+2)}, c_n) \mapsto s_{2^n-1}, \ldots, (s_{2^n-2}, c_1) \mapsto s_{2^n-1}\}$
    $F_k \leftarrow F_1 \cup \ldots \cup F_n$
    Add F_k to F
    Add $\{(s_j, c_1) \mapsto AG_k.s_1, \ldots, (s_j, c_n) \mapsto AG_k.s_n\}$ to F
    Add $(AG_k.s_{2^n-1}, b) \mapsto s_k$ to F
  else if $\Delta = $ SAND **then**
    for c_i in $kid(t)$ **do**
      Add s_{j+i} to Q and $(s_{j+i-1}, c_i) \mapsto s_{j+i}$ to F
    Add $(s_{j+n}, b) \mapsto s_k)$ to F
  $P \leftarrow P \cup Q$
  $Q \leftarrow \{\}$

---

graph. While processing the attack tree components in the radical dictionary, we add additional states and state transformations to the attack graph, until our attack graph fully represents the original attack tree.

The sequential construction of the attack tree follows from this intuition. We check the edges in the attack graph to see if they are a key for a radical in the radical dictionary. Once we find an edge that is a key to a radical in the radical dictionary, we remove this edge from the attack graph, and replace it with the relevant defined mapping from Sect. 5. The procedure of adding a radical to the attack graph is presented in Procedure 2. This expansion will cause new Q states to be generated, which will then become P states for other radicals. Additionally, these mappings will cause the keys to other elements of the radical dictionary to be added to the attack graph, which subsequently allow for the addition of every radical in the radical dictionary to be added to the attack graph. After a radical is added to the attack graph, it is removed from the radical dictionary. Once the radical dictionary is empty, all the radicals from the attack tree has been added to the attack graph, and the attack graph is thus a complete transformation from the original attack tree, representing similar information.

7 Discussion

Evaluation on the Running Example. If we return to the example found in Sect. 4, we can see that the application of the algorithm as described in Fig. 1 will exactly result in the attack graph shown in Fig. 2. For every attack vector represented in the attack tree, the same attack vector is represented similarly in the attack graph, only with the introduction of states. These states are not provided with specific meaning outside of numbering as our specific definition; however, the ability to assign further meaning to these states is not excluded by our methodology.

The running example shows that the approach can create attack graphs from attack trees. We now discuss the main benefits of our methodology, how can it be extended, and what measures have we taken to address the state explosion problem. For the lack of space, important semantical aspects of the OR decomposition and how does our approach relate to SP-graph semantics, the main semantics used for SAND-attack trees [9], are discussed in the appendix of the extended version [19].

Benefits of Our Approach. One of the immediate benefits of our technique is that now it is possible to generate attack graphs from all human-designed attack trees from the literature and attack tree libraries. Indeed, most attack trees are created by humans, but attack graphs for any interesting system are mostly generated automatically due to the state explosion problem, as discussed by Valmari [22]. Thus by enabling the transformation from a human-generated attack tree to a transformed attack graph, we create an attack graph structure for a scenario of interest that potentially can be enhanced with the methods and tools created specifically for attack graphs (e.g., transformation into Bayesian networks [5]). Moreover, typically attack trees use more abstract attack scenarios than attack graphs. Thus, it would be interesting to compare automatically generated attack graphs with the transformed attack graphs, to understand which attacks have been missed in both cases.

Another advantage of enabling a direct transformation between attack trees and attack graphs is that new, automated generation schemes for attack graphs could become possible. As we mentioned earlier, significant research has already been performed into novel generation schemes for attack trees. A major branch of current attack tree research is into generation schema, particularly focusing on automated generation [23]. Therefore, one advantage of being able to transform attack trees into attack graphs is the ability to use these novel generation methods to generate attack graphs.

Finally, thus far we have only concerned ourselves with SAND attack trees [9], but further expansion of attack trees are available. For instance, we could expand this transformation to use an attack-defense tree (AD Tree) as an input, and then created an expanded attack graph representing the defensive actions represented in the attack tree.

Addressing State Explosion Problem. A major consideration in any state-based model is the state explosion problem [22]. We thus want to define a sufficiently robust transformation that results in an attack graph that contains enough information (*i.e.* states) without containing too many states.

Our primary means of achieving a reduction in the state is to eliminate backtracking or partial attack paths. By maintaining the monotonicity in generated attack graphs, we can prevent a factorial number of states from being generated. Back to the example in Fig. 2, we have no state such that the same action has been taken multiple times. There is no state s_i such that a path from s_0 to s_i has two state transitions b_i and b_j where $i = j$. If we were to allow partial pathing, the attack graph couple potentially not terminate, or would have significant cycling.

Another mitigation strategy we take is treating the OR operator functions as more like an XOR operator. We can see this in action in Fig. 2, where there is no state s_i such that a path from s_0 to s_i has the state transitions C and D. If we were to understand that the OR operator was not an XOR, then we would have to add states to attack graphs to allow for each vector that includes multiple components from the OR radical. This directly increases the number of states for each child, given n children, from n to $n!$. We further discuss this choice in [19].

8   Conclusions and Future Work

In this work, we have laid out a structure of a transformation that will take an attack tree as input and return an attack graph. This style of transformation already exists in literature, albeit in the opposite direction as ours. We have evaluated our transformation approach on a case study.

In terms of expansion of our work, firstly we would wish to define a transformation of Attack-Defense Trees (AD Trees). Such a transformation would likely require an alternative definition of attack graphs; however, it may be possible to define a transformation such that we only use the definition of attack graphs that we use here. Furthermore, we would like to attempt to define a more efficient state creation schema, which would make the transformation algorithm more space and time efficient.

References

1. Barik, M.S., Sengupta, A., Mazumdar, C.: Attack graph generation and analysis techniques. Def. Sci. J. **66**(6), 559 (2016)
2. Dawkins, J., Hale, J.: A systematic approach to multi-stage network attack analysis. In: Second IEEE International Information Assurance Workshop (2004)

3. Feng, C., Han-Dong, M., Wei-Ming, Z.: Survey of attack graph technique. Comput. Sci. **38**(11), 12–18 (2011)
4. Gadyatskaya, O., Jhawar, R., Mauw, S., Trujillo-Rasua, R., Willemse, T.A.C.: Refinement-aware generation of attack trees. In: Livraga, G., Mitchell, C. (eds.) STM 2017. LNCS, vol. 10547, pp. 164–179. Springer, Cham (2017). https://doi.org/10.1007/978-3-319-68063-7_11
5. Haque, M.S., Atkison, T.: An evolutionary approach of attack graph to attack tree conversion. Int. J. Comput. Netw. Inf. Secur. **9**, 1–16 (2017)
6. Haque, S., Keffeler, M., Atkison, T.: An evolutionary approach of attack graphs and attack trees: a survey of attack modeling. In: International Conference Security and Management (2017)
7. Hong, J.B., Kim, D.S., Chung, C.J., Huang, D.: A survey on the usability and practical applications of graphical security models. Comput. Sci. Rev. **26**, 1–16 (2017)
8. Hong, J.B., Kim, D.S., Takaoka, T.: Scalable attack representation model using logic reduction techniques. In: 12th International Conference on Trust, Security and Privacy in Computing and Communications, pp. 404–411. IEEE (2013)
9. Jhawar, R., Kordy, B., Mauw, S., Radomirović, S., Trujillo-Rasua, R.: Attack trees with sequential conjunction. In: Federrath, H., Gollmann, D. (eds.) SEC 2015. IAICT, vol. 455, pp. 339–353. Springer, Cham (2015). https://doi.org/10.1007/978-3-319-18467-8_23
10. Kaynar, K.: A taxonomy for attack graph generation and usage in network security. J. Inf. Secur. Appl. **29**, 27–56 (2016)
11. Kordy, B., Pietre-Cambacedes, L., Schweitzer, P.: Dag-based attack and defense modeling: don't miss the forest for the attack trees. Comput. Sci. Rev. **13**, 1–38 (2014)
12. Lallie, H.S., Debattista, K., Bal, J.: A review of attack graph and attack tree visual syntax in cyber security. Comput. Sci. Rev. **35** (2020)
13. Lippmann, R., Ingols, K.: An annotated review of past papers on attack graphs. MIT Lincoln Laboratory (2005)
14. Mauw, S., Oostdijk, M.: Foundations of attack trees. In: Won, D.H., Kim, S. (eds.) ICISC 2005. LNCS, vol. 3935, pp. 186–198. Springer, Heidelberg (2006). https://doi.org/10.1007/11734727_17
15. Noel, S., Jajodia, S.: Managing attack graph complexity through visual hierarchical aggregation. In: Proceedings of VizSEC/DMSEC, pp. 109–118 (2004)
16. Ou, X., Boyer, W., McQueen, M.: A scalable approach to attack graph generation. In: Proceedings of CCS, pp. 336–345. ACM (2006)
17. Pinchinat, S., Acher, M., Vojtisek, D.: Towards synthesis of attack trees for supporting computer-aided risk analysis. In: Canal, C., Idani, A. (eds.) SEFM 2014. LNCS, vol. 8938, pp. 363–375. Springer, Cham (2015). https://doi.org/10.1007/978-3-319-15201-1_24
18. Pinchinat, S., Acher, M., Vojtisek, D.: ATSyRa: an integrated environment for synthesizing attack trees. In: Mauw, S., Kordy, B., Jajodia, S. (eds.) GraMSec 2015. LNCS, vol. 9390, pp. 97–101. Springer, Cham (2016). https://doi.org/10.1007/978-3-319-29968-6_7
19. Schiele, N., Gadyatskaya, O.: A novel approach for attack tree to attack graph transformation: extended version (2021). https://arxiv.org/abs/2110.02553
20. Schneier, B.: Attack trees. Dr. Dobbs J. **24**(12), 21–29 (1999)
21. Sheyner, O., Haines, J., Jha, S., Lippmann, R., Wing, J.: Automated generation and analysis of attack graphs. In: Proceedings of IEEE S&P, pp. 273–284. IEEE (2002)

22. Valmari, A.: The state explosion problem. In: Reisig, W., Rozenberg, G. (eds.) ACPN 1996. LNCS, vol. 1491, pp. 429–528. Springer, Heidelberg (1998). https://doi.org/10.1007/3-540-65306-6_21
23. Wideł, W., Audinot, M., Fila, B., Pinchinat, S.: Beyond 2014: formal methods for attack tree-based security modeling. ACM Comp. Surveys **52**(4), 1–36 (2019)
24. Zeng, J., Wu, S., Chen, Y., Zeng, R., Wu, C.: Survey of attack graph analysis methods from the perspective of data and knowledge processing. Secur. Commun. Netw. (2019)

Intelligent Decision Support
for Cybersecurity Incident Response
Teams: Autonomic Architecture
and Mitigation Search

Camilo Correa[1]([✉]), Jacques Robin[1], Raul Mazo[1,2,3], and Salvador Abreu[1,4]

[1] CRI, University of Paris 1 Panthéon-Sorbonne, Paris, France
{camilo.correa-restrepo,jacques.robin}@univ-paris1.fr
[2] Lab-STICC, ENSTA Bretagne, Brest, France
raul.mazo@ensta-bretagne.fr
[3] GIDITIC, Eafit University, Medellin, Colombia
[4] NOVA-LINCS, University of Évora, Évora, Portugal
spa@uevora.pt

Abstract. Critical infrastructures must be able to mitigate, at runtime, suspected ongoing cyberattacks that have eluded preventive security measures. To tackle this issue, we first propose an autonomic computing architecture for a *Cyber-Security Incident Response Team Intelligent Decision Support System (CSIRT-IDSS)* with a precise set of technologies for each of its components. We then zoom in on the component responsible for proposing to the CSIRT, automatically ranked sets of runtime actions to mitigate suspected ongoing cyber-attacks. We formalize its task as a *Constraint Optimization Problem (COP)*. We then propose to implement it by a *Constraint Object-Oriented Logic Program (COOLP)* deployed as a containerized web service through the integration of three orthogonal extensions of *Logic Programming (LP)*: *Web Service Oriented LP (WSOLP)*, *Constraint LP (CLP)* and *Object-Oriented LP (OOLP)*. This integration supports seamlessly reusing platform and task independent cybersecurity ontological knowledge to dynamically build a mitigation action search COP that is customized to an input suspected cyberattack action set. This customization then allows the COP, to be solved by a generic CLP engine efficiently enough to propose mitigation actions to the CSIRT team while they can still be effective. To validate this approach, we implemented a prototype called *CARMAS (Cyber Attack Runtime Mitigation Action Search)* and ran scalability tests on simulated attacks with various COP construction strategies.

This work was partially funded by *Fundação para a Ciência e Tecnologia* under grant UIDB/04516/2020 (NOVA-LINCS) and by the project C4IIoT funded by the European Commission under Grant Agreement No. 833828. It reflects the views only of the authors. The funding agencies cannot be held responsible for any use which may be made of the information it contains.

B. Luo et al. (Eds.): CRiSIS 2021, LNCS 13204, pp. 91–107, 2022.
https://doi.org/10.1007/978-3-031-02067-4_6

Keywords: Intelligent Decision Support System · Autonomic computing · Cybersecurity incident response · Object-oriented logic programming · Constraint logic programming

1   Introduction

Defending critical network infrastructures in industrial environments has become a pressing need in recent years. The ongoing transition, from custom-built control systems to the *Industrial Internet of Things (IIoT)* [29] based on low-cost, off-the-shelf, cloud connected devices, has considerably grown the attack surface exploitable by malicious agents [26]. Traditional approaches to cybersecurity emphasize attack prevention, laying out as many design-time defense mechanisms as is economically feasible. They sometimes add *post-mortem* analysis processes [7] to uncover and recover from attacks *after* they have occurred. These approaches are often insufficiently automated and, in a way, come too late. This leaves a large window of opportunity for attackers to continue causing damage. Some attacks may remain undetected for up to several months [2]. To tackle this problem, new approaches are needed to detect an attack and apply countermeasures *swiftly* or even *before* it has been fully completed to best minimize its impact.

In this paper, we make two original contributions towards solving this problem. We first propose a concrete architecture for a CSIRT-IDSS shown in Fig. 1 as an *Unified Modeling Language (UML)* [31] class diagram. This architecture refines, with a precise set of technologies, each abstract component of the classic autonomic computing architecture pattern ***MAPEK*** [16] shown on the top row of Fig. 1. It consists of a looping pipeline of *Monitor* (**M**), *Analyzer* (**A**), *Planner* (**P**) and *Executor* (**E**) components, sharing a common *Knowledge* (**K**) base, to autonomically manage a system.

Our second contribution focuses on the **P** step, leaving the details of the **M**, **A** and **E** steps for other publications. We show how **P** can be formalized as a COP and propose a specific COOLP architectural pattern to solve it with practical performance. It consists of generating, at runtime, a COP customized to the input attack to mitigate, for then solving this COP using a generic CLP solver. Thanks to the taxonomic knowledge representation features of OOLP, the COP generator reuses knowledge from the task-independent cybersecurity ontology that refines the **K** component of the MAPEK loop.

We describe the prototype implementation of this mitigation search engine architectural pattern as a COOLP. We also present scalability simulations comparing how various COP generation heuristics impact the performance of the combined COP generation and COP solving pipeline for attack action sets of increasing size and conceptual diversity. It shows that thanks to this approach, a declarative and generic CLP solver such as the CLP(FD) library of SWI-Prolog [34] can solve the generated COP efficiently enough to be usable in practice for cyberattack mitigation search.

2   Autonomic Architecture for CSIRT-IDSS

Our proposed MAPEK refinement for a CSIRT-IDSS is shown in Fig. 1. It focuses on a single autonomic self-management capability: self-protection. It is part of a larger *Security Orchestration, Automation and Response (SOAR)* [15] framework under development within the H2020 project *C4IIoT (Cybersecurity for the Industrial Internet of Things)*. This framework includes a variety of preventive and post-mortem components developed by project partners that are beyond the scope of the MAPEK architecture shown in Fig. 1, as they do not directly interact with our CARMAS component.

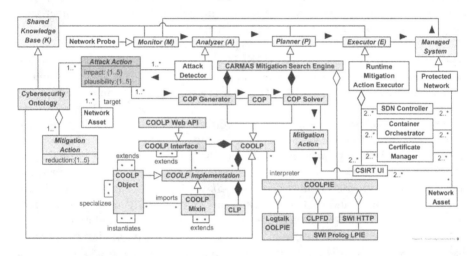

Fig. 1. MAPEK refinement for autonomic CSIRT-IDSS. (To avoid clutter, this diagram omits the UML stereotypes ≪component≫ and ≪interface≫. It uses the following color coding: *yellow* for the abstract MAPEK components, *orange* for the refinements of which we are the sole (CARMAS) or main (Ontology) developer, *grey* for the third-party *Inference Engines (IE)* and libraries reused by CARMAS, *red* for its input, *blue* for its output and *white* for the refinements developed by C4IIoT project partners that either generate this input or act upon this output.) (Color figure online)

The automation of the **K**-based **M, A, P** and **E** sub-task loop of an autonom*ic* system self-management capability is very similar to the knowledge-based *sense, reason, decide* and *act* loop of autonom***ous*** agents [25]. However, while the latter aims to perform all decision steps without requiring any human intervention, the former rather provides a very high-level *User-Interface (UI)* to a human-in-the-loop. Through this UI, this human expert can partition decisions between, on the one hand, those that the autonomic system can take without supervision, and, on the other hand, those for which the autonomic system proposes alternative, automatically executable, high-level plans for the human to choose from. Autonomic computing is inspired from the nervous system where

some functions are carried automatically without requiring conscious intervention (*i.e.,* heartbeat), whereas others are consciously triggered (*i.e.,* hyperventi-
lating). This automation continuum it a particularly good fit for a CSIRT-IDSS.

As shown in the second row of Fig. 1, at its highest level, our MAPEK refinement for a CSIRT-IDSS proposes that (a) **M** consists of probes that snoop
network packet traffic and host activities data (such as API and OS calls), (b)
A consists of attack detection from the probe generated data, (c) **P** (CARMAS)
consists of finding the network reconfiguration actions that can best mitigate the
suspected attack, (d) **E** consists of executing these actions and (e) the shared **K**
is a cybersecurity ontology. In this ontology, the choice of the bounded integer
values ranging from 1 to 5 shown in Fig. 1 for the attributes of the classes rooting
the attack and mitigation taxonomies were motivated by the requirement that
they be easy to estimate and understand by the CSIRT members.

A outputs a set of suspected ongoing attack actions targeting a set of network assets that it passes to CARMAS. The plausibility attribute of each action
comes from the attack detector while the impact attribute comes from the ontology. To mitigate the attack, CARMAS searches and ranks action sets and sends
them to the CSIRT UI. Among these ranked action sets, the CSIRT then chooses
which one to execute by calling sub-components of **E** (or none if it judges the
attack alert input to CARMAS to be a false positive). These sub-components are
general network management automation tools, already in place for normal operations, that **E** reuses for its specific cyberattack runtime mitigation purposes.
They include *Software Defined Network (SDN)* controllers [13] to reconfigure
network parameters and routes, container orchestrators [24] to reconfigure tech-
nological stacks installed on network hosts with alternative, updated elements
with no known vulnerabilities, and authentication certificate managers to reconfigure access rights to the hosted applications running on top of these stacks.
Note that only the **E** component of our proposed MAPEK refinement depends
on the use of these specific network management technologies. The CSIRT UI is
also a sub-component of **E** since it controls the calls to its other sub-components.

3   IIoT Cybersecurity Ontology

The shared ontology, refining **K**, provides a reusable, task-independent and
platform-independent reference conceptual model for the cybersecurity challenges in a given industry. The MAPEK refinement that we propose assumes
that both the managed system and its autonomic self-protection components
uniformly consist of containerized web services communicating through an SDN.
The payload schema of the communication API between these services can be
automatically generated from the ontology to support simultaneously rigorous
and agile API evolution.

While the top-level concepts of a cybersecurity ontology, such as
`Attack Action`, `Network Asset`, `Vulnerability` and `Mitigation Action` are
industry-independent, their refinements quickly become specific to a particular
industry, a set of technologies and even a specific network, for the main operating

mode of attackers is to spot the devil in the details. To illustrate such refinements, we show in Fig. 2 a snippet of the ontology under development for IIoT networks in the C4IIoT project. We are developing it in cooperation with the partners developing the refinements of the **M, A** and **E** components. It shows concepts from an `Attack Action` taxonomy (in red), a `Mitigation Action` taxonomy (in blue) and the many-to-many `mitigatedBy` role relations between them.

The C4IIoT ontology adopted a dual, synchronized representation: a high-level, graphical one in UML and a fully detailed, textual one as a COOLP. UML was a natural choice for both the overall architecture model of Fig. 1 and the shared conceptual model refining **K** because, while the components of the architecture run on different programming platforms, they all follow the OOP paradigm. Adopting a standard ontology language such as OWL [11], rather than UML, would have been a far steeper learning curve for a typical CSIRT. In addition, OWL's *Open-World Assumption (OWA)* is a semantic mismatch with OOP's *Closed-World Assumption (CWA)* [1]. However, while UML can intuitively represent taxonomies of concepts and local role relations between them, it cannot represent arbitrarily complex and possibly long-distance constraints among them. Nor does it provide formal semantics to support automated reasoning about them. This is why a refined, formal, executable, textual version of the ontology as a COOLP was also developed for components such as CARMAS that perform such reasoning. In the current implementation, we have so far synchronized the UML and COOLP versions of the ontology manually. We have however, specified a UML profile for COOLP as a first step towards automating it. The common OOP paradigm and

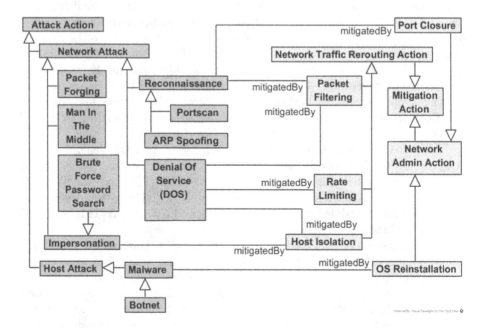

Fig. 2. Attack and mitigation action taxonomy snippet

CWA shared by the two languages make this translation far easier than a translation from UML to OWL would have been.

The snippet shown in Fig. 2 only aims to provide some illustrative context for the CARMAS running example presented in Sect. 6. The current attack taxonomy is primarily inspired by concepts proposed by MITRE [21] and Hindy et al. [14]. The current mitigation taxonomy is mostly inspired by the current focus of the project on (a) SDN controlled traffic rerouting actions and (b) network administration scripts remotely executable by the CSIRT.

4   Designing CARMAS as a COOLP Web Service

Let us now detail the design of CARMAS. Its main requirements are the following: (R1) solve a COP, formalized in Sect. 5, with practical performance, (R2) reuse the taxonomic knowledge of $\mathbf{K}$ for inheritance reasoning, (R3) be able to clearly explain its reasoning to the CSIRT and (R4) be deployed as a containerized web service inter-operating with the $\mathbf{A}$ and $\mathbf{E}$ components refinements. Each of these requirements suggest a different paradigm as the best fit to satisfy them: *Constraint Programming (CP)* [10] for R1, *Object-Oriented Programming (OOP)* for R2, rule-based LP [10] for R3 and *Web Service Oriented Programming (WSOP)* for R4. This led us to develop CARMAS as a COOLP integrating those four paradigms.

As its input is a suspected attack action set of *unknown size*, CARMAS cannot just instantiate a predefined parametric COP. We therefore decomposed CARMAS into a pipeline of two components as shown in Fig. 1. The first generates a COP problem instance from the output of the attack detector specializing $\mathbf{A}$. The second solves this COP and passes the solution as input to the runtime mitigation action executor specializing $\mathbf{E}$. As the $\mathbf{P}$ component of the MAPEK pattern, CARMAS has access to knowledge encapsulated in the $\mathbf{K}$ component, the cybersecurity ontology. Both its COP Generator and COP Solver components thus also have access to this knowledge through inheritance and composition. Both are declaratively implemented as a COOLP interpreted by a *COOLP Inference Engine (COOLPIE)* that answers COOLP queries.

This multi-paradigm COOLPIE that interprets both COP generation and COP solving COOLP queries is assembled by three orthogonal extensions to the LP engine SWI-Prolog [36]: the CLP library CLP(FD) [34], the WSOLP library HTTP [37] and the OOLP extension Logtalk [22]. This is seamlessly done by putting Prolog module import directives `use_module(library(clpfd))` and `use_module(library(http))` in a Logtalk source file.

Logtalk is an object-oriented extension of Prolog. It transpiles Logtalk programs and queries into Prolog programs and queries and reuses the Prolog engine to answer the queries given the program. Logtalk is itself implemented in Prolog. As shown in Fig. 1, a Logtalk program is composed of three main top-level code entities: *objects*, and what OOP languages usually call *interfaces* and *mixins* (respectively called *protocols* and *categories* in Logtalk). Faithful to the spirit of OOP, a Logtalk object or mixin represents both a concept in a generalization taxonomy and a unit of code encapsulation. But rather than encapsulating both a computation state and a set of state altering operations as in imperative OOP, Logtalk encapsulates a declarative LP, or a CLP when used with a CLP library. Both objects and mixins can realize interfaces. Logtalk objects and mixins can thus both be viewed as extensions of Prolog modules. Mixins can be imported into objects to support a simple form of reuse by composition. Like JavaScript, Logtalk supports both class-based and prototype-based inheritance by providing *specializes, instantiates* and *extends* relations between objects. It does not make *class* a first-class concept. Instead, it makes it a *role* that an object plays in an *instantiates* relation with another object, which allows Logtalk to easily support, like Python, both meta-classes and multiple inheritance. Similarly, the concept of *prototype* is a role that an object plays in an *extends* relation with another object. Logtalk also supports inheritance down extension hierarchies defined over interfaces and mixins. Logtalks thus allows combining JavaScript and/or Python style OOP for structural code with the declarative, formal yet executable rule-based specification of CLP for behavioral code.

Using COOLP rather than CLP alone, allows simultaneously leveraging the built-in inheritance reasoning services provided by OOLP, down the cybersecurity ontology taxonomies, with the built-in heuristic optimization reasoning services provided by CLP. It also allows following a model-driven, object-oriented development methodology [11]. This is handy in the software engineering context of CARMAS, as a component in an heterogeneous, multi-platform framework such as C4IIoT. The web server built in SWI Prolog's HTTP library and its seamless integration with Logtalk ease the deployment of CARMAS as a web service. Its built-in JSON serialization and deserialization predicates facilitate programming the data exchange between the inward-facing Logtalk interfaces of CARMAS and its outward-facing Web API interface to the other C4IIoT components. CARMAS is provided as a Docker image stacking two COOLPs, the COP Generator and the COP Solver, on top of Logtalk, CLP(FD) and SWI-HTTP, all three stacked on top of SWI-Prolog, itself stacked on top of Linux.

5 Formalizing Attack Mitigation Search

The following definitions formalize the attack mitigation search task.

- Set definitions:
  1. A: the possible attack actions;
  2. $A_p \subset A$: input attack actions to a given mitigation search problem p;
  3. T: possible network assets targeted by members of A;
  4. $T_p \subset T$: target assets for a given problem p;
  5. M: the possible mitigation actions;
  6. $M(a_i) \subset M$ with $a_i \in A_p$, the possible actions to mitigate a given attack action a_i
  7. $M(t_i) \subset M$ with $t_i \in T_p$, the possible actions to mitigate the attack actions targeting a given asset t_i.

8. $A_p(t_i) \subset A_p$ with $t_i \in T_p$, the attack actions targeting a given asset t_i.
- Function definitions:
  1. $at\colon A_p \to T_p$, asset target of a given attack action;
  2. $cl_A\colon A \to \mathscr{P}(A)$ (respectively $cl_M\colon M \to \mathscr{P}(M)$, $cl_T\colon T \to \mathscr{P}(T)$) onto-logical class of a given attack action (respectively mitigation action, target asset);
  3. $p\colon A_p \to \{1, ..., 5\}$ plausibility of an attack action suspicion;
  4. $i\colon \mathscr{P}(A) \times \mathscr{P}(T) \to \{1, ..., 5\}$ negative business impact, if left unmitigated, of an attack of a given action class targeting a given asset class;
  5. $r\colon \mathscr{P}(M) \times \mathscr{P}(A) \times \mathscr{P}(T) \to \{1, ..., 5\}$: negative business impact *reduction* of a given mitigation action class to a given attack class targeting a given asset class;
  6. $u\colon \mathscr{P}(M) \times \mathscr{P}(A) \to \mathbb{N}$: utility of mitigation action set $M' \subset M$ for attack action set $A' \subset A$ s.t.

$$u(M', A') = \sum_{m_i \in M', a_j \in A'} 5 - |p(a_j) - r(cl_M(m_i), cl_A(a_j), cl_T(at(a_j)))|.$$

- Relation definition: $mtg \subset \mathscr{P}(M) \times \mathscr{P}(A) \times \mathscr{P}(T)$, a given mitigation action class can mitigate a given attack action class targeting a given network asset class;

- Definition of integrity constraints for input problem instance and the ontology:
  1. $\forall a_i \in A_p, \exists (x, y) \in \{1, ..., 5\}^2 \ [x = p(a_i) \wedge y = i(cl_A(a_i), cl_T(at(a_i)))]$ (each attack action must have a plausibility and an impact);
  2. $\forall a_i \in A_p, \exists (m_j, x) \in M \times \{1, ..., 5\} \ x = r(cl_M(m_j), cl_A(a_i), cl_T(at(a_i)))$ (each attack action must have mitigation actions with an impact reduction);
  3. $\forall a_i \in A_p, \forall m_j \in M, \exists (x, y) \in \{1, ..., 5\}^2 \ [mtg(cl_M(m_j), cl_A(a_i), cl_T(at(a_i))) \wedge x = r(cl_M(m_j), cl_A(a_i), cl_T(at(a_i))) \wedge y = i(cl_A(a_i), cl_T(at(a_i)))] \Rightarrow x < y$ (a mitigation action cannot reduce the impact of an attack action below zero)
- Definition of output solution sets:
  1. $\mathscr{F}_M(A_p) = \{M_{sat} \subset M \mid \forall a_i \in A_p, \exists! m_j \in M_{sat}[mtg(cl_M(m_j), cl_A(a_i), cl_T(at(a_i)))]\}$ family of all solution mitigation action sets;
  2. $M_{max}(A_p) = \underset{M_{sat} \in \mathscr{F}_M(A_p)}{\arg\max} \ u(M_{sat}, A_p)$ maximum utility solution set.

The formal notation just defined relates to the UML model elements of Fig. 1 as follows. The Attack Action set that the Attack Detector component passes as input to the COP Generator is formalized by the sets A_p and T_p, and the functions at and p. The knowledge encapsulated in the ontology that enriches this input is formalized by the sets A, M and T, the functions cl_A, cl_M, cl_T, i and r, the relation mtg and the three integrity constraints. The Mitigation Action set output by the COP Solver is formalized by the $M_{max}(A_p)$ function.

The u function is constructed by the COP Generator and used by the COP Solver. Its formula favors choosing mitigation actions with higher (respectively mid-range, lower) reduction impact r for suspected attack actions with higher (respectively mid-range, lower) plausibility p. The rationale behind this choice is that mitigations with higher attack impact risk reduction generally tend to come with a higher negative impact on other factors such as service availability. Consider for example a DOS attack; the ontology snippet of Fig. 2 shows three possible mitigations for it: host isolation, rate limiting and packet filtering. While the first one has a higher attack risk impact reduction that the two others, it also more severely reduces the availability of the service running on the host suspected as the attack source. Thus, when the plausibility of this host being the source of a DOS attack targeting another network host is low, choosing packet filtering and/or rate limiting over host isolation is better for the overall availability of the network services. The u formula allows CARMAS to implicitly carry out such trade-off while still only building and solving a single objective COP, rather than a more complex multi-objective COP.

COP generation starts by creating the variable set:

$$V = D \cup R \cup P \cup \{u_p\}$$

where:

$$D = \left\{ d(m_j, a_i) \in \{0, 1\} \mid a_i \in A_p \wedge m_j \in M' \right\}$$
$$M' = \left\{ m_j \in M \mid a_i \in A_p \wedge mtg(cl_M(m_j), cl_A(a_i), cl_T(at(a_i))) \right\}.$$
$$P = \left\{ p(a_i) \in \{1, ..., 5\} \mid a_j \in A_p \right\}$$

$$R = \left\{ r(cl_M(m_j), cl_A(a_i), cl_T(at(a_i))) \in \{1, ..., 5\} \right.$$
$$\left. \mid a_i \in A_p \wedge m_j \in M' \wedge mtg(cl_M(m_j), cl(a_i), cl(at(a_i))) \right\}$$
$$u_p = \sum_{\delta \in D, \rho \in R, \pi \in P} \delta * (5 - |\pi - \rho|)$$

In the set definitions above, $d(m_j, a_i) = 1$ when the COP solver selects m_j to mitigate a_i among the set M' of candidates, and $d(m_j, a_i) = 0$ otherwise. D is thus a set of *decision* Boolean variables that represents the COP solver's mitigation action choices. P and R are sets of *parameter* integer variables with values in $\{1, ..., 5\}$. P contains the plausibility of each input suspected attack action to mitigate. R contains variables that comes from the ontology and contains the expected business impact reduction of each mitigation action on the attack action it is selected to mitigate. u_p is a positive integer *optimization* variable that the COP solver tries to maximize to guide its choices of value for the decision variables. With the variable defined above, the COP consists in choosing the allocation of *decision variables* D that maximizes the *optimization variable* u_p given the values of *parameter* variables P and R.

The worst-case complexity of a Boolean COP is 2 to the power of the number of its decision variable (*cf.* [25] p. 199). The most straightforward COP generation strategy yields a COP with $\sum_{a_i \in A_p} |M(a_i)|$ decision variables. Its complexity is thus: $SF = O(2^{\sum_{a_i \in A_p} |M(a_i)|})$.

To improve the performance of the COP solver we propose two simple heuristics to generate equivalent COPs with less variables. The first is *asset-based decomposition*. It consists of building one sub-COP per targeted asset in the input, solving each of them and taking the union of the solutions as the global COP solution. With this heuristic, the number of variables for each sub-COP is upper-bounded by $\max_{t \in T_P} |M(t)|$. The total complexity of the union of all the sub-COPs is thus upper-bounded by: $ABD = O((2^{\max_{t \in T_P} |M(t)|}).(\sum_{a_i \in A_p} |M(a_i)|)/(\max_{t \in T_P} |M(t)|)))$ (*cf.* [25] p.199 again) whose growth rate is less than that of SF since $\max_{t \in T_P} |M(t)| \leq \sum_{a_i \in A_p} |M(a_i)|$. This is because the set of actions attacking a given asset is a subset of the whole attack action input set. Thus, the size of the search space of the sub-problems will necessarily be smaller than or equal to that of the whole problem. This heuristic can be used by CARMAS because, in the COP that it must generate and solve, the value choice for any given decision variable is independent from the choices for all other decision variables.

The second heuristic is *uniform mitigation* where the following constraint is added to the COP: all actions that mitigate attack actions of a given class must all belong to the same mitigation class. Or formally:

$$\forall a_i \in A_p, \forall m_j \in M' \Big[[d(m_j, a_i) = 1 \wedge cl_M(m_j) = c_m \wedge cl_A(a_i) = c_a]$$

$$\Rightarrow \forall a_l \in A_p, \forall m_q \in M' \setminus \{m_j\} [(d(m_q, a_l) = 1 \wedge cl_M(m_q) = c_m) \Rightarrow cl_A(a_l) = c_a] \Big]$$

It assumes that if a given mitigation action is appropriate for an attack action of a given attack class, actions of the same mitigation class are likely to be effective for all other actions of that attack class. When this holds, this heuristic dramatically reduces the number of decisions to be taken by the COP solver from $\sum_{a_i \in A_p} |M(a_i)|$ to just $d = \sum_{k_A \in \{cl(a_i)|a_i \in A_p\}} |\{k_M | \exists t \in T_p[mtg(k_M, k_A, cl_t(t))]\}|$, where $(k_M, k_A) \in \mathscr{P}(M) \times \mathscr{P}(A)$; that is, the sum, over the classes of attacks given as input, of the number of classes that can mitigate them. The resulting COP complexity is thus $UM = O(2^d)$. The price to pay for this performance gain is to give up the guarantee that the solver always return at the top of its list of proposed mitigation action sets, the one that maximizes the reduction of the attack impact.

6   CARMAS Running Example

To illustrate how our CARMAS prototype implementation works, at a very high-level, we now provide and explain four code listings. Listing 1.1 shows a snippet of the top-level CARMAS COOLP web service object that generates an HTTP response from an HTTP request. Listing 1.2 shows a request payload: a JSON object containing an example input set of two reconnaissance attack actions, one targeting an Android tablet and the other a Linux server. Listing 1.3 contains a snippet from a logged trace of the logical variable bindings resulting from the

COOLPIE evaluating the goals of line 7 in Listing 1.1. Listing 1.4 shows the JSON payload generated by CARMAS as answer to the request. It contains the actions to mitigate the attack actions from the client's request.

Let us now explain each listing a bit further in turn. In Listing 1.1, lines 1 and 11 show that the CARMAS web server is encapsulated in a COOLP object. Line 2 routes the request URL to the appropriate predicate handler of that object. Lines 4 to 10 show the COOLP rule defining this predicate. Lines 5 and 6 extract the JSON payload from the request and convert it to a SWI-Prolog logical term. On line 7, the web server invokes the COP generation and COP solving predicates of the **carmas** COOLP object. The arguments DVars and U of these predicates respectively contain the decision variable set D and the optimization variable u_p defined in Sect. 5. Line 8 builds a term containing the mitigation action set chosen by the decision variables and line 9 converts it to a JSON object. Line 10 sends the object as payload of the HTTP response.

In Listing 1.3, lines 1–4 show the COP logical variable bound by the COOLPIE after evaluating the **gen_cop** goal predicate of the **carmas** object on line 7 of Listing 1.1. It contains a set of candidate actions, retrieved from the ontology, to mitigate the input attack action set shown in Listing 1.2. Each such candidate action is associated with a pair of logical variables, one, DVarN representing the choice of this action, and the other, IVarN, representing the contribution of this choice to the optimization variable. In this example, COP contains two candidate actions to mitigate each attack action from Listing 1.2: one **port closure** and one **packet filtering**. Continuing with Listing 1.3, lines 5 and 8 of show DVars before and after the COOLPIE evaluates the **solve_cop** goal predicate of the **carmas** object on line 7 of Listing 1.1. Also in Listing 1.3, lines 6–7 show the mitigation action set logical variable Ms bound by the COOLPIE by evaluating the **solve-cop** goal predicate of the **carmas** object on line 7 of Listing 1.1. Ms then contains the choice of a **port closure** action to mitigate the **reconnaissance** action targeting the Android tablet and of a **packet filtering** action to mitigate the **reconnaissance** targeting the Linux server.

Listing 1.1. CARMAS COOLP web service code snippet

```
1   :- object(server).
2      {:- http_handler(root(ap), [Request]>>(server::handle_attack(Request)),
       ↪   [])}.
3      ...
4      handle_attack(Request) :-
5         {http_json:http_read_json(Request, Data, [json_object(dict),
          ↪   value_string_as(atom)])},
6         serialization::deserializeAttackActionSet(Data, AASetTerm),
7         carmas::gen_cop(AASetTerm, COP, DVars, U), carmas::solve_cop(DVars,U)
          ↪   ,
8         carmas::selectMitigationActions(COP, Ms), carmas::mitigationTerm(Ms,
          ↪   MASetTerm),
9         serialization::serialize(MASetTerm, MADict),
10        {http_json:reply_json(MADict, [status(200), json_object(term)])}.
11  :- end_object.
```

Listing 1.2. CARMAS COOLP web service JSON input example

```
1  {"attack_actions": [
2     {"plausibility": 4, "attack_type": "reconnaissance", "attack_id": 1,
3       "target": {"target_id": "tt", "os": "android", "ip":"1.1.1.1", "
          ↪ target_type":"tablet"}},
4     {"plausibility": 5, "attack_type": "reconnaissance", "attack_id": 2,
5       "target": {"target_id": "td", "os": "linux", "ip": "1.1.1.2", "
          ↪ target_type":"appServer"}}],
6   "attack_id": "ap1"}
```

Listing 1.3. CARMAS COOLP internal logical variable binding log snippet for example input/output

```
1  COP = [[portClosure(tablet(tt, "1.1.1.1", android), 1, reconnaissance)-(
         ↪ DVar1-IVar1),
2          packetFiltering(tablet(tt, "1.1.1.1", android), 1, reconnaissance)
            ↪ -(DVar2-IVar2)],
3         [portClosure(appServer(td, "1.1.1.2", linux), 2, reconnaissance)-(
            ↪ DVar3-IVar3),
4          packetFiltering(appServer(td, "1.1.1.2", linux), 2, reconnaissance
            ↪ )-(DVar4-IVar4)]],
5  DVars = [DVar1, DVar2, DVar3, DVar4],
6  Ms = [portClosure(tablet(tt, "1.1.1.1", android), 1, reconnaissance),
7        packetFiltering(appServer(td, "1.1.1.2", linux), 2, reconnaissance)
         ↪ ],
8  DVars = [1, 0, 0, 1], U = 23,
```

Listing 1.4. CARMAS COOLP web service JSON output example

```
1  {"mitigationActions": [
2     {"mitigation_action_type": "portClosure", "attack_type": "
          ↪ reconnaissance", "attack_id": 1,
3       "target": {"target_id": "tt", "os": "android", "ip":"1.1.1.1", "
          ↪ target_type":"tablet"}},
4     {"mitigation_action_type": "packetFiltering", "attack_type": "
          ↪ reconnaissance", "attack_id": 2,
5       "target": {"target_id": "td", "os": "linux", "ip": "1.1.1.2", "
          ↪ target_type":"appServer"}}],
6   "id": "mp1"}
```

7   Experimental Evaluation

To empirically evaluate the scalability of CARMAS, we carried out a set of execution time measurements with synthetic input attack sets of growing size in terms of number of attack actions and/or number of assets targeted by these attacks. Those two numbers are not always aligned. Although we assume that each input attack action only targets a single asset, multiple input attacks actions can however target the same asset. The synthetic attack sets were randomly generated from the classes of the attack taxonomy while ensuring that they satisfied all the integrity constraints of the ontology. To draw practical usability conclusions from the measurements presented below, one must note that in the current version of C4IIoT, CARMAS is used in a *reactive* manner, searching for a mitigation action set as soon as an attack is suspected and assuming that some of these actions will be immediately carried out by the CSIRT. Therefore, it does not reason on a *history* of attack actions, but rather only considers newly arriving attack actions. This considerably limits the current practical size of its input. However, we felt it was interesting to assess its scalability to larger inputs, if it becomes required to take as input the attack history in a future version of C4IIoT.

In the first experiment, we compared the time CARMAS takes to propose to the CSIRT from one to six alternative action sets to mitigate attack action sets of growing size. For an IDSS such as CARMAS performing heuristic search on the basis of an uncertain input, providing a few alternatives to human experts to choose from is important. However, too many alternatives is counterproductive to support a swift choice by the CSIRT. For single attack inputs, CARMAS took 0.06 s to propose a one solution and 0.13 s to propose six alternative solutions. Its response time remains practical up to about 10 attack inputs with 5.26 s for one solution and 13.32 s for six solution.

In the second experiment we compared execution time without and with the uniform-mitigation heuristic described in Sect. 5. Unsurprisingly, both these times grow exponentially with input size but with a different exponent. Using this heuristic reduces the response time for input of size 1, 5, 10 and 15 from 0.06s, 0.44 s, 5.26 s and 51 s down to 0.07 s, 0.074 s, 0.105 s and 0.134 s respectively.

Table 1. Asset-based decomposition heuristic performance

Actions/Asset	Number of assets				
	1 Asset	2 Assets	5 Assets	10 Assets	15 Assets
1 Action	0.001(s)	0.002(s)	0.004(s)	0.009(s)	0.117(s)
2 Actions	0.002(s)	0.004(s)	0.011(s)	0.019(s)	0.090(s)
5 Actions	0.020(s)	0.041(s)	0.112(s)	0.121(s)	0.222(s)
10 Actions	0.545(s)	1.977(s)	3.260(s)	6.692(s)	7.355(s)
15 Actions	18.746(s)	25.360(s)	181.974(s)	293.632(s)	476.140(s)

In the third experiment, we compared execution time with the asset-based decomposition heuristic described in Sect. 5 for both a growing number of target assets and a growing number of attack actions for each target. The results are shown in Table 1. The main take away from this table is that with this heuristic, CARMAS responds quickly even for inputs much larger than expected in practice. While encouraging, the general validity of these experimental results is limited by the fact that it is based on simulated data rather than real-world attack data.

8   Related Work

To show the originality of our proposal, we now compare it with previous work closely related to either (a) its application, namely runtime cyberattack mitigation or (b) its approach, namely leveraging ontological knowledge to dynamically build a COP so as to solve it efficiently by a generic solver.

Concerning (a), we only found four previous works that propose and evaluate an approach to search a many-to-many mapping space from attack action classes to mitigation action classes. Nespoli et al. [23] presents a runtime mitigation *local* search approach based on the artificial immune system metaphor. In contrast, CARMAS performs *global* optimization search. Samarji et al. [27] proposes an approach to respond to complex coordinated attacks based on the Situation Calculus [32]. A strength of their approach, as compared to CARMAS, is that it addresses the parallel nature of simultaneous attacks and ensures that the mitigations separately chosen for each attack are not mutually incompatible. However, they do not model preferences among multiple possible mitigations. In contrast, Gonzales-Granadillo et al. [12], propose a multi-criteria cost function for mitigations taking into account an economic model, the history of past mitigations and the network topology. Vieira et al. [35] propose a preference model for mitigation choices taking into account their probability of success and the computational cost of their execution. CARMAS currently misses such rich input model which would be interesting to incorporate in future work. All the other previous works did not tackle many-to-many mappings from attacks to mitigations (Marsa-Maestre et al. [20]), (Sandor et al. [28]), (Lysenko et al. [18], Huertas-Celdran et al. [5,19]).

Concerning (b) we only found a single previous work by Zhu et al. [38] similar to our approach. Taking as input an F-Logic [17] ontology that models a database schema evolution, their approach translates it into a Prolog and *Constraint Handling Rules* [9] CLP that declaratively models, as a COP, a wrapper allowing database queries following a new schema to be run on historical data that follow an old schema. The similarity with our approach is that both their ontology and ours are specified in an OOLP language under CWA, F-Logic for them and Logtalk for us. The key design difference between these two languages is that in F-Logic, *objects appear inside rules* taking the place of Prolog atomic formulas, whereas in Logtalk, it is the other way around, as *rules appear inside objects* which replace Prolog modules. Another difference between this previous work and ours is that while we leverage the seamless *integration* of OOLP with CLP provided by Logtalk and CLP(FD), they, in contrast, implemented a *translation* from OOLP to CLP. Furthermore, they build then solve a COP for a completely different application than ours. In all other previous works leveraging ontologies and COPs in concert, the respective roles of the former, the latter and the combination differ notably from our proposal. Camacho et al. [4] use an ontology to represent the state of a smart home and specify as a COP the resolution of user preferences conflicts on such states. Fowler et al. [8] follow a similar approach for a mechanical engineering design assistant. In both these works, ontological knowledge merely instantiates parameters of a fixed structure COP rather than dynamically generating that structure as we do. Chesani et al. [6] use an ontology for pre-processing and validating requests, formulated as COPs, to aid in the management of food items in a smart warehouse. Torta et al. [33] encode constraints directly into their ontology, to filter geographic information system queries.

9   Conclusion

In this paper, we made four original contributions to advance the state-of-the-art in CSIRT-IDSS. The first is a detailed architecture pattern for such system with runtime attack detection and mitigation capabilities. It is a refinement of the classic **MAPEK** autonomic architecture in which **M** is a set of network traffic and host activity data probes, **A** is an attack detector, **P** is a mitigation search engine, **E** is a mitigation executor that reuses SDN, container orchestration and certificate management tools, and **K** is a cybersecurity ontology. In this architectural context, we then made three more contributions focused on the mitigation search engine. The first is a formal definition of its task as a COP. The second is its decomposition into a COP generator, that heavily relies on knowledge from the ontology, pipelined into a COP solver. The third is the proposal of COOLP as a parsimonious unifying paradigm implementing both the generator and the solver. We showed the practical efficiency of this approach through a set of scalability experiments for runtime attack mitigation searches.

One limitation of our approach is that it formalizes mitigation search as a single objective COP: maximizing the business impact reduction of the attack. In future work, we intend to rethink this task as a *multi-objective* COP taking into account other criteria to choose among mitigation actions such as the cost of their execution and their impact on the availability of the various services deployed on the network to protect.

Another limitation is that both the attack action input set and the mitigation action output set are unstructured. In future work, we intend to extend our cybersecurity ontology to include temporal and causal relations between these actions, as well as spatial relations in terms of network topology. This will allow the CSIRT-IDSS to (a) represent and reason about the spatio-temporal progression of a complex, coordinated multi-stage attack, (b) hypothesize the plan behind the observed anomalies and (c) in some cases mitigate some attack plan actions before they are executed. This is a major endeavor since leveraging such richer ontology will require both extending the attack detector with a probabilistic adversarial plan recognition capability and extending CARMAS with a probabilistic adversarial planning capability [3]. This will pursue the line of research pioneered by Samarji et al. [27] who proposed parallel attack mitigation planning in a *purely logic* action calculus [32]. We intend to improve such an approach by using instead a *probabilistic* action calculus [30] to better model the inescapable uncertainty concerning the ongoing attacks to mitigate against.

References

1. Baset, S., Stoffel, K.: Object-oriented modeling with ontologies around: a survey of existing approaches. Int. J. Softw. Eng. Knowl. Eng. **28**(11n12), 1775–1794 (2018)
2. Bilge, L., Dumitraş, T.: Before we knew it: an empirical study of zero-day attacks in the real world. In: Proceedings of the 2012 ACM Conference on Computer and Communications Security, pp. 833–844 (2012)

3. Braynov, S.: Adversarial planning and plan recognition: two sides of the same coin. In: Secure Knowledge Management Workshop, vol. 3, pp. 67–70 (2006)
4. Camacho, R., Carreira, P., Lynce, I., Resendes, S.: An ontology-based approach to conflict resolution in home and building automation systems. Expert Syst. Appl. **41**(14), 6161–6173 (2014)
5. Huertas Celdrán, A., Karmakar, K.K., Gómez Mármol, F., Varadharajan, V.: Detecting and mitigating cyberattacks using software defined networks for integrated clinical environments. Peer-to-Peer Network. Appl. **14**(5), 2719–2734 (2021). https://doi.org/10.1007/s12083-021-01082-w
6. Chesani, F., Cota, G., Lamma, E., Mello, P., Riguzzi, F., et al.: A decision support system for food recycling based on constraint logic programming and ontological reasoning. In: 33rd Italian Conference on Computational Logic, vol. 2214, pp. 117–131. CEUR-WS.org (2018)
7. Cichonski, P., Millar, T., Grance, T., Scarfone, K., et al.: Computer security incident handling guide. NIST Spec. Publ. **800**(61), 1–147 (2012)
8. Fowler, D.W., Sleeman, D., Wills, G., Lyon, T., Knott, D.: The designers' workbench: using ontologies and constraints for configuration. In: Macintosh, A., Ellis, R., Allen, T. (eds.) International Conference on Innovative Techniques and Applications of Artificial Intelligence. pp. 209–221. Springer, London (2004). https://doi.org/10.1007/1-84628-103-2_15
9. Frühwirth, T.: Constraint Handling Rules. Cambridge University Press, Cambridge (2009)
10. Frühwirth, T., Abdennadher, S.: Essentials of Constraint Programming. Springer, Heidelberg (2003). https://doi.org/10.1007/978-3-662-05138-2
11. Gašević, D., Djuric, D., Devedžic, V.: Model Driven Engineering and Ontology Development. Springer, Heidelberg (2009). https://doi.org/10.1007/978-3-642-00282-3
12. Gonzalez-Granadillo, G., Doynikova, E., Garcia-Alfaro, J., Kotenko, I., Fedorchenko, A.: Stateful RORI-based countermeasure selection using hypergraphs. J. Inf. Secur. Appl. **54**, 102562 (2020)
13. Goransson, P., Black, C., Culver, T.: Software Defined Networks: A Comprehensive Approach. Morgan Kaufmann, San Francisco (2016)
14. Hindy, H., et al.: A taxonomy of network threats and the effect of current datasets on intrusion detection systems. IEEE Access **8**, 104650–104675 (2020)
15. Islam, C., Babar, M.A., Nepal, S.: A multi-vocal review of security orchestration. ACM Comput. Surv. (CSUR) **52**(2), 1–45 (2019)
16. Kephart, J.O., Chess, D.M.: The vision of autonomic computing. Computer **36**(1), 41–50 (2003)
17. Kifer, M., Lausen, G.: F-Logic: a higher-order language for reasoning about objects, inheritance, and scheme. In: Proceedings of the 1989 ACM SIGMOD International Conference on Management of Data, pp. 134–146 (1989)
18. Lysenko, S., Savenko, O., Bobrovnikova, K., Kryshchuk, A.: Self-adaptive system for the corporate area network resilience in the presence of botnet cyberattacks. In: Gaj, P., Sawicki, M., Suchacka, G., Kwiecień, A. (eds.) CN 2018. CCIS, vol. 860, pp. 385–401. Springer, Cham (2018). https://doi.org/10.1007/978-3-319-92459-5_31
19. Maati, B., Saidouni, D.E.: CioTAS protocol: CloudIoT available services protocol through autonomic computing against distributed denial of services attacks. J. Ambient Intell. Humanized Comput., 1–30 (2020)
20. Marsa-Maestre, I., Gimenez-Guzman, J.M., Orden, D., de la Hoz, E., Klein, M.: REACT: reactive resilience for critical infrastructures using graph-coloring techniques. J. Netw. Comput. Appl. **145**, 102402 (2019)

21. MITRE: Att&ck® for industrial control systems (2021). https://collaborate.mitre.org/attackics/index.php/Main_Page
22. Moura, P.: Logtalk-design of an object-oriented logic programming language. Ph.D. thesis, Department of Computer Science, University of Beira Interior, Portugal (2003)
23. Nespoli, P., Mármol, F.G., Vidal, J.M.: A bio-inspired reaction against cyberattacks: AIS-powered optimal countermeasures selection. IEEE Access **9**, 60971–60996 (2021)
24. Rice, L.: Container Security: Fundamental Technology Concepts that Protect Containerized Applications. O'Reilly Media, Sebastopol (2020)
25. Russel, S., Norvig, P.: Artificial Intelligence; A Modern Approach, 4th edn. Pearson, Upper Saddle River (2020)
26. Sadeghi, A.R., Wachsmann, C., Waidner, M.: Security and privacy challenges in industrial internet of things. In: 2015 52nd ACM/EDAC/IEEE Design Automation Conference (DAC), pp. 1–6. IEEE (2015)
27. Samarji, L., Cuppens-Boulahia, N., Cuppens, F., Papillon, S., Kanoun, W., Dubus, S.: On the fly design and co-simulation of responses against simultaneous attacks. In: Pernul, G., Ryan, P.Y.A., Weippl, E. (eds.) ESORICS 2015. LNCS, vol. 9327, pp. 642–661. Springer, Cham (2015). https://doi.org/10.1007/978-3-319-24177-7_32
28. Sándor, H., Genge, B., Szántó, Z., Márton, L., Haller, P.: Cyber attack detection and mitigation: software defined survivable industrial control systems. Int. J. Crit. Infrastruct. Prot. **25**, 152–168 (2019)
29. Serpanos, D., Wolf, M.: Industrial Internet of Things. In: Internet-of-Things (IoT) Systems, pp. 37–54. Springer, Cham (2018). https://doi.org/10.1007/978-3-319-69715-4_5
30. Skarlatidis, A., Artikis, A., Filippou, J., Paliouras, G.: A probabilistic logic programming event calculus. Theory Pract. Logic Program. **15**(2), 213–245 (2015)
31. The Object Management Group: Unified modeling language (UML) version 2.5.1. Standard, December 2017. Accessed 21 Apr 2021
32. Thielscher, M.: Action Programming Languages, vol. 2. Morgan & Claypool Publishers (2008)
33. Torta, G., Ardissono, L., Fea, D., La Riccia, L., Voghera, A.: A semantic approach to constraint-based reasoning in geographical domains. In: Fred, A., Salgado, A., Aveiro, D., Dietz, J., Bernardino, J., Filipe, J. (eds.) IC3K 2018. CCIS, vol. 1222, pp. 202–227. Springer, Cham (2020). https://doi.org/10.1007/978-3-030-49559-6_10
34. Triska, M.: The finite domain constraint solver of SWI-prolog. In: Schrijvers, T., Thiemann, P. (eds.) FLOPS 2012. LNCS, vol. 7294, pp. 307–316. Springer, Heidelberg (2012). https://doi.org/10.1007/978-3-642-29822-6_24
35. Vieira, K., Koch, F.L., Sobral, J.B.M., Westphall, C.B., de Souza Leão, J.L.: Autonomic intrusion detection and response using big data. IEEE Syst. J. **14**(2), 1984–1991 (2019)
36. Wielemaker, J., Huang, Z., Van Der Meij, L.: SWI-prolog and the web. Theory Pract. Logic Program. **8**(3), 363–392 (2008)
37. Wielemaker, J., Schrijvers, T., Triska, M., Lager, T.: SWI-prolog. Theory Pract. Logic Program. **12**(1–2), 67–96 (2012)
38. Zhu, H., Madnick, S.E., Siegel, M.D.: Reasoning about temporal context using ontology and abductive constraint logic programming. In: Ohlbach, H.J., Schaffert, S. (eds.) PPSWR 2004. LNCS, vol. 3208, pp. 90–101. Springer, Heidelberg (2004). https://doi.org/10.1007/978-3-540-30122-6_7

Using Garbled Circuit for Secure Brokering

Lotfi Ben Othmane[1]([✉]) and Noor Ahmed[2]

[1] Iowa State University, Ames, IA, USA
othmanel@iastate.edu
[2] Air Force Research Lab/RISD, Rome, NY, USA

Abstract. Many domains such as military and agriculture collect data from sensors and other trusted applications, process them, and distribute them according to predetermined rules to interested entities. These systems need to trust the data broker, which could be hosted in a public environment. This paper assesses the use of garbled circuits technique to protect the collected time-sensitive data and filtering and distribution policy from suspicious brokers. It reports about the design of a secure brokering protocol and preliminary performance evaluation of the implementation.

1 Introduction

Current information systems collect data from sensors and other trusted applications, process them, and distribute them according to predetermined rules within given time-constraints to interested entities. Figure 1 shows an example of such systems, an area monitoring system. The parties of the scenario are: data broker B, data producers P_i and data consumers C_i, where index i refers to the ith participant. Let P_1 be a drone that takes photos and sends them along with its ID P_1 and its latitude and longitude position (L_1, L_2) to a broker B. Let the consumer C_1 sends a request to the broker to get photos collected in the area (L_A^1, L_B^2) and (L_B^1, L_B^2), where (L^i, L^j) are the latitude and longitude of area limit point A.

The broker needs often to be located close to the time-sensitive data producer entities and may need to operate in a suspicious or malicious environment, e.g., to serve a ground monitoring mission. To address this requirement, the broker needs to operate such that it applies the filtering and distribution policy without understanding the data and the policy.

The threat model is as follow: The broker could intercept the execution of the filtering policy and/or apply arbitrary function on the data received from the producers and send the results to the consumers. The producers are trusted to send "good" data. The consumers are trusted to send "good" filtering policy predicate. The broker, however, must know nothing about the application of the filtering policy.

© The Author(s), under exclusive license to Springer Nature Switzerland AG 2022
B. Luo et al. (Eds.): CRiSIS 2021, LNCS 13204, pp. 108–117, 2022.
https://doi.org/10.1007/978-3-031-02067-4_7

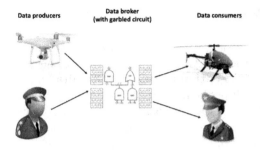

Fig. 1. Secure evaluation of access and dissemination policy on untrusted environments.

The issue of secure enforcement of access control policies in cross-domain system is applicable to wide-range of domains including e-commerce, supply-chain, and cyber-physical systems. The common approach is to use Attribute-Based Encryption (ABE) [1,2]. However, this approach requires mechanisms to distribute and manage the public/private keys for each participant, which makes it difficult to apply in data dissemination scenarios, where the data senders and receivers do not know each others at the setup phase. In addition, the performance of the proposed homomorphic schemes that address the problem makes them not practical.

An alternative approach is to use the Garbled Circuit (GC) [3] technique to ensure the secure execution of brokering algorithm. GC is not commonly used because most of the constructions require its size to grow exponentially to the size of the input, includes big number of encryption/decryption operations, and requires extensive exchange between the two parties contributing to evaluate the circuit. For instance, Carter et al. evaluated the execution time of garbled circuit for a set of algorithms including Dijkstra with 50 vertices and 100 vertices, which take about 6 h and 47 h respectively [4]. Recent work focus on developing non-interactive evaluation of garbled circuit [5,6], which allows to reduce the cost of communication between the two parties participating on evaluating the garbled circuit. These work focused on the security of the algorithms and did not provide empirical performance evaluations.

The contributions of this paper are:

- Design and implementation of a GC-based brokering protocol for protecting input data and filtering policy from suspicious brokers for time-sensitive information sharing application.
- Preliminary security analysis and performance evaluations of the protocol.

The paper is organized as follows. Section 2 discusses related work. Section 3 describes the protocol of using Garbled Circuit (GC) for brokering data that we propose. Section 4 describes the prototype of the protocol *SFEDataShare*. Section 5 discusses the evaluation of SFEDataShare and Sect. 6 concludes the paper.

2   Related Work

We discuss in this section examples of work on attribute-based encryption of circuits, implementations of GC and non-interactive constructions of GC.

Attribute-based Encryption (ABE) for Circuits. In ABE scheme, a ciphertext is associated with public indexes of the attributes ind, a message m, a private/public key, and Boolean predicate P over the attributes ind [7]. Several ABE schemes have been proposed. For instance, Gorbunov et al. [1] proposed a construction that uses the Learning With Errors (LWE) assumption [8], which allows a receiver to decrypt only data that comply with its predicate and no more. The scheme uses the public key to encrypt the wires inputs and allows to compute the ciphertext and the circuit representing the predicates over the attributes at the same time. In this scheme, the parameters and ciphertext grow linearly with the depth of the circuit. Garg et al. proposed another construction of ABE scheme but using multilinear maps [2].

Bonah et al. [9] proposed an attribute based encryption systems that relies on LWE problems [8] and supports functions representing arithmetic circuits. This scheme allows to transform an encryption c of message m with attribute vector x into an encryption under public key $< f(x), f >$. It can then decrypt the result only if $f(x) = 0$, that is, the policy is valid. The performance of the scheme is expected to be not practical for time critical data sharing in military applications.

Implementations of Garbled Circuit. Fairplay is the first known implementation of garbled circuit for two-party computation system [10]. Several implementations have been published since then, which provide better performance and security. We report about the main ones in the following.

Kreuter et al. implemented the garbled circuit protocol for the malicious model [11] in the two-party context using multiple-copies to detect malicious GC evaluator. They were able to execute secure AES in 1.4 s and 4095-bit edit distance circuit in about 8.2 h on 256 cores for each of the two parties. We note, however, that about 40% of the execution time is spent on the communication between the parties.

Bellare et al. [12] implemented the primitives of GC using AES to generate the tokens for the wire signals. They also improved their implementation to benefit from the free-xor [13] and garbled row reduction [14] performance improvement techniques. The performance of the implementation [15] was assessed using AES circuit and showed excellent performance: 637 µs for the circuit garbling primitive and 264 µs for the evaluation primitive.

Almeida et al. [16] proposed a software stack for Secure Function Evaluation (SFE) that consists of a verified compiler that translates C programs into Boolean circuits, a verified implementation of Yao's SFE protocol based on GCs and oblivious transfer [17], and a transparent application integration and communications. The security of the protocol implementation is formally verified using EasyCrypt [18], a tool-assisted framework for building high-confidence cryptographic proofs.

Non-interactive GC. Bellare et al. [19] proposed a security formulation of GC as four algorithms: garble the circuit, encrypt input, evaluate GC, and decrypt the results. In addition, they formulated three security properties for GCs: (1) privacy – the host shouldn't learn anything impermissible beyond that which is revealed by knowing just the final output, (2) obliviousness–leaks nothing about the original function and input beyond known information such as the topology of the circuit and (3) authenticity–inability of adversary to create an output from the GC and input that is different from its output. The authors provided one garbling scheme that comply with the security property and could be instantiated using AES.

Goldwasser et al. proposed a construction of an encrypted decryption function that decrypts an encrypted message without a key [20]–they embed the key in the GC. The construction uses GC of the decryption algorithm and LWE-based ABE [1]. The construction uses the encrypted message to identify recursively the labels to be used in evaluating the GC and outputs the plain-text message.

3   Design of the Secure Brokering Protocol

Garbled Circuit (GC) has been proposed as an approach for secure function evaluation [3,21]. A short description of garbled circuit follows. Let C be a circuit that implements function f. A garbled circuit of C is an "encryption" of C such that the decryption of its output using input x is equivalent to the output of function f using the same input x. The steps of the algorithm are [3,22,23]:

1. $Gb(1\lambda, f) \rightarrow (F, e, d)$ – The garbling algorithm Gb takes in the security parameter λ and a circuit f, and returns a garbled circuit F, encoding information e, and decoding information d.
2. $En(e, x) \rightarrow X$ – The encoding algorithm En takes in the encoding information e and an input x, and returns a garbled input X.
3. $Ev(F, X) \rightarrow Y$ – The evaluation algorithm Ev takes in the garbled circuit F and the garbled input X, and returns a garbled output Y.
4. $De(d, Y) \rightarrow y$ – The decoding algorithm De takes in the decoding information d and the garbled output Y, and returns the plain text output y.

Figure 2 shows the GC of a simple circuit. In this construction, we associate to each of the wires two labels, e.g., wire 2 is associated with label C for signal value 1 and label D for value 0. We also provide the truth table of each of the garbled gates and associate the labels for outputs 0 and 1, where the values 0 indicates that the predicate is valid and 1 indicates otherwise. We observe that in the basic construction, the encoding algorithm generates labels for the input wires signals and associates them to the wire input and the decoding algorithm generates labels for output wires signals and associates them to the output values [19].

We propose the use of GC [3,21] for the secure evaluation of policy functions in malicious environments. Figure 3 depicts the adapted protocol that we propose

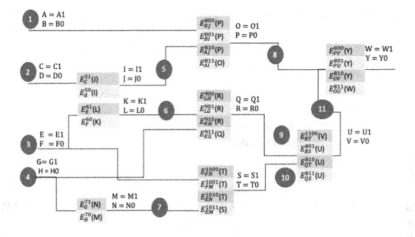

Fig. 2. An illustration of garbled circuit for a simple circuit

for secure brokering. The protocol uses the four roles: (1) the *Owner*, (2) the *Produce*, (3) the *Broker*, and (4) the *Consumer*. The *Owner* generates the input labels using the key SK_i and the GC using the key SK_v and sends the key SK_i to the *Producer*, and the GC and the key SK_v to the *broker*. In addition, the *Owner* constructs a decoding map that matches the possible output of the circuit to the possible output labels of the GC, which it sends to the *Consumer*. The *Producer* uses the key SK_i to generate the input labels associated with its input, which it sends to the *Broker*. The *Broker* evaluates the GC using the input labels it receives from the *Producer* and the key SK_v and sends the output labels of the GC to the *Consumer*. The *Consumer* uses the output map to decode the output labels it receives from the *Broker* and generates the plain-text data of the circuit.

We adapt the cryptographic primitives of Bellare et al. [19] to generate and evaluate the GC for our use case as illustrated in the Procedure Gb and Procedure Ev respectively. Procedure Gb generates a GC from function f. The first loop sets up the GC in line 2 and 3, and the second loop computes the q garbled tables for each gate g in $P[g, b, a]$ in lines 4 to 5, where the set garbled tables F is given to the broker. Figure 4 shows the partial content of GC at the Owner, including the parameters of the circuit, and a part of the garbled table.

For the evaluation of the GC, The procedure Ev evaluates the GC F using encrypted input X by extracting the labels X_a and X_b of the inputs to each of the gates and uses them to compute the output labels. Then, the output labels are given to the consumer to decrypt them.

A short security analysis of our GC weaknesses is as follows: Each of the producers receives a secret key to encrypt its data then send to the broker. An attacker who compromises a producer can impersonate the producer by using the producers' secret key to send data of their choice to the broker. Another weakness of the first version of our solution is that the size of a predicate could

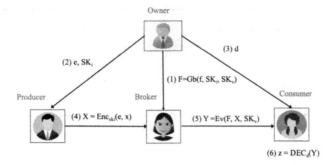

Fig. 3. Secret-key-based protocol for secure data dissemination. Note: f: function, F: garbled function, e: encoding alg., SKi: secret key for generating input labels, SKv: secret key for garbling circuit C representing f, input labels x: producer input, X: encryption of x, y: output, Y: encrypted output, and d: map of possible circuit outputs to possible GC output labels.

Procedure $Gb(1^k, f)$ [19]

---

1   $(n, m, q, A', B', G) \leftarrow f$

2   **for** $i \in \{1, ..., n+q-m\}$ **do**

3     $t \leftarrow \{0, 1\}, X_i^0 \leftarrow \{0, 1\}^{k-1} t, X_i^1 \leftarrow \{0, 1\}^{k-1} \bar{t}$

4   **for** $(g, i, j) \in n+1, ..., n+q \times 0, 1 \times 0, 1$ **do**

5     $a \leftarrow A'(g), b \leftarrow B'(g) \; A \leftarrow X_a^i, a \leftarrow lsb(A), B \leftarrow X_b^j, b \leftarrow lsb(B)$

6     $T \leftarrow g \,\|a\| \, b, P[g, a, b] \leftarrow E_{A,B}^T(X_g^{G^{(i,j)}})$

7   $F \leftarrow (n, m, q, A', B', P)$

8   $e \leftarrow (X_1^0, X_1^1, ..., X_n^0, X_n^1)$

9   $d \leftarrow (X_{n+q-m+1}^0, X_{n+q-m+1}^1, ..., X_{n+q}^0, X_{n+q}^1)$

10   **return** (F, e, d)

---

be small enough for a malicious broker to bypass it by mapping the input and the output. We consider to address these limitations in our future work.

4   Description of SFEDataShare Framework

We developed a framework for secure brokering, referred to as *SFEDataShare*. We use *JustGarble* [12, 15, 19, 24], an open source code base for garbling and evaluating Boolean circuits, as the core component of the framework. *JustGarble* [15] uses two AES keys in constructing the GC. The first key is used to generate the input labels that correspond to possible inputs to the circuit. The second key is used to generate the GC wires labels and to evaluate the GC using the provided input labels.

Procedure $\text{Ev}(F, X)$ [19]

---

1 $(n, m, q, A', B', P) \leftarrow F, (X_1, ..., X_n) \leftarrow x$

2 **for** $g \leftarrow n + 1$ **to** $n + q$ **do**

3 $\quad \Big|\quad a \leftarrow A'(g), b \leftarrow B'(g)\ A \leftarrow X_a, a \leftarrow lsb(A), B \leftarrow X_b, b \leftarrow lsb(B)$
$\quad \Big\lfloor\quad T \leftarrow g \,\|a\|\, b, Xg \leftarrow \mathbb{D}^T_{A,B}(P\,[g, a, b])$

4 **return** $x_{n+q-m+1}, ..., x_{n+q}$

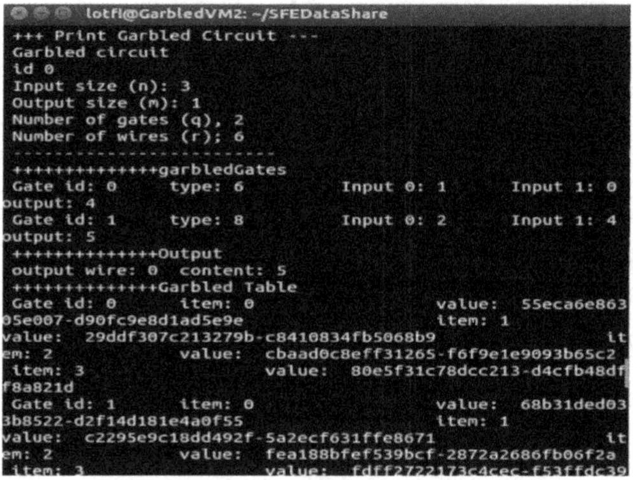

Fig. 4. Data owner GC output

justGarble allocates memory for the GC dynamically. The operating system allocates a big memory size for the GC as the memory is fragmented. For instance, the OS reserves effectively 2 GB memory (considering memory fragmentation) for a garbled circuit of 51 input wires while the effective needed memory is 9544 bytes, excluding the memory for storing the input labels. This problem prevented us from easily serializing the GC. Thus, we developed serialization and deserialization functions for the GC, input labels, and output labels. The serialization consists of performing a memory copy of the data in its data type form to a reserved memory of type void. The deserialization consists of performing a memory copy of the received data of type array of voids to the variables addresses and performing type casting of the variables or using function __mmload_si128() [25] to store the data into __m128i variables. This solves the problem as we are consuming only the needed memory zones.

Figure 4 shows part of the log of the *Owner* module. The log shows the input/output labels of a circuit composed of three input wires and two gates XOR(.) and AND(.).

Table 1. Performance of the protocol.

# Of inputs wires	# Of gates	GC size (in bytes)	Garbling time (in ticks)	Evaluation time (in ticks)
3	2	520	80584	569
10	9	1836	81076	1137
15	14	2776	82134	901
22	21	4092	171404 (0.017 s)	1990 (0.2 msec)

*10.000 ticks correspond to 1 millisecond

5   Performance Evaluation

We evaluated the framework using a MacBook Air laptop of 1.1 GHz Dual-Core Intel i3 processor with 16 GB RAM. The framework's modules run in a virtual box VM that runs Ubuntu 14.04.6 LTS. Table 1 provides the GC serializing size, circuit garbling time, and GC evaluation time. We observe that garbling a circuit of 21 gates and 22 wires takes about 17 milliseconds to garble and 0.2 milliseconds to evaluate. The timing values are considered acceptable, compared to the timing of e.g., the construction of Carter et al. [4], although the sizes of the circuits are small.

The time to send GC from the *Owner* to the *Broker* depends mainly on the size of the serialized GC. Equation 1 provides the size of the serialized garbled circuit, where q is the number of gates, n is the number of input wires, and m is the number of output wires of the circuit. Column 3 of Table 1 provides examples of the sizes the serialized GCs. We believe that the time to send GC will be reasonably low.

$$s = (84 \times q) + ((n + q + 1) \times 52) + (4 \times m) + 16 + 20.$$
where:
q: number of gates.   (1)
n: number of input wires.
m: number of output wires.

The framework crashes when we use circuits of large size because of the enormous effective size of the memory allocated to the GC in `justGarble`. This issue requires further debugging of the code to make it more robust and useful.

We note that the implemented protocol uses two AES keys to construct the labels for the GC. The schema is secure because the broker, who evaluates the GC, cannot associate the input to the input labels and cannot associate the output of the circuit to the output labels generated from the GC.

6   Conclusion

We discussed in this paper the results of assessing the use of Garbled Circuit (GC) to protect time-sensitive input data and filtering and distribution rules from suspicious brokers. We designed a protocol for secure data dissemination that uses GC and implemented a prototype of it, *SFEDataShare*. Then, we evaluated the framework using a small randomly generated circuits of up to about 21 gates.

We found that the size of data exchanged between the parties is small and the time to garble a circuit and evaluate it are also reasonably small. The results show that GC could be used for secure data brokering with acceptable performance.

Acknowledgement. This work is supported by the Air Force Research Lab, Rome, USA.

References

1. Gorbunov, S., Vaikuntanathan, V., Wee, H.: Attribute-based encryption for circuits. J. ACM **62**(6), 1–33 (2015)
2. Garg, S., Gentry, C., Halevi, S., Sahai, A., Waters, B.: Attribute-based encryption for circuits from multilinear maps. In: Canetti, R., Garay, J.A. (eds.) CRYPTO 2013. LNCS, vol. 8043, pp. 479–499. Springer, Heidelberg (2013). https://doi.org/10.1007/978-3-642-40084-1_27
3. Yao, A.C.: How to generate and exchange secrets. In: Proceedings of the 27th IEEE Symposium on Foundations of Computer Science, pp. 162–167 (1986)
4. Carter, H., Mood, B., Traynor, P., Butler, K.: Secure outsourced garbled circuit evaluation for mobile devices. J. Comput. Secur. **24**(2), 137–180 (2016)
5. Badrinarayanan, S., Jain, A., Ostrovsky, R., Visconti, I.: Non-interactive secure computation from one-way functions. In: IACR Cryptology ePrint Archive (2018)
6. Morgan, A., Pass, R., Polychroniadou, A.: Succinct non-interactive secure computation. Cryptology ePrint Archive, Report 2019/1341 (2019). https://eprint.iacr.org/2019/1341
7. Boneh, D., Sahai, A., Waters, B.: Functional encryption: definitions and challenges. In: Ishai, Y. (ed.) TCC 2011. LNCS, vol. 6597, pp. 253–273. Springer, Heidelberg (2011). https://doi.org/10.1007/978-3-642-19571-6_16
8. Regev, O.: On lattices, learning with errors, random linear codes, and cryptography. J. ACM **56**(6), 1–40 (2009)
9. Boneh, D., et al.: Fully key-homomorphic encryption, arithmetic circuit ABE and compact garbled circuits. In: Nguyen, P.Q., Oswald, E. (eds.) EUROCRYPT 2014. LNCS, vol. 8441, pp. 533–556. Springer, Heidelberg (2014). https://doi.org/10.1007/978-3-642-55220-5_30
10. Malkhi, D., Nisan, N., Pinkas, B., Sella, Y.: Fairplay-a secure two-party computation system. In: Proceedings of the 13th Conference on USENIX Security Symposium, SSYM 2004, vol. 13, p. 20, USA, USENIX Association (2004)
11. Kreuter, B., Shelat, A., Hao Shen, C.: Billion-gate secure computation with malicious adversaries. In: Presented as part of the 21st USENIX Security Symposium (USENIX Security 12), Bellevue, WA, pp. 285–300. USENIX (2012)
12. Bellare, M., Hoang, V.T., Keelveedhi, S., Rogaway, P.: Efficient garbling from a fixed-key blockcipher. In: 2013 IEEE Symposium on Security and Privacy, pp. 478–492 (2013)
13. Kolesnikov, V., Schneider, T.: Improved garbled circuit: free XOR gates and applications. In: Aceto, L., et al. (eds.) ICALP 2008. LNCS, vol. 5126, pp. 486–498. Springer, Heidelberg (2008). https://doi.org/10.1007/978-3-540-70583-3_40

14. Pinkas, B., Schneider, T., Smart, N.P., Williams, S.C.: Secure two-party computation is practical. In: Matsui, M. (ed.) ASIACRYPT 2009. LNCS, vol. 5912, pp. 250–267. Springer, Heidelberg (2009). https://doi.org/10.1007/978-3-642-10366-7_15

15. Bellare, M., Hoang, V.T., Keelveedhi, S., Rogaway, P.: Get justgarble. http://cseweb.ucsd.edu/groups/justgarble/. Accessed Jul 2020

16. Almeida, J.B., et al.: A fast and verified software stack for secure function evaluation. In: Proceedings of the 2017 ACM SIGSAC Conference on Computer and Communications Security, CCS 2017, pp. 1989–2006 (2017)

17. Rabin, M.O.: How to exchange secrets with oblivious transfer, technical report TR-81, Aiken Computation Lab, Harvard University (1981)

18. Barthe, G., Dupressoir, F., Grégoire, B., Kunz, C., Schmidt, B., Strub, P.-Y.: Foundations of Security Analysis and Design VII FOSAD 2012-2013 Tutorial Lectures, EasyCrypt: A Tutorial, pp. 146–166 (2014)

19. Bellare, M., Hoang, V.T., Rogaway, P.: Foundations of garbled circuits. In: Proceedings of the 2012 ACM Conference on Computer and Communications Security, CCS 2012, pp. 784–796 (2012)

20. Goldwasser, S., Kalai, Y., Popa, R.A., Vaikuntanathan, V., Zeldovich, N.: Reusable garbled circuits and succinct functional encryption. In: Proceedings of the Forty-Fifth Annual ACM Symposium on Theory of Computing, STOC 2013, pp. 555–564 (2013)

21. Goldreich, O., Micali, S., Wigderson, A.: How to play any mental game. In: Proceedings of the Nineteenth Annual ACM Symposium on Theory of Computing, STOC 1987, pp. 218–229 (1987)

22. Kiss, Á., Schneider, T.: Valiant's universal circuit is practical. Cryptology ePrint Archive, Report 2016/093 (2016). https://eprint.iacr.org/2016/093

23. Othmane, L.B.: Active Bundles for Protecting Confidentiality of Sensitive Data throughout Their Lifecycle. PhD thesis, Western Michigan University, USA (2010)

24. Keelveedhi, S., Bellare, M.: Justgarble, March 2014. https://github.com/irdan/justGarble

25. Intel Corporation, Intel® C++, intrinsic reference, document number: 312482-003us, September 2021

Network and Data Security

Path-Preserving Anonymization for Inter-domain Routing Policies

Xiaozhe Shao$^{(\boxtimes)}$, Hossein Pishro-Nik, and Lixin Gao

Department of Electrical and Computer Engineering,
University of Massachusetts Amherst, Amherst, USA
{xiaozheshao,pishro,lgao}@engin.umass.edu

Abstract. The Internet consists of tens of thousands of autonomous systems (ASes), which exchange routing information through policy-based routing protocols, such as Border Gateway Protocol (BGP). BGP allows network administrators/operators to configure routing policies independently. The routing result is derived from complex interactions controlled by the configured policies. Thus, the routing policies of all networks are essential to understand which network a packet uses to reach a destination or whether there is a path to reach a destination. However, the routing policies of a network are proprietary information. The majority of networks in the Internet do not publicly share their routing policies. In this paper, we anonymize the routing policy with the aim to preserve the utility to understand the routing system. To this end, we perturb both the routing policies and the AS-level topology. We propose a series of anonymization schemes that perturb the AS-level topology to derive a k-anonymity graph. We further perturb routing policies to preserve the best path. We evaluate the anonymization schemes against sophisticated de-anonymization attacks exploiting rich structural information of AS-level topologies, such as neighborhood and reference distance. The experimental result shows that the de-anonymization attack exploiting rich structural information can identify less than 1% of nodes.

Keywords: Graph anonymization · K-anonymity · Network verification

1 Introduction

The Internet consists of tens of thousands of autonomous systems (ASes), each of which belongs to an organization such as an Internet Service Provider (ISP), a university, a company, or an Internet Exchange Point (IXP). The interconnections in the Internet have a hierarchical structure, where tier-1 ISPs provide settlement-free services among each other, and provide transit services to regional ISPs or stub networks, and regional ISPs provide transit services to even smaller ISPs or stub networks. BGP is a policy-based protocol used for routing among ASes.

The route taken by a packet to traverse in the Internet is determined by the route selection process, and a result of complex interactions controlled by

© The Author(s), under exclusive license to Springer Nature Switzerland AG 2022
B. Luo et al. (Eds.): CRiSIS 2021, LNCS 13204, pp. 121–136, 2022.
https://doi.org/10.1007/978-3-031-02067-4_8

the configured routing policies of all networks. Knowing routing policies of all networks allow us to answer a broad set of what-if questions [11,18]. For example, if a network wants the inbound traffic from Google to go through a specific provider, then before changing its routing configuration the operator wants to verify that the configuration indeed leads to the desired outcome.

Routing policies are considered to be proprietary by their networks. Each network administrator/operator configures its routing policy independently. The routing policy of a network reveals how the network exchanges routes with neighbors. Thus, the commercial agreement (*e.g.*, provider-customer relationships) between neighboring ASes can be inferred through their routing policies. Further, the routing policy of a network reveals that which neighbor is more preferred than others. Therefore, routing policies should be anonymized before sharing.

A trivial method of anonymizing routing policies is to anonymize IDs of all networks, *e.g.* AS Numbers, in the routing policies. Namely, each original AS Number is transformed into a unique ID. However, anonymizing IDs alone is not sufficient. The number of neighbors of a network can be inferred from the anonymized routing policy of the network, even if all network IDs contained in the routing policy are anonymized.

In the Internet, tier-1 ISPs have a large number of neighbors (customers and peers) and the number of neighbors follow power-law distribution [12]. The ASes with a large number of neighbors are few and their degrees (*e.g.* the number of neighbors) are usually unique. The AS-level topology can be derived from the publicly available routing tables of RouteViews [14] and RIPE RIS [9]. The degrees in the AS-level topology can be used to identify the AS. Even if the derived AS-level topology does not exactly reflect the AS-level topology in reality, the ranking of these large ISPs in terms of degree will be same. Thus, these Tier-1 ISPs can still be identified. Identifying a few tier-1 networks can lead to identifying tier-2 networks by what tier-1 neighbors they have. Progressively, more and more ASes might be identified when their higher-tier neighbors have been identified. Therefore, anonymizing the AS-level topology is the key in anonymizing routing policies.

Anonymizing graphs have been studied at the area of online social networks [2,3,6,8,10,17,19–21]. These schemes perturb the graph through adding and/or removing nodes and/or edges in social networks, so that the adversaries can not identify users from the social network. These schemes focus on preserving social network structural properties. However, these schemes do not maintain the best paths derived from the routing policies. The applications exploiting the inter-domain routing policy are very sensitive to the best paths derived from the routing policy. Therefore, these schemes can not be directly applied to the anonymization of routing policies.

In this paper, we propose a path-preserving anonymization scheme for sharing inter-domain routing policies. We anonymize the routing policies so that the best paths can be maintained after anonymization. To do that, we first perturb AS-level topology by adding fake networks and connection between fake networks and between fake and real networks. We then establish routing policies for these newly-added links.

To perturb the AS-level topology, one anonymization scheme is adding neighborhood relationships between pairs of networks. However, simply adding fake edges between networks is not sufficient to maintain the best path utility. The reason is that the local preferences on the fake edge between two networks can not be properly assigned. When network u is connected to network v through a fake edge, to avoid the fake edge being included in the best paths, all real edges should be preferred over the fake edge. Thus, network u and network v should give each other the lowest local preference. In practice, a network assigns the lowest local preference to its provider and a pair of neighboring ASes can not be the provider of each other. Therefore, the fake edges between a pair of ASes, such as network u and network v, can be identified by using the local preferences assigned to the fake edge.

We propose to add fake networks into the AS-level topology and then add the connection between fake networks and real networks to perturb the AS-level topology. In the topology perturbation, we first consider to avoid being identified through the number of neighbors. We propose a deterministic anonymization scheme which derives a k-anonymity graph. As a result, the probability of identifying a network by the degree information is at most $\frac{1}{k}$. However, the resulting k-anonymity graph is deterministic. We further propose the probabilistic anonymization scheme to generate the k-anonymity graph with higher randomness. To anonymize the AS-level topology, the probabilistic anonymization scheme might significantly enlarge the graph with fake networks. Adding too many fake networks might make the scheme infeasible in practice. Finally, we propose the hybrid anonymization scheme to take advantage of the strengths of both the deterministic anonymization scheme and the probabilistic anonymization scheme.

After fake networks and fake edges are added, we propose to generate the associated routing policies for those fake networks and edges. To avoid de-anonymization, in the anonymized routing policies, the local preferences assigned to real neighboring ASes and fake neighboring ASes have the same distribution.

We evaluate the proposed anonymization schemes against de-anonymization attacks exploiting rich structural information, such as neighborhood and reference distance. The experimental result shows that the structure-based de-anonymization attacks can identify less than 1% networks from the anonymized AS-level topology. In addition, we use Closeness Centrality as an example metrics to illustrate how hard to identify a network through the structural information. We also show that the forged routing policies of networks added by the anonymization schemes will not be used to identify the added networks from the original networks.

The rest of this paper is organized as follow: In Sect. 2, we illustrate background and formally define the problem. In Sect. 3, we discuss the preliminaries necessary for preserving utility to construct the anonymization schemes. To perturb the AS-level topology, in Sect. 4 we propose the deterministic anonymization scheme, the probabilistic anonymization scheme and the hybrid anonymization scheme respectively. In Sect. 5, we propose to perturb the routing policies through a local preference assignment scheme. We describe the experiment in Sect. 6, related work in Sect. 7, and make the conclusion of the paper in Sect. 8.

2   Background and Problem Formulation

2.1   Routing Policies and AS-level Topology

BGP is the de-facto standard for inter-domain routing in the Internet. BGP allows network operators to configure the routing policy of their own networks. The routing policies of those networks together determine the best routes from source to destination networks. In BGP, a network assigns a local preference to each of its neighbors respectively and prefers the routes from a neighbor network with a larger local preference.

Listing 1.1. A snippet of the routing policy

```
router bgp 45000
   neighbor 192.168.1.2 remote-as 40000
   neighbor 192.168.1.2 route-map SET-LOCAL-PREF-CUST in
   neighbor 192.168.1.3 remote-as 50000
   neighbor 192.168.1.3 route-map SET-LOCAL-PREF-PEER in
!
route-map SET-LOCAL-PREF-CUST
   set local-preference 200
route-map SET-LOCAL-PREF-PEER
   set local-preference 100
```

In Listing 1.1, we illustrate a snippet of the routing policy for AS 45000. The routing policy of AS 45000 indicates the neighborhood relationships of AS 45000. According to the routing policy, AS 45000 has two neighboring ASes, AS 40000 and AS 50000. This snippet also indicates that AS 45000 sets up the local preference 200 for its customer, AS 40000, and the local preference 100 for its peer, AS 50000. As a result, AS 45000 prefers routes from AS 40000 over that from AS 50000.

The routing policy of a network indicates the neighboring ASes of the network. The routing policies of all networks together implies the AS-level topology of the Internet. Let us denote the AS-level topology by a graph, $G = \{V, E, R\}$, where V is the set of nodes, E is the set of edges and R is the set of all routing policies. Each node represents an AS in the Internet. The edge between two nodes represents the link between two networks.

2.2   Path-preserving Anonymization

To protect the routing policies, we can obfuscate the key information in the routing policies. One of the most trivial one is pseudonymization. We can replace

AS numbers in the routing policies by a pseudo ID, so that the routing policies can not be identified through the AS numbers directly. Let us denote the pseudonymization as a network mapping function, π, that maps the original AS number to the anonymized AS number (the pseudo ID).

Anonymizing IDs only is not enough for the anonymization of routing policies. The neighboring relationship with the real preference and the real neighbor ID implied by the routing policies can be used for identification as we state in the introduction. Beyond pseudonymization, we might also change the neighboring ASes and local preferences for these neighboring ASes in a routing policy. As for the routing policy in Listing 1.1, we might switch the local preferences of AS 40000 and AS 50000. However, the obfuscation might not preserve the best paths derived by the routing policies. For example, after switching the local preferences in the routing policy of Listing 1.1, AS 45000 prefers routes from AS 50000 over that from AS 40000.

Answering what-if questions by exploiting the inter-domain routing policy relies on the best paths derived from the routing policies. If the best paths of the anonymized routing policy is different from the best paths of the original routing policy, then the anonymized routing policy might not be useful to answer what-if questions. In order to preserve the utility of the routing policy, a best path derived by the original routing policy should be a best path derived by the anonymized routing policy. We say that the anonymization scheme preserves the *best path utility*, if, for an AS-level topology $G = \{V, E, R\}$, $\forall i, j \in V$, $\pi(Path(i, j)) = Path(\pi(i), \pi(j))$, where $Path(i, j)$ indicates the best path from network i to network j and $\pi(Path(i, j))$ maps all original AS numbers of ASes in the best path to their anonymized AS numbers.

In this paper, we propose the anonymization schemes that preserve the best path utility. To do so, all networks and the neighboring relationships are maintained after the routing policy anonymization. Namely, the anonymization schemes should not remove nodes or edges from the AS-level topology. Instead, the anonymization schemes can add new nodes and new edges into the AS-level topology. In addition, the local preferences of neighboring ASes can be changed but the ranking of these local preferences should be maintained. Thus, after the anonymization, a network ranks the neighboring ASes in the same way as before the anonymization.

2.3   Threat Model

After the anonymization, the routing policies of all networks are publicly available. The adversary can access the anonymized routing policies of all networks and try to figure out the routing policy for each network. Given an AS number, the adversary needs to identify the routing policy of this AS and discovers how this AS ranks its neighboring ASes from the routing policy. To preserve the best path utility, how an AS ranks its neighboring ASes is maintained in the anonymized routing policy. Therefore, the key of this de-anonymization procedure is to infer the network mapping function, π.

The AS-level topology implied by the anonymized routing policies can be used to identify the routing policy of each network. The routing tables of Route-Views [14] and RIPE RIS [9] are publicly available. The adversary can get the AS-level topology of the Internet by using the routing tables. To preserve the best path utility, all networks and their connections are maintained in the anonymized AS-level topology. We consider that the adversary tries to use the AS-level topology of the Internet to identify the networks in the anonymized AS-level topology and figure out the routing policy of the networks.

3   Anonymization Scheme Overview

To anonymize the routing policies, we first consider how to perturb the AS-level topology implied by the routing policies, so that the networks are hard to be identified through the number of neighbors. Then, we modify the routing policies of these networks accordingly, so that the networks are hard to be identified through the local preferences in the anonymized routing policies.

3.1   Anonymizing Graph Structure

To perturb the AS-level topology, we consider to generate *k-anonymity* graphs. A k-anonymity graph is a graph that, for any node, there are at least $k-1$ other nodes sharing the same degree with the node. If only the degree information is used by the adversary, the probability that the adversary can correctly identify a real node from the k-anonymity graph is at most $\frac{1}{k}$.

An anonymized graph that is not *k*-anonymity can also guarantee that the adversary can not correctly identify a real node with the probability higher than $\frac{1}{k}$. Following this idea, we extend the definition of k-anonymity graph as follows. Given an anonymized graph derived from the original graph, the anonymized graph is a k-anonymity graph, if the probability that the adversary can correctly identify a real node is no more than $\frac{1}{k}$ when the original graph size goes to infinity. Formally, $\forall u \in V$ and $\forall v \in V'$,

$$\lim_{|V|\to\infty} P\big(P(\pi(u) = v|\mathbf{Y} = \mathbf{y}) \leq \frac{1}{k}\big) = 1, \tag{1}$$

where V and V' are the sets of nodes in the original graph and the anonymized graph respectively and $\mathbf{y}$ is the degree sequence of nodes in the anonymized graph. In Sect. 4, we propose three graph anonymization schemes to generate *k*-anonymity graph.

Although *k*-anonymity with a small k is vulnerable to de-anonymization attacks, the schemes proposed in this paper can select a large k, such as k equals the number of real nodes. The reason is that the schemes in this paper preserve the best path utility. Selecting a large k does not impact the utility of the anonymized graph. In the experiment, we will show that selecting a large k can achieve pretty good anonymization performance.

To preserve the best path utility, all nodes and edges in the original graph should be maintained in the anonymized graph. Therefore, the anonymization schemes should not remove nodes or edges. In this paper, we propose to add fake nodes into the graph. Then, fake nodes and real nodes are connected by a set of fake edges to perturb the graph structure.

3.2 Local Preference Assignment for Fake Edges

After the graph anonymization, we need to modify all routing policies for newly-added nodes and edges. For each fake node added into the topology, we need to create a new routing policy for the node. For each fake edge added into the topology, the local preferences should be properly assigned to the edge. In Sect. 5, we propose a local preference assignment scheme to determine local preferences for these fake edges, so that the fake nodes can not be identified through their local preferences.

4   Node Anonymization

In this section, we propose three anonymization schemes to perturb the AS-level topology. In Sect. 4.1, we first propose the deterministic anonymization scheme which generates a k-anonymity graph. However, the resulting graph is determined by the Internet topology and lacks of randomness. To increase the randomness of the resulting graph, we propose the probabilistic anonymization scheme in Sect. 4.2. The probabilistic anonymization scheme might significantly enlarge the graph with fake networks. Finally, in Sect. 4.3, we propose the hybrid anonymization scheme that takes the advantages of both the deterministic and probabilistic anonymization schemes.

4.1   Deterministic Anonymization Scheme

In the deterministic anonymization scheme, we partition all nodes of the original graph into several groups, where each group contains at least k nodes. Then, we add fake edges between these real nodes and fake nodes to make these real nodes in the same group have the same degree. Finally, fake edges are added between fake nodes to make all fake nodes have the same degree.

4.1.1   Node Grouping

Given a graph with n nodes, we partition all real nodes into $\lfloor \frac{n}{k} \rfloor$ groups, where each group at least has k nodes. To do so, we sort the nodes of the original graph in the descending order of their degrees. For the first $\lfloor \frac{n}{k} \rfloor - 1$ group, the group i is composed of the $(i*k-k+1)$-th node to the $(i*k)$-th node. The last group is composed of the $(\lfloor \frac{n}{k} \rfloor * k - k + 1)$-th node to the n-th node.

For each group, we select a target degree. All real nodes in the group are supposed to reach the target degree of this group after the anonymization. To increase the degree of real nodes, we add fake nodes and fake edges. We also select a target degree for all fake nodes. When every node reaches their target degrees, we get a k-anonymity graph. Please refer to the technical report[1] for how we select the target degrees and the number of fake nodes added into the anonymized graph.

4.1.2   Graph Construction

Given the number of fake nodes and the target degrees, we add fake edges to generate k-anonymity graph. We define *degree gap* of a node as the target degree of this node minus its degree. We use g_i to denote the degree gap of node i. The degree of fake nodes in the original graph are zero. Through adding fake edges, we will make the degree gaps of all nodes be zero. To do so, we select one node with the largest degree gap and make the node reach its target degree in each step. We show the details as follows.

Increasing Real Node Degree. To increase the degree of real nodes, we always select the real node that has the largest degree gap. Suppose that we select node i with the degree gap g_i. Then, we select g_i fake nodes that have the largest degree gap and connect these g_i fake nodes with node i with fake nodes.

Increasing Fake Node Degree. To increase the degree of fake nodes, we always select the fake node that has the largest degree gap. Suppose that we select node i with the degree gap g_i. Then, besides node i, we select g_i fake nodes that have the largest degree gap and connect these g_i fake nodes with node i with fake nodes.

4.1.3   Privacy Guarantee

Theorem 1. *The deterministic anonymization scheme can generate a k-anonymity graph.*

Please refer to the technical report for the proof of this Theorem.

4.2   Probabilistic Anonymization Scheme

The deterministic scheme lacks of uncertainty. The regularity of the anonymized graph generated by the deterministic scheme can be used for de-anonymization. In order to increase the uncertainty of the anonymization scheme, we propose probabilistic anonymization scheme. In probabilistic scheme, we add randomness during the graph anonymization so that the resulting graph is not deterministic.

4.2.1   Graph Anonymization

The basic idea of the graph anonymization is to connect a real node and a fake node with the probability, p. For each real node, the number of its fake neighbors is a random variable that follows binomial distribution with the average as $m * p$

---

[1] Please access to the technical report through http://rio.ecs.umass.edu/mnilpub/papers/crisis2021-shao-tr.pdf.

and the variance as $m*p(1-p)$. When the difference between the degrees of two real nodes in the original graph is insignificant comparing to $m*p(1-p)$, these two real nodes can not be identified through their degrees.

Given a graph G, we refer to a group with k nodes in G as k-node group. In a graph G, we define k-node degree delta of a k-node group as the difference between the maximal and the minimal degrees of nodes in the group. Then, for a specific node, there are a number of k-node groups that contain this node. We define minimal k-node degree delta of a node as the minimal k-node degree delta of k-node groups that contain the node. We use $\delta_{(i,k)}$ to denote the minimal k-node degree delta of node i. We refer to that k-node group as minimal k-node group of this node. We construct the k-anonymity graph as follows.

Adding Fake Nodes. We add $m = max(\delta_{(max,k)}^2 \ln n, n)$ fake nodes into the graph, where $\delta_{(max,k)}$ is the maximal $\delta_{(i,k)}$ for $\forall i \in [1,n]$, n is the number of nodes in G and d_{max} is the maximal degree in the graph G. We will show that m is sufficient in Theorem 2.

Connecting Real Nodes with Fake Nodes. For each real node, we add a fake edge between this real node and each fake node with a probability p, where $0 < p < 1$. On average, each real node will connect to $m*p$ fake nodes.

Connecting Fake Nodes with Fake Nodes. Then, we connect fake nodes with fake nodes. The goal is to make the expected degree of fake nodes be the expected degree of the real node with the highest degree in the original graph. To do that, each fake node connects to another fake node with the probability $q = \frac{(m-n)p+d_{max}}{m-1}$.

4.2.2 Probabilistic Privacy Guarantee

Theorem 2. *The probabilistic scheme generates a k-anonymity graph.*

We provide the proof of this Theorem in the technical report. In the following, we just illustrate the intuitive idea that the anonymization method can generate a k-anonymity graph. In the anonymization procedure, a number of fake edges are added to each real and fake node. With a higher probability (the probability goes to one when the graph size goes to infinity), the k nodes in the minimal k-node group of each node will have very similar degrees in the anonymized graph. Because, the minimal k-node degree delta will be asymptotically smaller than the variance for the number of the fake edges connected to each real node. Apparently, it is more likely that the node with higher degree in original graph has the higher degree in the anonymized graph. However, when the degree of a node in the anonymized graph is dominated by the fake edges added in the anonymization procedure, the degree delta of the nodes in the original graph are insignificant. Then, the k nodes in each group have similar degrees. The probability of successfully identifying nodes by their degrees is $1/k$.

4.3   Hybrid Anonymization Scheme

In the probabilistic anonymization scheme, the number of fake nodes needed to perturb the graph rises rapidly with the increasing of the degree difference. In order to reduce the number of added faked nodes, we propose the hybrid anonymization scheme. We will first use the deterministic anonymization scheme to reduce the degree difference in the graph. After that we derive probabilistic k-anonymity graph by using the probabilistic anonymization scheme.

4.3.1   Graph Construction

Hybrid anonymization scheme guarantees to generate a k-anonymity graph. The key idea is to reduce the degree difference through the technique of the deterministic anonymization scheme and then apply the probabilistic anonymization scheme. We describe the two phases as follows.

Reducing Degree Delta through Deterministic Anonymization Scheme. Given a graph with n nodes, to reduce the degree delta, we first partition the nodes into $\lfloor \frac{n}{k} \rfloor$ groups, where each group at least has k nodes. In this phase, our aim is to make sure that the degree delta of each group is less than a target degree delta, δ_{target}. We select $\delta_{target} = \lfloor \sqrt{n/\ln n} \rfloor$. When $\delta_{max,k}$ is less than δ_{target}, in a graph with n nodes, according to Theorem 2 , n fake nodes are enough to generate a k-anonymity graph in the next phase. The detailed steps of this phase is similar to the deterministic anonymization scheme.

Perturbing Node Degrees through Probabilistic Anonymization Scheme. In this phase, we randomly increase the node degrees by using the same technique of the probabilistic anonymization method. We treat both the real nodes and the fake nodes added by the last phase as the real nodes. Then, we can use the probabilistic anonymization scheme to anonymize the graph.

4.3.2   Algorithm Analysis

Theorem 3. *The hybrid anonymization scheme generates a k-anonymity graph.*

Proof. When the degree delta of each group is reduced into $\lfloor \sqrt{n/\ln n} \rfloor$, the minimal k-node degree delta of each node is equal to or less than $\lfloor \sqrt{n/\ln n} \rfloor$. According to Theorem 2, we can prove this theorem.

5   Routing Policy Anonymization

In this section, we propose a local preference assignment scheme for fake edges. We aim to guarantee that the real nodes and fake nodes have the similar local preferences, so that fake nodes can not be identified by the local preferences. We consider both *outgoing preference* and *incoming preference*. The outgoing preference of a node is the average of local preferences that are assigned to its neighbors by this node. The incoming preference of a node is the average of local preferences that are assigned to this node by its neighbors. The proposed scheme generates local preferences so that the distribution of the outgoing preferences and the incoming preferences for real nodes are same with that for fake nodes.

The best paths are determined by the ranking of the local preferences instead of the exact value of the local preferences. In this paper, we use the ranking number of these local preferences to represent the original values of these local preferences. For example, if a node assigns local preferences to its four neighbors as 100, 200, 200 and 400, then the associated ranking numbers are 3, 2, 2 and 1 respectively.

5.1   Accommodating the Distribution of Outgoing Preference

To adjust the outgoing preferences of a node, we need to determine ranking number for neighbors. Namely, how many neighbors have the ranking number 1, how many neighbors have the ranking number 2 and so on. We refer to the set of neighbors with the ranking number i as the i-th ranking set of the node. The union of all ranking sets of a node should be the neighbor set of the node. Note, in this step, we determine how many fake edges will be assigned with a ranking number instead of assigning the ranking number to specific fake edges. In the following, we illustrate how we determine the size of the ranking sets for each node.

In each step, we randomly select a node and determine the size of the ranking sets. For each node, we initiate the procedure from determining the size of first ranking set and finish the procedure until the total size of ranking sets equals the number of neighbors. To preserve the best path utility, a real node will not change the local preference for its real neighbors and will not prefer fake neighbors over real neighbors. Namely, the top ranking sets of a real node are already determined by the original routing policy. For these real nodes, we select the size of ranking sets for their fake neighboring relationships only.

To determine the size of i-th ranking set for a node, we investigate the size of i-th ranking sets of the other nodes. If the size of i-th ranking sets of the other nodes are all zero, then we just pick the size for i-th ranking set of this node. Therefore, the total size of ranking sets of this node equals to the node degree. Otherwise, we select an existing size for i-th ranking set of this node. More specifically, the probability of selecting the size of i-th ranking set as s is as follows.

$$p(s,i) = \begin{cases} 0 & \forall k, N(k,i) = 0 \\ \frac{1/N(s,i)}{\sum_{(k|N(k,i)\neq 0)} 1/N(k,i)} & N(s,i) \neq 0. \end{cases} \qquad (2)$$

where s is the size of a ranking set and $N(s,i)$ is the number of i-th ranking sets with the size s.

5.2   Accommodating the Distribution of Incoming Preference

Given the size of all ranking sets, we select specific neighbors for each ranking set. The goal is to make the incoming preference of real nodes have the same distribution with that of fake nodes. To preserve the best path utility, real nodes always prefer their real neighbors over fake neighbors. To avoid fake nodes having large incoming preference, we make fake nodes prefer fake neighbors over real neighbors.

The maximal degree of real nodes, d_{max}, can be used by the adversary to remove fake edges. For a node i, only if node j is one of its top d_{max} neighbors in the ascending order of local preferences, then the edge (i, j) could be a real edge. Otherwise, the edge (i, j) has to be a fake edge. To avoid an edge (i, j) from being identified as a fake edge, node i and node j should treat each other as top d_{max} neighbors. To do so, before assigning the local preference value to each fake edge, for each node, we select a set of neighbors as its top d_{max} neighbors. We refer to those neighbors of the node as *high-ranking neighbors*. Apparently, for a node, there are at most d_{max} high-ranking neighbors. The rest neighbors are *low-ranking neighbors*. Only the edges between the node and its low-ranking neighbors are identified as fake edges.

6   Experiment

6.1   Datasets

To evaluate the proposed anonymization schemes, we anonymize a series of graphs through these schemes. Since Internet topologies are power-law graphs, we synthesize power-law graphs with various sizes for evaluation. In order to generate power-law graphs that have the same properties with Internet topologies, we exploit the graph generation algorithm in [4]. We also use the Internet AS-level topologies in CAIDA AS Relationship Database [1] to evaluate the performance of these schemes on Internet topologies.

6.2   Robustness Against De-anonymization Algorithm

There are a number of de-anonymiztion algorithms which exploit structural information to identify nodes from the anonymized graph. Most of them are seed-based. Those algorithms rely on a seed graph which already maps a subset of real nodes in the original graph to the nodes in the anonymized graph. However, in the context of de-anonymizing network graph, it is hard to get a set of seed nodes. Therefore, in the experiment, we consider the seedless de-anonymization algorithm to identify the real nodes in the anonymized graph. We exploit the state-of-the-art seedless de-anonymization algorithm [5] to identify the nodes from the anonymized graphs.

Table 1 illustrates the number of real nodes identified through de-anonymization algorithm. In this experiment, we synthesize power-law graphs of various size and perform the anonymization and de-anonymization algorithms. For each size, we generate five graphs and illustrate the average number of real nodes that are correctly identified in Table 1. Although the anonymization schemes aim to perturb the degree of each nodes, to some extent, they can defend the de-anonymization algorithm using structural information. When k is n, $\sqrt{n}$ or $\ln n$, more than 90% real nodes can not be correctly identified.

Table 1. Percentage of real nodes that are identified by seedless de-anonymization algorithm [5].

Number of nodes	100	400	700	1,000
Hybrid n-anonymity	0%	0%	0%	0%
Hybrid $\sqrt{n}$-anonymity	0.2%	0.1%	0.03%	0%
Hybrid $\ln n$-anonymity	1.2%	0.15%	0%	0.1%
Deterministic n-anonymity	0%	0%	0%	0.02%
Deterministic $\sqrt{n}$-anonymity	2.4%	1.05%	0.94%	0.92%
Deterministic $\ln n$-anonymity	7.2%	5.1%	7.31%	7.28%

6.3   Potential De-anonymization Using Local Preference

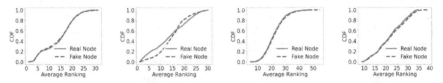

(a) Outgoing Prefer- (b) Incoming Prefer- (c) Outgoing Prefer- (d) Incoming Preference (DAS).   ence (DAS).   ence (HAS).   ence (HAS).

Fig. 1. Distribution of local preferences with deterministic anonymization scheme (DAS) and hybrid anonymization Scheme (HAS).

The local preference of nodes in the anonymized graph might be used to separate real and fake nodes. In this experiment, we investigate the distribution of outgoing and incoming preferences of real nodes and fake nodes. When the distribution for real nodes are similar with that for fake nodes, the local preference is hard to be used to identify real nodes.

We illustrate CDF of outgoing and incoming after deterministic and hybrid anonymization schemes in Fig. 1 and Fig. 2 respectively. As Fig. 1 shows, the distributions for real and fake nodes are very similar. The adversary might or might not use the local preference and the maximal degree to identify fake edges. Namely, for each AS, only the d_{max} top-ranking links can be real links while the other links have to be fake. These fake edges can be removed. Thus, in the experiments, we consider the scenarios where the adversary uses or does not use fake edge removal. As Fig. 2 shows, the distributions for real and fake nodes are still very similar after removing fake edges.

Fake edges in the anonymized graph can be removed through observing the outgoing local preference of each node. Even after removing fake edges, the seedless de-anonymization attack can not identify real nodes from the anonymized graphs. The result is similar to Table 1. Due to the space limit, we do not list the result.

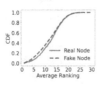

(a) Outgoing Preference.

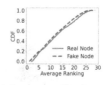

(b) Incoming Preference.

Fig. 2. Distribution of local preferences with hybrid anonymization scheme after fake node removal.

7   Related Work

7.1   Internet-Wide Network Verification

A number of formal methods have been exploited to verify properties for inter-domain routing. To study the safety property of BGP systems, Satisfiable Module Theories (SMT) [16] and Rewriting Logic [15] are used to verify the convergence conditions. A model checking tool is used to search possible attraction attacks on the Internet [13]. A policy-aware model [11] is proposed for routing verification at Internet scale. Those verification schemes need both the Internet topologies and the routing policies of networks for the verification. To preserve the confidentiality of routing policies, the anonymization schemes proposed in this paper can generate anonymized graphs for those verification schemes.

7.2   Graph Anonymization

A series of graph anonymization mechanisms have been proposed at the area of online social networks [2,3,6,8,10,17,19–21]. One large class of anonymization mechanisms exploits k-anonymity, where k nodes in the anonymized graph can not be separated from each other. The first approach in this direction is proposed in [6], where each node shares the same degrees with at least $k-1$ other nodes. At the same time, Zhou and Pei [20] propose the concept of k-neighborhood anonymity to defend against neighborhood attacks. To defend against more sophisticated structural attacks, k-automorphism [21] and k-isomorphism [2] are proposed. Our schemes follow k-anonymity as well as preserve the best path utility for routing verification.

Another class of anonymization mechanisms use the Differential Privacy technique to provide strong privacy guarantee [3,8,10,17,19]. Those mechanisms generate a synthetic graph which maintains structural similarity to the original graph. However, the best paths of the synthetic graph will be different from that of the original graph, since there is not an injective function mapping from nodes of the original graph to nodes of the synthetic graph.

To preserve edge privacy, Mittal et al. proposed a Random Walk based anonymization technique [7]. Although the preserving edge privacy can avoid local preferences from being revealed, the best paths in the anonymized graph are changed and the graph utility can not be preserved.

8 Conclusion

In this paper, we anonymize the inter-domain routing policies. We design the anonymization schemes to guarantee the policy privacy of networks without jeopardizing the best path utility of the routing policies. To perturb the Internet topology, we propose deterministic, probabilistic and hybrid anonymization schemes. These three schemes guarantee that degree-based de-anonymization can not be identified network from the anonymized graph with a probability higher than $\frac{1}{k}$. Even if the de-anonymization attack using structural information can not identify more than 1% of networks. After topology anonymization, we anonymize the routing policies accordingly. To do so, we propose a local preference assignment scheme. The resulting local preferences in the anonymized graph preserve the best path utility and can not be used to identify networks.

Acknowledgement. This work was supported in part by NSF grants CNS-1900866 and CCF-1918187, and the Radcliffe fellowship. We thank Catherine Greenhill for many helpful discussions.

References

1. CAIDA: the caida as relationships dataset. <1998–2020>, October 2019. http://www.caida.org/data/as-relationships/
2. Cheng, J., Fu, A.W.C., Liu, J.: K-isomorphism: privacy preserving network publication against structural attacks. In: Proceedings of the 2010 ACM SIGMOD International Conference on Management of Data, pp. 459–470 (2010)
3. Dwork, C., McSherry, F., Nissim, K., Smith, A.: Calibrating noise to sensitivity in private data analysis. In: Halevi, S., Rabin, T. (eds.) TCC 2006. LNCS, vol. 3876, pp. 265–284. Springer, Heidelberg (2006). https://doi.org/10.1007/11681878_14
4. Elmokashfi, A., Kvalbein, A., Dovrolis, C.: On the scalability of BGP: the role of topology growth. IEEE J. Sel. Areas Commun. **28**(8), 1250–1261 (2010)
5. Ji, S., Li, W., Srivatsa, M., Beyah, R.: Structural data de-anonymization: quantification, practice, and implications. In: Proceedings of the 2014 ACM SIGSAC Conference on Computer and Communications Security, CCS 2014, pp. 1040–1053. Association for Computing Machinery, New York (2014). https://doi.org/10.1145/2660267.2660278
6. Liu, K., Terzi, E.: Towards identity anonymization on graphs. In: Proceedings of the 2008 ACM SIGMOD International Conference on Management of Data, pp. 93–106 (2008)
7. Mittal, P., Papamanthou, C., Song, D.: Preserving link privacy in social network based systems. arXiv preprint arXiv:1208.6189 (2012)
8. Proserpio, D., Goldberg, S., McSherry, F.: A workflow for differentially-private graph synthesis. In: Proceedings of the 2012 ACM Workshop on Workshop on Online Social Networks, pp. 13–18 (2012)
9. RIPE Ncc: routing information service. https://www.ripe.net/analyse/internet-measurements/routing-information-service-ris
10. Sala, A., Zhao, X., Wilson, C., Zheng, H., Zhao, B.Y.: Sharing graphs using differentially private graph models. In: Proceedings of the 2011 ACM SIGCOMM Conference on Internet Measurement Conference, pp. 81–98 (2011)

11. Shao, X., Gao, L.: Verifying policy-based routing at internet scale. In: IEEE INFO-COM 2020 - IEEE Conference on Computer Communications, pp. 2293–2302 (2020)
12. Siganos, G., Faloutsos, M., Faloutsos, P., Faloutsos, C.: Power laws and the as-level internet topology. IEEE/ACM Trans. Netw. **11**(4), 514–524 (2003)
13. Sosnovich, A., Grumberg, O., Nakibly, G.: Analyzing internet routing security using model checking. In: Davis, M., Fehnker, A., McIver, A., Voronkov, A. (eds.) LPAR 2015. LNCS, vol. 9450, pp. 112–129. Springer, Heidelberg (2015). https://doi.org/10.1007/978-3-662-48899-7_9
14. University of Oregon: Route Views (2021). www.routeviews.org
15. Wang, A., et al.: A reduction-based approach towards scaling up formal analysis of internet configurations. In: IEEE INFOCOM 2014 - IEEE Conference on Computer Communications, pp. 637–645, April 2014. https://doi.org/10.1109/INFOCOM.2014.6847989
16. Wang, A., et al.: FSR: formal analysis and implementation toolkit for safe inter-domain routing. IEEE/ACM Trans. Netw. **20**(6), 1814–1827 (2012)
17. Wang, Y., Wu, X.: Preserving differential privacy in degree-correlation based graph generation. Trans. Data Priv. **6**(2), 127 (2013)
18. Weitz, K., Woos, D., Torlak, E., Ernst, M.D., Krishnamurthy, A., Tatlock, Z.: Scalable verification of border gateway protocol configurations with an SMT solver. In: Proceedings of the 2016 ACM SIGPLAN International Conference on Object-Oriented Programming, Systems, Languages, and Applications, OOPSLA 2016, pp. 765–780. Association for Computing Machinery, New York (2016). https://doi.org/10.1145/2983990.2984012
19. Xiao, Q., Chen, R., Tan, K.L.: Differentially private network data release via structural inference. In: Proceedings of the 20th ACM SIGKDD International Conference on Knowledge Discovery and Data Mining, pp. 911–920 (2014)
20. Zhou, B., Pei, J.: Preserving privacy in social networks against neighborhood attacks. In: 2008 IEEE 24th International Conference on Data Engineering, pp. 506–515. IEEE (2008)
21. Zou, L., Chen, L., Özsu, M.T.: K-automorphism: a general framework for privacy preserving network publication. Proc. VLDB Endowment **2**(1), 946–957 (2009)

Policy Modeling and Anomaly Detection in ABAC Policies

Maryam Davari$^{(\boxtimes)}$ and Mohammad Zulkernine

School of Computing, Queen's University, Kingston, Canada
{maryam.davari,mz}@queensu.ca

Abstract. Sensitive data is available online through web and distributed protocols that highlight the need for access control mechanisms. System designers write access control policies to represent conditions on accessing data. Access control policies can contain anomalies (redundancy, inconsistency, irrelevancy, and incompleteness) that can lead to security vulnerabilities. Detecting anomalies in large and complex policies is challenging due to the lack of effective analysis mechanisms and tools. In this paper, we introduce a formal tree-based policy modeling technique to represent, update, and analyze access control policies. Based on the proposed formal policy modeling, we propose an anomaly detection technique. Our approach focuses on Attribute Based Access Control (ABAC) policies as they are widely adopted. Also, they can provide high flexibility and enhance security and information sharing. The effectiveness of our policy modeling and anomaly detection technique has been demonstrated through experimental evaluation.

Keywords: Access control policies · Security · Attribute based access control · Policy modeling · Policy anomalies · Anomaly detection and Resolution

1 Introduction

With the massive growth of online data ranging from web interfaces to web services, access control has become a critical part of systems. Access control policies are used to control which users (e.g., human, process, application) have access to which protected resources (e.g., databases, files) for performing which actions (e.g., write, read) under which environment conditions (e.g., time, location). A vital requirement to assure correct enforcement of access control policies is that policies have high qualities. Weak policies lead to conflicts at the policy enforcement phase that can result in availability issues (i.e., rejecting a legitimate user to access a resource) and security problems (i.e., allowing an illegitimate user to access a resource) [20]. Different methods (including matrix, event calculus, mathematics, and tree) have been used as policy modeling techniques to represent, update, and analyze access control policies [16]. However, these methods were developed in the network, EXtensible Access Control Markup Language (XACML) [3], and Role Based Access Control (RBAC) [25] domains rather than the Attribute Based Access Control(ABAC) [15] domain.

© The Author(s), under exclusive license to Springer Nature Switzerland AG 2022
B. Luo et al. (Eds.): CRiSIS 2021, LNCS 13204, pp. 137–152, 2022.
https://doi.org/10.1007/978-3-031-02067-4_9

Access control policies can contain different types of anomalies. One of the critical problems of ABAC policies is redundancy detection and removal. Redundancy can be considered as an anomaly when the response time of access requests relies on the number of policies to be parsed. It affects the performance of policy evaluation. Redundancy detection and elimination is an optimized solution to improve the performance of policies as they are growing fast in size and complexity. In a policy set, multiple policies might overlap which means one access request matches more than one policy. In addition, policies conflict with each other which means that the policies not only overlap but also yield different decisions. This issue is referred to as inconsistency.

Irrelevancy and incompleteness are other problems with ABAC policies. Irrelevancy refers to a situation that a given policy is not suitable for any users' request. Incompleteness refers to a scenario when the current policies cannot cover an access request. In an access control system, it is important to assure that the access control policies do not result in permission leakage to unauthorized principals. For instance, an incomplete policy might lead to granting access to an intruder unintentionally. Detecting and removing irrelevant and incomplete policies can considerably enhance the security, performance, and usability of the system.

Anomaly detection in large and complicated policies is not easy as there are not enough effective analysis mechanisms and tools. Policy anomaly detection has attracted the attention of many researchers [1,6,13,35]. Different policy analysis tools such as FIREMAN [1], Firewall Policy Advisor [35], FAME [13], and Capretta et al. [6] have been developed that focused on detecting firewall policy anomalies. They may not be directly applied to ABAC policies as some policy anomaly analysis mechanisms still need improvement [2]. Policy fields should be considered as a whole piece; while most of the existing approaches detect pairwise policy anomalies. Furthermore, ABAC policies can be multi-valued while the firewall policies are specified by fixed fields.

In this paper, we propose an access control policy modeling technique that includes a formalization of policy anomalies (redundancy, inconsistency, irrelevancy, and incompleteness). The technique adopts a tree data structure to represent ABAC policies. The policy tree maintains different information about users, resources, actions, environments, effects, and policy ids. Based on this modeling technique, policy anomalies are detected. We attempt to develop an approach not only for accurate anomaly detection but also for efficient anomaly resolution that checks if policies permit legitimate users to reach their goals and whether policies prevent intruders from reaching malicious goals.

The major contributions of this paper can be summarized as follows:

- The formalization of policy anomalies (redundancy, inconsistency, irrelevancy, and incompleteness) for the ABAC model.
- The design and implementation of the tree-based policy modeling for representing, updating, and analyzing access control policies.
- The design and implementation of anomaly detection and resolution techniques according to the anomaly formalization and policy modeling.

We deal with the lack of a large real dataset of ABAC policies to evaluate the proposed model. For this purpose, we generate different datasets of ABAC policies for experimental purposes. The experimental results show that our approach is efficient to detect anomalies in large-size policy sets. In addition, our approach simplifies policy insertion, modification, and deletion.

The rest of the paper is organized as follows: Sect. 2 overviews the ABAC model. Section 3 describes the policy anomaly formalization, access control policies modeling, and policy updating. In Sect. 4, we present anomaly mitigation techniques (detection and resolution). In Sect. 5, we discuss the experiments and analyze the results. Section 6 presents the related work. Finally, Sect. 7 outlines conclusions and future work.

2   Overview of ABAC

In what follows, we provide background information about the Attribute Based Access Control (ABAC) model and define notations for ABAC attributes. The ABAC model has been used for over two decades and different ABAC-based models have been developed. The flexibility features of ABAC make it a powerful access control model to promote security.

ABAC attributes. Attributes are the basic unit of ABAC policies:

User Attributes. Attributes that describe the characteristics of a user. Let U be a finite set of users and Att_u is a finite set of user attributes. The value of attribute $a \in Att_u$ for user $u \in U$ is represented by the function $d_u(a, u)$. Some user attributes have a single value and some contain multiple values. Single value attributes $(Att_{u,1})$ have a unique value for each user (e.g., user id), and multiple value attributes $(Att_{u,m})$ are a set of single values (e.g., university courses).

Resource Attributes. Attributes that describe characteristics of resources. Let R be a finite set of resources and Att_r is a finite set of resource attributes. The value of attribute $a \in Att_r$ for resource $r \in R$ is represented by the function $d_r(a, r)$.

Environment Attributes. Attributes that represent the current states of system environments (Att_{env}) such as time, date, and date-time. The environment attributes help in achieving dynamic access decisions. In addition to providing more fine-grained access control, the value of attribute $a \in Att_{env}$ for environment $env \in Env$ is represented by the function $d_{env}(a, env)$.

There are users, user attributes, resources, resource attributes, actions (i.e., operations on resources), environments, environment attributes, and effects (decisions). The simplest form of a policy instance in ABAC is a tuple: $< U, Att_u, d_u,$ $R, Att_r, d_r, action, Att_{env}, d_{env}, effect >$. The following grammar can specify a policy.

$$policy ::= < expression \; [; expression], \; effect > \quad expression ::= u.Att_u = val \mid$$
$$r.Att_r = val \mid$$
$$action = val \mid$$
$$env.Att_{env} = val$$
$$effect := Permit \mid Deny$$

Attribute Hierarchies. We consider hierarchies in user, resource, and environment attributes of ABAC [5,19,26] that can enhance access control flexibility and attribute management. This hierarchy can be a tree or forest without cycles. Hierarchy can be written as $\succeq_{att}$ that implies if attribute values of a child node are assigned to a user (resource or environment), all the attribute values of its parent nodes are acquired by the user (resource or environment). The user attribute hierarchy is defined such that a user c is a child of user p ($c.Att_u \succeq_u p.Att_u$) if and only if

$$\forall a \in p.Att_u, \exists \, ! \, a' \in c.Att_u \mid Att_u(a) = Att_u(a') \land d_u(a) \subseteq d_u(a').$$

For each user attribute of p, there must be a user attribute for c such that the attributes have the same name, and the attribute value of p is a subset of the attribute value of c. The resource and environment attribute hierarchies are similarly defined.

3   Policy Modeling

In this section, policy anomalies are illustrated and formalized for ABAC policies. Then, the structure of the policy modeling that is necessary for policy analysis is described along with the complexity of the model in terms of time. Our policy modeling makes policy updating (insertion, modification, and deletion) more efficient as described in this section.

Table 1. ABAC sample policies.

Policy	Description
P_1	$<r.type=budget; u.projectLed=r.project; action=write; Permit>$
	A project leader can write the project budget
P_2	$<r.type=schedule; u.projectLed=r.project; action=read; Permit>$
	A project leader can read the project schedule
P_3	$<u.project=r.project; r.type=schedule; action=read; Permit>$
	A user working on a project can read the project schedule
P_4	$<u.adminRole=auditor; r.type=budget; u.project=r.project; action=read; Permit>$
	An auditor assigned to a project can read the budget
P_5	$<r.type=budget; u.projectLed=r.project; u.department=dep1; action=request; Permit>$
	The project leader of the department of "dep1" can request to know the budget of a project assigned to her
P_6	$<u.adminRole=auditor; r.type=budget; u.project=r.project; u.department= dep\_security; action=read; Deny>$
	An auditor assigned to a project of the department "dep_security" cannot read the budget

3.1 Formalization of Policy Anomalies

We formalize policy anomalies (redundancy, inconsistency, irrelevancy, and incompleteness) that are utilized for policy analysis. For illustration, we use some sample policies (from [34]) that are shown in Table 1 (with the description for each policy). These policies focus on project management that controls access by the project leaders, department managers, employees, contractors, auditors, accountants, and planners to manage tasks, schedules, and budgets.

1) Redundancy Anomaly (RED). Redundancy indicates similarities among policies. The policies may not exactly match but every field in one policy is a part of or equal to the corresponding field in another policy. Detecting and removing redundancies can help in decreasing the policy set size and enhancing policy evaluation performance. An access control policy P_j is redundant if and only if

$$P_i.Att_u \succeq_u P_j.Att_u \wedge P_i.Att_r \succeq_r P_j.Att_r \wedge P_i.action = P_j.action \wedge P_i.Att_{env}$$
$$\succeq_{env} P_j.Att_{env} \wedge P_i.effect = P_j.effect.$$

For example, P_2 in Table 1 specifies that a project leader can read the project schedule and P_3 specifies that any user working on the project can read the project schedule. Therefore, P_2 is redundant in the case of the project leader.

2) Inconsistency Anomaly (INCON). Inconsistency refers to a situation when there are at least two policies that conflict with each other. Reducing the number of inconsistencies can mitigate the need for conflict resolution activities. Consider access control policies P_i and P_j. These two policies are inconsistent if and only if

$$P_i.Att_u \succeq_u P_j.Att_u \wedge P_i.Att_r \succeq_r P_j.Att_r \wedge P_i.action = P_j.action \wedge P_i.Att_{env}$$
$$\succeq_{env} P_j.Att_{env} \wedge P_i.effect \neq P_j.effect.$$

As an example, P_4 specifies that an auditor assigned to a project can read the budget, while P_6 specifies that an auditor assigned to a project of the department "dep_security" cannot read the budget. P_4 and P_6 are inconsistent.

3) Irrelevancy Anomaly (IRR). Irrelevancy refers to a scenario where a policy is never triggered or required for any kind of access request. An access control policy is irrelevant if and only if

$$\nexists req_i \in Req \mid req_i.Att_u \succeq_u P.Att_u \wedge req_i.Att_r \succeq_r P.Att_r \wedge req_i.action =$$
$$P.action \wedge req_i.Att_{env} \succeq_{env} P_i.Att_{env}.$$

As an example, P_5 indicates that a project leader of the department "dep1" can request the budget of a project assigned to her. However, this policy is irrelevant as a team leader already has access and can write to the budget of a project assigned to her based on P_1.

4) Incompleteness Anomaly (INCOM). A set of access control policies is incomplete when an access request cannot be covered by the current policies. A set of policies is incomplete if and only if

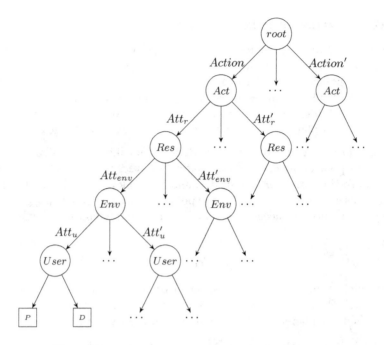

Fig. 1. The policy tree structure for ABAC policies.

$\exists req_i \in Req \mid req_i = att_{ui} \in Att_u,\ att_{ri} \in Att_r,\ a_i \in action, att_{envi} \in Att_{env}.$

$\nexists P \in ACP \mid req_i.Att_u \succeq_u P.Att_u \wedge req_i.Att_r \succeq_r P.Att_r \wedge req_i.action = P.action \wedge req_i.Att_{env} \succeq_{env} P_i.Att_{env}.$

As an example, assume a contractor working on a project asks for information about the project budget, but there is no policy to address the request.

3.2   Policy Modeling Structure

In this model, access control policies are represented by a single-rooted tree named policy tree. The policy tree prepares a simple representation of access control policies that makes the policy updating and anomaly detection technique easier (that will be discussed in the next section). This is a scalable representation for the analysis of access control policies. The tree is a type of decision diagram.

As shown in Fig. 1, the first level of the tree is action nodes that represent all distinct actions of the system. Each action node points to the second level of the tree containing resource nodes. Then each resource node points to environment nodes in the third level of the tree. Each environment node points to the fourth level of the tree containing user nodes. Each user node can have one or two leaf nodes depending on effect value. The leaf nodes contain a counter variable (that shows the frequency of policy references) and policy ids. The policy ids indicate a policy that is represented by that path and other policies that might be in anomaly with it.

To compute the time cost of constructing a policy tree, we consider the number of policies (n) and the number of node fields (p), where $p = max(num_u, num_r, num_a, num_{env})$. Num_u, num_r, num_a, and num_{env} are the number of user nodes, the number of resource nodes, the number of action nodes, and the number of environment nodes, respectively. The time cost of building a policy tree is $O(n\log_p n)$ and the time complexity of inserting a policy in the policy tree is $O(\log_p n)$.

3.3   Policy Updating

Policies are written by system administrators and updated (inserted, modified, and deleted) occasionally. To insert a new policy into the policy tree, the tree nodes are searched and compared with the new policy components to find an appropriate position in the tree for the new policy. If a node is exactly matched with the policy components (reaches the effect node), the counter value increases, and the policy id is added to the leaf node. Otherwise, a node is added and the component is inserted. The ordering of policies is crucial when policy components are supersets (i.e., general) or subsets (i.e., specific) of corresponding fields of the policy tree. Otherwise, the ordering is insignificant. In the case of disordered policies, some policies might not be used at all. When a policy component is a superset of a node value, the policy component is inserted in a node that is added right before the subset node. If a policy component is a subset of a node value, the policy component is inserted in a node that is added right after the superset node. To modify or delete a policy in a policy tree, a similar process is applied to the policy tree. In case of deletion, the corresponding node is updated by decreasing the counter value and removing the policy id. If the counter value reaches zero, the path is deleted from the tree.

4   Anomaly Mitigation

Policy anomaly formalization and policy modeling are developed for the ABAC model to achieve the goal of effective anomaly mitigation (detection and resolution) as described in this section.

4.1   Anomaly Detection

The policy tree construction and update (described in Sect. 3.3) may avoid initiating anomalies in the system. They check for anomalies in the insertion time and store information (counter value, policy id) in leaf nodes that can help to identify anomalies. However, anomalies that may still exist in the policy tree can be detected by Algorithm 1.

The algorithm detects anomalies of access control policies by traversing the policy tree from the root to the leaf nodes. One simple approach to detect redundancy, inconsistency, and irrelevancy anomalies in the policy tree is to keep track

---

Algorithm 1. Anomaly Detection in the Policy Tree.

  Input: policy_tree
  RED ← {} , INCON ← {} , IRR ← {}
  Output: RED, INCON, IRR
  node ← {*policy_tree.root*}
 1: **for each** fnode ∈ node.children **do**
 2:    **if** fnode = "Permit" **OR** fnode = "Deny" **then**
 3:       **if** fnode.counter = 0 **then**
 4:          IRR ← fnode
 5:       **else if** Number of (fnode.policy_id) > 1 **then**
 6:          RED ← fnode
 7:       **end if**
 8:    **else if** fnode.level = 4 **then**
 9:       P' ← fnode.children
10:       **if** there exists p_i ∈ P' **AND** p_j ∈ P' such that $p_i.effect \neq p_j.effect$
    then
11:          INCON ← fnode
12:       **end if**
13:    **end if**
14: **end for**
15: **Return** RED, INCON, IRR

---

of the counter variable (described in Sect. 3.2). If the counter value of a path is zero, it means that the policy was not referenced at all, and the policy is irrelevant (lines 3–4). If the number of store policy ids is more than one (lines 5–7), it means that the policy was defined several times. If a user node has more than one child node, the policy is considered inconsistent (lines 8–12). Information about the corresponding policy ids is stored in the leaf node of the tree that can help to find anomaly policies in the policy set. Incompleteness anomalies cannot be detected by the policy tree as they can be detected by analyzing transactions (i.e., actions executed) in the system.

4.2   Anomaly Resolution

To have an anomaly-free policy tree, the detected anomalies (described in Sect. 4.1) should be resolved. Redundant policies can be safely removed that boost the runtime performance of the policy evaluator. Our policy tree can identify redundant policies at the insertion time simultaneously (described in Sect. 3.3). To detect a list of redundant policies in the policy tree, all the tree paths are traversed to reach the leaf nodes. When the leaf node contains more than one policy id, the policy is identified as redundant.

   Eliminating policy conflicts by modifying policies is an intuitive solution by policy developers. However, it is remarkably difficult because of the following reasons [14]. The chance of conflicts in ABAC is high as it contains hundreds or thousands of policies. Conflicts are complicated; one policy may conflict with more than one policy. Moreover, in the distributed application, policies might

Algorithm 2. Policy Inconsistency Detection and Removal.

Input: P_i, P_j

1: **if** $P_j.effect \neq P_i.effect$ **then**
2:    **if** $P_j.Att_u \succeq_u P_i.Att_u \wedge P_j.Att_r \succeq_r P_i.Att_r \wedge P_j.action = P_i.action \wedge$
      $P_j.Att_{env} \succeq_{env} P_i.Att_{env}$ **then**
3:       $u_k = (\forall u_f \in P_j.Att_u) - (\forall u_g \in P_i.Att_u)$
4:       Update(P_j, u_k)
5:       $r_k = (\forall r_f \in P_j.Att_r) - (\forall r_g \in P_i.Att_r)$
6:       Update(P_j, r_k)
7:       $env_k = (\forall env_f \in P_j.Att_{env}) - (\forall env_g \in P_i.Att_{env})$
8:       Update(P_j, env_k)
9:    **else if** $P_i.Att_u \succeq_u P_j.Att_u \wedge P_i.Att_r \succeq_r P_j.Att_r \wedge P_i.action = P_j.action \wedge$
      $P_i.Att_{env} \succeq_{env} P_j.Att_{env}$ **then**
10:       Repeat lines 3-8 with swapping indexes j and i.
11:    **end if**
12: **end if**

aggregate. More than one administrator might maintain policies. Changing a policy might not resolve conflicts correctly, while it might modify the policy's semantics. The inconsistency issue can be addressed by eliminating the corresponding policies or limiting their applicability.

A policy might have an unintentional wide scope and cover policies that should be defined separately. The algorithm for inconsistency detection and removal is presented in Algorithm 2. Given two policies, the similarities between policy components (user attributes, resource attributes, actions, and environment attributes) are identified. In the case of similarity, redundant attributes are removed from the policy. In the case of irrelevancy, the service recommends deleting irrelevant policies. Incompleteness can be satisfied by adding incomplete policies or extending existing policies to cover incomplete policies.

5   Experimental Evaluation

The primary goal of this experiment is to evaluate the effectiveness and efficiency of our policy modeling and anomaly detection. As data sets may contain sensitive information, organizations are reluctant to share real-world policy sets. We perform our experiment on the project management policies adapted from [34] (described in Sect. 3.1) and extend it to support our work.

We create five synthetic datasets of policies (referenced as $DS1$, $DS2$, $DS3$, $DS4$, $DS5$) for the above-mentioned project management with different numbers of attributes and policies. Each policy can contain multiple users (maximum m), resources (maximum n), actions (maximum l), and environments (maximum k) and each one can have several attributes. Each user is uniformly and randomly assigned multiple attributes (maximum r). Similar to the user, each resource is uniformly and randomly assigned multiple attributes (maximum s). Likewise, each environment can have (maximum t) random attributes. The effect of each policy is uniformly and randomly selected as either Permit or Deny. Hierarchical relations between user attributes, resource attributes, and environment attributes are created. To generate user attribute hierarchies, some (about a quarter) of the user attributes are selected as parent nodes and the rest of the user attributes are considered child nodes. The child nodes are appended to the parent nodes. Similarly, resource and environment attribute hierarchies are generated. The anomaly detection algorithm is implemented in Java 11. The experiments and analyses were performed on an Intel Core i7 1.99 GHz processor with 16 GB of RAM and they do not require any specific architecture support.

Based on the above-mentioned parameters, we generate all combinations (referenced as P) of the users, user attributes, resources, resource attributes, actions, and environment attributes for each dataset. Other techniques (human experts) are used to identify true anomaly types (RED, INCON, and IRR) of each policy. The anomaly type is used in the evaluation part (described in the following paragraphs). Then, a subset of P refers to Q is uniformly and randomly selected (referenced as $Q \subset P$). This subset of policies is used for evaluating the anomaly detection technique. The policies might not be based on the specific real-world case study. However, they are intended to be analogous with policies in the application domain. Our modest size dataset can present the effectiveness of our algorithm as they contain anomalies that we discussed. In addition, they are complicated since each rule has lots of structures.

Table 2. Access control policy datasets.

	$DS1$	$DS2$	$DS3$	$DS4$	$DS5$
$\mid U \mid$	50	100	150	200	250
$\mid Att_u \mid$	4	8	7	5	9
$\mid R \mid$	1000	2000	3000	4000	5000
$\mid Att_r \mid$	5	6	4	7	8
$\mid Env \mid$	10	20	30	40	50
$\mid Att_{env} \mid$	7	5	6	4	8
$\mid Q \mid$	50000	250000	500000	750000	1000000

Table 2 summarizes the size of sample datasets in terms of the number of users ($\mid U \mid$), the number of user attributes ($\mid Att_u \mid$), the number of resources ($\mid R \mid$), the number of resource attributes ($\mid Att_r \mid$), the number of environments ($\mid Env \mid$), the number of environment attributes ($\mid Att_{Env} \mid$), and the number of randomly selected policies ($\mid Q \mid$). To assess the efficiency of our anomaly detection technique, we report accuracy, precision, recall, and False Negative Rate (FNR) defined as follows:

$$Accuracy = \frac{TP + TN}{TP + TN + FP + FN} \tag{1}$$

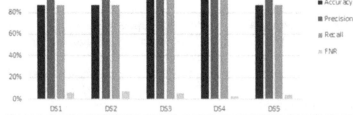

Fig. 2. Accuracy, Precision, Recall, and FNR values using the datasets.

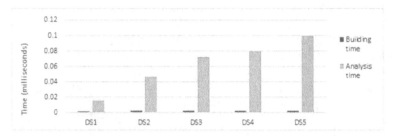

Fig. 3. Average building time and analysis time per policy.

$$Precision = \frac{TP}{TP + FP} \quad (2)$$

$$Recall = \frac{TP}{TP + FN} \quad (3)$$

$$FNR = \frac{FN}{TP + FN} \quad (4)$$

Our techniques must achieve high accuracy, precision, and recall and a very low FNR to be usable in practice. Policy trees are constructed for the generated datasets. Then, the anomaly detection technique is executed on each tree to detect anomalies. To calculate True Positive (TP), False Positive (FP), True Negative (TN), and False Negative (FN), the detected anomalies are compared with the true anomaly types of policies. TP is the number of policies that are predicted as anomalies, and are truly anomalies. Furthermore, the type of detected anomalies and true anomalies should be identical. FP is the number of policies that are predicted as anomaly, while they are truly valid. FN is the number of policies that are predicted as valid, while they are truly anomalous. TN is the number of policies that are predicted as valid, and they are truly valid. As Fig. 2 shows, the accuracy, recall, and precision of all five datasets are above 87%. Some datasets like DS3 achieved the maximum accuracy, recall, and precision of 99%. Moreover, the observation shows that the FNRs are between 0–7%. It indicates that the anomaly detection technique can detect almost all anomalies and the overall performance is high. These promising results indicate the efficiency of our policy modeling and anomaly detection technique, especially in large datasets.

Furthermore, the building time of policy trees and analysis time of anomaly detection are shown in Fig. 3. In general, the analysis time takes a longer time than the building time of the policy tree that is reasonable, especially for the large datasets. The negligible building time and reasonable analysis time make the tree-based policy modeling very efficient with respect to memory space and time.

6   Related Work

In the context of policy analysis, policies can be represented as graphs or trees to efficiently analyze and verify policies by using the tree or graph operations or features (e.g., graph traversal, graph union). Graph-based anomaly detection and resolution have been used for ensuring that policy specification fulfills system requirements and goals [17,24].

Davy et al. [8] proposed a policy conflict algorithm by using an efficient policy selection process. The algorithm leveraged the information model to select an efficient set of deployed policies for analysis. They stored histories of previous policy comparisons in multiple tree data structures. Their goal was to improve the performance that relies on the relationships between deployed or newly added policies. However, their approach was not efficient and smart. It repeated over all deployed policies to make sure that they did not cause potential conflict. Mohan et al. [23] determined conflicts and inconsistencies in policies to protect biomedical data. They viewed biomedical ontology as a resource tree.

The formal method for policy analysis has been investigated [12,30,31]. Cuppens et al. [7] proposed a management mechanism for conflicts happening among permissions and prohibitions. In this approach, rules were grouped based on the organizations emitting them. This approach can effectively reduce the number of redundant policies. The model-checking technique that characterizes the system's model and specification into mathematical representation was also used to verify the correctness of system properties. First-order logic language Alloy [18] and formulae were used to detect security properties, conflicts, and inconsistencies [4,21]. Another technique to support consistency checking of policies was Satisfiability Modulo Theories (SMT) solver. The SMT logic solvers separated the Boolean part of satisfiability checking from algorithms used property checking [32]. In addition, mutation testing [9] has been adopted for policy correctness [22]. Martin et al. [22] proposed a mutation verification to measure qualities specified for policy properties. After generating mutant policies having issues, it was verified if properties were held. When the properties did not hold, it meant the verification process detected faults in the faulty policies.

Some researchers [10, 27–29] applied data mining techniques (data classification and clustering) to detect policy conflicts. Shaikh et al. [29] used a modified C4.5 classification algorithm that has linear computational complexity to detect inconsistencies in access control policies. Moreover, Shaikh et al. [28] adopted different data classification techniques to detect incompleteness in access control policies. This approach consisted of three steps. First, attributes were ordered and Boolean expressions were normalized. Second, a decision tree (which was a modification of C4.5) was generated. Third, the proposed anomaly detection algorithm was executed on the decision tree. In clustering-based anomaly detection and resolution, policies were decomposed into clusters of rules, then the proposed approach was applied to each cluster [11].

Different techniques (graph-based, formal method, model-checking, mutation, and data mining) [16] have been explored to solve the problem of conflict and anomalies in access control policies. However, the computational complexity of some of these approaches had exponential growth and it could not deal with numerical and continuous values. In contrast, our policy anomaly detection and resolution techniques are not expensive in terms of time and space. In addition, most of the existing approaches were developed in the network management and RBAC domains rather than the ABAC domain. Although these works are useful in general, they are not suitable for anomaly detection and resolution in the ABAC domain. Furthermore, the previous works on policy analysis focused on some of the anomalies (inconsistency was the most investigated), while the primary goal of our approach is to detect all types of anomalies (redundancy, inconsistency, and irrelevancy).

7   Conclusion and Future Work

Enabling internet-based devices with a large number of access control policies might not provide appropriate security necessarily. One reason for this is the complexity of managing a large number of policies and potential vulnerabilities. Policies can contain different anomalies (redundancy, inconsistency, irrelevancy, and incompleteness). In this work, we have formalized policy anomalies and proposed a tree-based policy modeling that represents, updates, and analyzes ABAC policies. The policy insertion approach is considerably efficient as it can check for anomalies in the insertion time and facilitate policy updating. In addition, we have developed anomaly mitigation techniques based on anomaly formalization and policy tree modeling to detect and resolve policy anomalies. The experimental results show that the anomaly detection technique can achieve accuracy, recall, and precision of 87%. These promising results indicate the significant effect of the tree-based policy modeling. Moreover, short anomaly detection time illustrates the efficiency and effectiveness of our anomaly detection technique. As a part of future work, we will expand our policy modeling and anomaly detection technique to support other policy models [33].

Acknowledgment. This work was supported in part by the Natural Sciences and Engineering Research Council of Canada (NSERC) and the Canada Research Chairs (CRC) Program.

References

1. Al-Shaer, E.S., Hamed, H.H.: Discovery of policy anomalies in distributed firewalls. In: IEEE Infocom 2004, vol. 4, pp. 2605–2616. IEEE (2004)
2. Alfaro, J.G., Boulahia-Cuppens, N., Cuppens, F.: Complete analysis of configuration rules to guarantee reliable network security policies. Int. J. Inf. Secur. **7**(2), 103–122 (2008)
3. Anderson, A., et al.: Extensible access control markup language (XACML) version 1.0. OASIS (2003)
4. Bandara, A., Calo, S., Lobo, J., Lupu, E., Russo, A., Sloman, M.: Toward a formal characterization of policy specification & analysis. In: Annual Conference of ITA (ACITA), University of Maryland, USA. Citeseer (2007)
5. Bhatt, S., Patwa, F., Sandhu, R.: ABAC with group attributes and attribute hierarchies utilizing the policy machine. In: Proceedings of the 2nd ACM Workshop on Attribute-Based Access Control, pp. 17–28 (2017)
6. Capretta, V., Stepien, B., Felty, A., Matwin, S.: Formal correctness of conflict detection for firewalls. In: Proceedings of the 2007 ACM Workshop on Formal Methods in Security Engineering, pp. 22–30 (2007)
7. Cuppens, F., Cuppens-Boulahia, N., Ghorbel, M.B.: High level conflict management strategies in advanced access control models. Electron. Notes Theoret. Comput. Sci. **186**, 3–26 (2007)
8. Davy, S., Jennings, B., Strassner, J.: Efficient policy conflict analysis for autonomic network management. In: Fifth IEEE Workshop on Engineering of Autonomic and Autonomous Systems (ease 2008), pp. 16–24. IEEE (2008)
9. DeMillo, R.A., Lipton, R.J., Sayward, F.G.: Hints on test data selection: help for the practicing programmer. Computer **11**(4), 34–41 (1978)
10. El Hadj, M.A., Ayache, M., Benkaouz, Y., Khoumsi, A., Erradi, M.: Clustering-based approach for anomaly detection in XACML policies. In: SECRYPT, pp. 548–553 (2017)
11. El Hadj, M.A., Khoumsi, A., Benkaouz, Y., Erradi, M.: Formal approach to detect and resolve anomalies while clustering ABAC policies. EAI Endorsed Trans. Secur. Saf. **5**(16), e3 (2018)
12. Garcia-Alfaro, J., Cuppens, F., Cuppens-Boulahia, N., Preda, S.: MIRAGE: a management tool for the analysis and deployment of network security policies. In: Garcia-Alfaro, J., Navarro-Arribas, G., Cavalli, A., Leneutre, J. (eds.) DPM/SETOP -2010. LNCS, vol. 6514, pp. 203–215. Springer, Heidelberg (2011). https://doi.org/10.1007/978-3-642-19348-4_15
13. Hu, H., Ahn, G.J., Kulkarni, K.: Fame: a firewall anomaly management environment. In: Proceedings of the 3rd ACM Workshop on Assurable and Usable Security Configuration, pp. 17–26 (2010)
14. Hu, H., Ahn, G.J., Kulkarni, K.: Discovery and resolution of anomalies in web access control policies. IEEE Trans. Dependable Secure Comput. **10**(6), 341–354 (2013)
15. Hu, V.C., et al.: Guide to attribute based access control (ABAC) definition and considerations (draft). NIST Spec. Publ. **800**(162), 1–54 (2013)

16. Jabal, A.A., Davari, M., Bertino, E., Makaya, C., Calo, S., Verma, D., Russo, A., Williams, C.: Methods and tools for policy analysis. ACM Comput. Surv. (CSUR) **51**(6), 1–35 (2019)
17. Jabal, A.A., et al.: Profact: a provenance-based analytics framework for access control policies. IEEE Trans. Serv. Comput. **14**(6), 1914–1928 (2019)
18. Jackson, D.: Alloy: a lightweight object modelling notation. ACM Trans. Softw. Eng. Methodol. (TOSEM) **11**(2), 256–290 (2002)
19. Kolovski, V., Hendler, J., Parsia, B.: Analyzing web access control policies. In: Proceedings of the 16th International Conference on World Wide Web, pp. 677–686 (2007)
20. Li, N., Wang, Q., Qardaji, W., Bertino, E., Rao, P., Lobo, J., Lin, D.: Access control policy combining: theory meets practice. In: Proceedings of the 14th ACM Symposium on Access Control Models and Technologies (SACMAT), pp. 135–144 (2009)
21. Mankai, M., Logrippo, L.: Access control policies: modeling and validation. In: 5th NOTERE Conference (Nouvelles Technologies de la Répartition), pp. 85–91 (2005)
22. Martin, E., Hwang, J., Xie, T., Hu, V.: Assessing quality of policy properties in verification of access control policies. In: 2008 Annual Computer Security Applications Conference (ACSAC), pp. 163–172. IEEE (2008)
23. Mohan, A., Blough, D.M., Kurc, T., Post, A., Saltz, J.: Detection of conflicts and inconsistencies in taxonomy-based authorization policies. In: 2011 IEEE International Conference on Bioinformatics and Biomedicine, pp. 590–594. IEEE (2011)
24. Biskup, J., López, J. (eds.): ESORICS 2007. LNCS, vol. 4734. Springer, Heidelberg (2007). https://doi.org/10.1007/978-3-540-74835-9
25. Sandhu, R.S.: Role-based access control. In: Advances in Computers, vol. 46, pp. 237–286. Elsevier (1998)
26. Servos, D., Osborn, S.L.: HGABAC: towards a formal model of hierarchical attribute-based access control. In: Cuppens, F., Garcia-Alfaro, J., Zincir Heywood, N., Fong, P.W.L. (eds.) FPS 2014. LNCS, vol. 8930, pp. 187–204. Springer, Cham (2015). https://doi.org/10.1007/978-3-319-17040-4_12
27. Shaikh, R.A., Adi, K., Logrippo, L.: A data classification method for inconsistency and incompleteness detection in access control policy sets. Int. J. Inf. Secur. **16**(1), 91–113 (2017)
28. Shaikh, R.A., Adi, K., Logrippo, L., Mankovski, S.: Detecting incompleteness in access control policies using data classification schemes. In: 2010 Fifth International Conference on Digital Information Management (ICDIM), pp. 417–422. IEEE (2010)
29. Shaikh, R.A., Adi, K., Logrippo, L., Mankovski, S.: Inconsistency detection method for access control policies. In: 2010 Sixth International Conference on Information Assurance and Security, pp. 204–209. IEEE (2010)
30. Spanoudakis, N.I., Kakas, A.C., Moraitis, P.: Gorgias-b: argumentation in practice. In: COMMA, pp. 477–478 (2016)
31. Turkmen, F., den Hartog, J., Ranise, S., Zannone, N.: Analysis of XACML policies with SMT. In: Focardi, R., Myers, A. (eds.) POST 2015. LNCS, vol. 9036, pp. 115–134. Springer, Heidelberg (2015). https://doi.org/10.1007/978-3-662-46666-7_7
32. Turkmen, F., den Hartog, J., Ranise, S., Zannone, N.: Formal analysis of XACML policies using SMT. Comput. Secur. **66**, 185–203 (2017)

33. Verma, D., et al.: Generative policy model for autonomic management. In: 2017 IEEE SmartWorld, Ubiquitous Intelligence & Computing, Advanced & Trusted Computed, Scalable Computing & Communications, Cloud & Big Data Computing, Internet of People and Smart City Innovation (Smart-World/SCALCOM/UIC/ATC/CBDCom/IOP/SCI), pp. 1–6. IEEE (2017)
34. Xu, Z., Stoller, S.D.: Mining attribute-based access control policies. IEEE Trans. Dependable Secure Comput. **12**(5), 533–545 (2014)
35. Yuan, L., Chen, H., Mai, J., Chuah, C.N., Su, Z., Mohapatra, P.: Fireman: a toolkit for firewall modeling and analysis. In: 2006 IEEE Symposium on Security and Privacy (S&P 2006), p. 15. IEEE (2006)

Short Papers

Designing a Service for Compliant Sharing of Sensitive Research Data

Aakash Sharma$^{(\boxtimes)}$, Thomas Bye Nilsen , Sivert Johansen ,
Dag Johansen , and Håvard D. Johansen

UiT The Arctic University of Norway, Tromsø, Norway
aakash.sharma@uit.no

Abstract. Data-driven research is increasingly becoming fueled by access to open datasets, often shared publicly on the Internet. However, many research projects study sensitive data. They cannot easily participate in this shift as access to their data is significantly controlled by ethical and regulatory constraints. This paper discusses the requirements for building a service that enables sensitive data for sharing between collaborators in a controlled manner. We argue that a decentralized service that maintains metadata, a global view on all data usage, and active policy combined with local monitoring and security enforcement can provide automated compliance checking. With such a service, researchers can share sensitive data with a broader community rather than limiting access to core project members.

Keywords: Open data · Data-sharing · Compliance · Sensitive data

1 Introduction

The Internet has changed the way researchers work, collaborate, and disseminate. Open Science is a cultural change [2]. The arguments concerning the benefits of Open Data are well established; for example allowing researchers to explore existing datasets in new ways [1,4,10]. Volunteers (hereafter written as *subjects*) contribute their data for research. The trustworthiness of the institution conducting the research plays a key role in a subject's willingness to contribute [17]. Privacy leaks or misuse can damage the reputation and affect future research studies [1,4]. Fears of misuse of data may also restrict many researchers from sharing data openly [4,20].

Researchers argue that these concerns can be mitigated by building accountability in research data sharing and processing [8]. Recent regulations, such as General Data Protection Regulation (GDPR) require researchers to abide by a subject's consent for data processing. GDPR also provides workarounds for public-funded research by entrusting a Regional Ethics Committee (REC) or an Institutional Review Board (IRB) to protect subjects' privacy. The public's trust in researchers is fragile [1]. The growing concerns regarding data breaches, data

B. Luo et al. (Eds.): CRiSIS 2021, LNCS 13204, pp. 155–161, 2022.
https://doi.org/10.1007/978-3-031-02067-4_10

brokers, and indiscriminate profiling of users might change subjects' willingness to participate or continue participating in a research project.

The guidelines and complexity of compliance is a tedious job and requires a complex understanding of legal, ethical, and regulatory issues [5]. Often institutions employ large teams to assist researchers in making their data openly available [18]. Researchers' concern about misuse of their data is the leading reason given for not sharing data [4,20]. As a result, research data may end up in silos accessible only to a limited few. A lot of work has been done for simplifying regulatory requirements, easy-to-create toolkits [5,18,21] and metadata formats for making research openly accessible [7,12,21]. However, additional regulations like *data sovereignty* [13] may further restrict Open Data. For example, medical research data is heavily regulated. Often movement of such sensitive data is restricted outside a nation's physical boundaries.

Open science and data-based collaboration require access to the same data regardless of international borders [2,11]. As argued earlier, there might be regulatory restrictions limiting the sharing of sensitive data. The cloud provides an interesting platform for Open Data access to researchers with manageable services. Our contribution is a scalable cloud-based service that allows researchers to analyze sensitive data regardless of their location. We discuss related works in Sect. 2, and present the requirements for the service in Sect. 3. Later in Sect. 4, we present our system's design, key features, and limitations.

2   Related Work and Discussion

Dataverse [7] is a well-known data repository for sharing research data, which currently hosts tens of thousands of datasets. However, Dataverse does not support sensitive data. Datatags system [18] translates security and access requirements for sensitive data into a model set of six tags. Their approach simplifies the complex workings and guidelines for sharing datasets responsibly as they provide a decision tree for picking a correct tag for different requirements. The Datatags approach simplifies complex information flows for IRBs and RECs without specifying mechanisms for automated audits or enforcement.

Automatable Discovery and Access Matrix (A-DAM) [21] provides a *profile* as regulatory metadata for responsible sharing of biomedical assets. A-DAM provides a semi-automated approach for analyzing ethical and regulatory requirements for sharing and processing research data. Policy changes require a newer profile and reevaluation. Maguire et al. [9] proposed a metadata-based architecture for accountability. Similar to A-DAM, Maguire et al.'s approach attaches a static policy to a dataset, which is verified by a gatekeeper service. Their approach introduces validation against *context* by the gatekeeper. For sensitive data, they only briefly discuss adding encryption and keeping the keys under the control of the gatekeeper. In our earlier work Lohpi [15,16], we argued that the changes occurring during a project's life cycle might affect its data security policies. Thus, we built support for accountability by keeping data security policies up to date securely and efficiently. We build upon existing works to semi-automate regulatory, ethical, and legal requirements. Our contribution is a scalable cloud-based service that allows researchers to analyze sensitive data regardless of their location. The service provides transparency to stakeholders, such as subjects regarding data sharing and data use.

Axelsson and Schroeder [1] argue that public trust is fragile, and once broken, might take years to re-build. Compliance and transparency are crucial for maintaining the fragile public trust in researchers. The complex set of guidelines, regulatory and legal requirements, and consent management increase complexity for data curators and researchers. And keeping sensitive data open is a challenging [1]. Even experts in various fields feel the lack of assurances [6] in existing practices. We provide compliance with audit-able data sharing of sensitive datasets. Our approach simplifies access to such datasets by automating compliance while maintaining compliance. The compliance requirements are derived from applicable regulatory and legal requirements. Many researchers have argued for building transparency for data-sharing, usage, and privacy protections [8,14]. Along with these themes, our approach addresses the compliant sharing of sensitive data, especially data sovereignty. Thus, allowing sensitive datasets to reach a broader audience while fulfilling regulatory and legal compliance requirements. The built-in transparency allows stakeholders, such as subjects, to understand the usage of their data and answer questions like who, whom, and where, about their contributed data. Such transparency may improve the public's trust and participation in studies that rely heavily on volunteers.

3 Requirements for the Service

As argued earlier, Open Data should be able to reach a broader audience. Our goal is to build a service that supports sharing of sensitive data and addresses the compliance requirements. We now discuss the requirements for building services for researchers to share sensitive research data. The regulations, re-identification attack methods, and legal and ethical requirements may change over time. We conjecture that the following requirements are essential for building a service compliant with the legal, regulatory, and ethical requirements stipulated by concerned authorities/stakeholders. The service can adapt to changes that may affect data sensitivity and a subject's preference. Existing works like Datatags [18] and A-DAM [21] provide methods for computable ethical, legal, and regulatory requirements. Different security mechanisms can enforce these requirements [18]. Additionally, we include the *data sovereignty* requirement for sensitive data, which restricts the movement of data outside a nation's physical boundaries, even if the data are hosted, by a cloud service provider (CSP).

RQ 1 (Timely Dissemination of Data Policies). Data policies define the ethical, legal, and regulatory requirements attached with a dataset. The service should disseminate changes to data policies within a predefined time τ. Each dissemination should be secure, maintain integrity, and be logged, for auditing. Consent revocations and new approvals from an IRB or a REC can result in such changes. A change in laws, regulations and institutional guidelines may result in a policy change as well.

RQ 2 (Data Sovereignty).   The service should ensure data sovereignty by verifying data residency. Any attempt of data movement which violates data sovereignty should be prevented and logged.

RQ 3 (Garbage Collection).   Once completed with the task, copies of data should be securely deleted and logged. No residual copies of the data or the dataset remain on an unsolicited location or machine.

RQ 4 (Auditing).   The service should log each operation and action in a distributed log. These operations and actions must be available for auditing by an IRB, REC or an independent auditing authority.

RQ 5 (Secure Computation).   The continuous access evaluation should be securely computed at the CSP. The attack surface for tampering with the data access policy should be limited.

4   System Overview

We now describe our approach and discuss how different components will fulfill the requirements discussed earlier (Sect. 3). We assume that each dataset has a unique identifier. Researchers who are interested in accessing a dataset can authenticate themselves. The existing data security policy allows authenticated researchers to access the dataset. The dataset in this example has data sovereignty constraints. A CSP has a data center in the same region as the dataset.

4.1   Workflow

Figure 1 shows the system architecture with an example workflow. A researcher or simply a *user* is interested in analyzing a dataset hosted at an institution in another country. After authenticating herself using the web portal, the user configures a machine for her analysis (RQ4). The user can decide from multiple pre-configured container images which contain different data analysis software packages. These container images enable communication with a trusted substrate for exchanging data policy updates and logs (RQ1, RQ4). The daemon software is pre-installed and configured in these container images. For enhanced security, the container images are pre-configured to limit data egress and allow only a set of pre-approved packages. As the last step, the user chooses the dataset that she is interested in (RQ5).

Once configured, a new container instance with chosen software packages runs in the cloud which, exists in the same country as the dataset (RQ2). The user obtains access to the container running in the cloud. Upon initialization, the user needs to authenticate herself again for obtaining a copy of the dataset (RQ4). The instance also receives policy changes that might arrive while the user is working on the dataset after the initialization (RQ1).

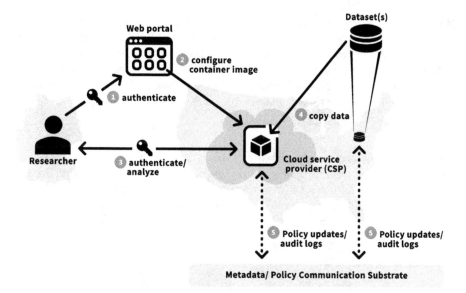

Fig. 1. An example workflow: a researcher from Germany wants to access a sensitive dataset from an institute in the USA. The movement of the data outside the USA is restricted. By leveraging a CSP, we facilitate sharing of the dataset for research without moving the data outside the USA. The accesses are logged for audit and transparency reports. The data security policies are updated using the communication substrate.

The instance enforces *use-based* policies using Intel's software guard extensions (SGX) using approaches like [3] (RQ5). In-line monitoring using SGX can result in a performance penalty. For performance reasons, we use the delegated monitoring architecture proposed in Birrel et al. [3]'s work. The instance communicates with the metadata communication substrate and keeps the metadata/policy up-to-date (RQ1). The changes to a checked-out dataset's policy are disseminated through the substrate. Both the original dataset and the copy in the container receive the changes via the substrate. After receiving metadata updates, the compliance and access are reevaluated (RQ5). The daemon process routinely checks for compliance with the latest data security policies. These work behind the scenes and notify the user if additional inputs are required. Thus, making compliance easier for the user. In case of non-compliance, the user may lose access to the machine while saving the image to save her work-in-progress. After resolving the non-compliance issue, the user can regain access. The user can export the analysis' results in different pre-approved file formats to the web portal (RQ3). Through the portal, the user can obtain the results later. The results can be archived at the portal for cross-examination by auditors and reviewers for scientific peer-review processes.

At the end of the analysis, the user can terminate the instance, and the analysis scripts and the dataset copy are securely destroyed (RQ3). A user may also choose to save the current state of the container for reproducibility of results [19]. The sharing and accesses generate logs containing sanitized information for audits. The stakeholders (subjects, REC or IRB) can also view reports on data use and sharing and intervene if necessary. Oversight committees (RECs or IRBs) can review non-compliance incidents and take necessary actions. These actions can be in the form of policy updates propagated to every copy of the dataset. Securing a container image while preserving reproducibility is beyond the scope of this paper.

Limitations. Our approach protects against a benign threat model and assumes an accountable adversary. The system may not protect against a sophisticated attacker. The availability of a cloud service provider (CSP)'s container services in the same administrative region as of a dataset's location is crucial for the data sovereignty requirements.

5   Conclusion

Regulatory compliance in research data sharing is a developing problem with newly introduced regulations and growing concerns about individual privacy. The relationship between subjects and research institutions relies heavily on trust for voluntary participation. Data sharing and use, compliant with the subjects' wishes is crucial for continued participation and sustaining trust. We discussed the requirements for building a service enabling compliant data use and sharing sensitive research data. We further presented our approach for building such a service and how it addresses those requirements. We plan to test the system with our partners from sports sciences and medical science, creating policy templates for legal and regulatory requirements for sensitive research data.

Acknowledgements. We thank Katja Pauline Czerwinska for her assistance with the graphics. This work was funded in part by Research Council of Norway project numbers 263248 and 274451.

References

1. Axelsson, A.S., Schroeder, R.: Making it open and keeping it safe: e-enabled data-sharing in Sweden. Acta Sociologica **52**(3), 213–226 (2009). https://doi.org/10.1177/0001699309339799. ISSN 00016993
2. Bartling, S., Friesike, S.: Opening Science: the Evolving Guide on how the Web is Changing Research, Collaboration and Scholarly Publishing, vol. 51. Springer, Berlin (2014). https://doi.org/10.5860/choice.51-6715
3. Birrell, E., Gjerdrum, A., Van Renesse, R., Johansen, H., Johansen, D., Schneider, F.B.: SGX enforcement of use-based privacy. In: Proceedings of the ACM Conference on Computer and Communications Security, pp. 155–167 (2018). https://doi.org/10.1145/3267323.3268954, ISBN 9781450359894, ISSN 15437221
4. Borgman, C.L.: Open data, grey data, and stewardship: universities at the privacy frontier. Berkeley Tech. Law J. **33**, 365 (2018). http://arxiv.org/abs/1802.02953

5. Braunschweig, K., Eberius, J., Thiele, M., Lehner, W.: The state of open data. Limits Curr. Open Data Platforms Www 2012 (2012)
6. Hammack, C.M., Brelsford, K.M., Beskow, L.M.: Thought leader perspectives on participant protections in precision medicine research. J. Law Med. Ethics **47**(1), 134–148 (2019). https://doi.org/10.1177/1073110519840493. ISSN 1748720X
7. King, G.: An introduction to the dataverse network as an infrastructure for data sharing (2007). https://doi.org/10.1177/0049124107306660
8. Kroll, J.A., Kohli, N., Laskowski, P.: Privacy and policy in polystores: a data management research agenda. In: Gadepally, V., et al. (eds.) DMAH/Poly -2019. LNCS, vol. 11721, pp. 68–81. Springer, Cham (2019). https://doi.org/10.1007/978-3-030-33752-0_5
9. Maguire, S., Friedberg, J., Nguyen, M.-H.C., Haynes, P.: A metadata-based architecture for user-centered data accountability. Electron. Mark. **25**(2), 155–160 (2015). https://doi.org/10.1007/s12525-015-0184-z
10. Molloy, J.C.: The open knowledge foundation: open data means better science. PLoS Biol. **9**(12), (2011). https://doi.org/10.1371/journal.pbio.1001195, ISSN 15449173
11. Mulligan, A., Mabe, M.: The effect of the internet on researcher motivations, behaviour and attitudes. J. Documentation **67**(2), 290–311 (2011). https://doi.org/10.1108/00220411111109485. ISSN 00220418
12. Pampel, H., et al.: Making research data repositories visible: the re3data.org registry. PLoS ONE **8**(11), e78080 . https://doi.org/10.1371/journal.pone.0078080. ISSN 19326203
13. Peterson, Z.N., Gondree, M., Beverly, R.: A position paper on data sovereignty: the importance of geolocating data in the cloud. In: 3rd USENIX Workshop on Hot Topics in Cloud Computing, HotCloud 2011 (2011)
14. Schneider, G.: Disentangling health data networks: a critical analysis of articles 9(2) and 89 GDPR. Int. Data Priv. Law **9**(4), 253–271 (2019). https://doi.org/10.1093/idpl/ipz015. ISSN 20444001
15. Sharma, A., Nilsen, T.B., Brenna, L., Johansen, D., Johansen, H.D.: Accountable human subject research data processing using lohpi. In: Proceedings of the ICTeSSH 2021 Conference (2021). https://doi.org/10.21428/7a45813f.80ebd922
16. Sharma, A., et al.: Up-to-the-minute privacy policies via gossips in participatory epidemiological studies. Front. Big Data **4**, 14 (2021). https://doi.org/10.3389/fdata.2021.624424. ISSN 2624909X
17. Slegers, C., et al.: Why do people participate in epidemiological research? J. Bioethical Inquiry **12**(2), 227–237 (2015). https://doi.org/10.1007/s11673-015-9611-2
18. Sweeney, L., Crosas, M., Bar-Sinai, M.: Sharing sensitive data with confidence: the datatags system. Technol. Sci. 1–34 (2015). http://techscience.org/a/2015101601/
19. Trisovic, A., et al.: Advancing computational reproducibility in the dataverse data repository platform. In: P-RECS 2020 - Proceedings of the 3rd International Workshop on Practical Reproducible Evaluation of Computer Systems, pp. 15–20 (2020). ISBN 9781450379779, https://doi.org/10.1145/3391800.3398173
20. Winthrop, S.: Social considerations to make data FAIR-er: understanding researchers' views on data "misuse" and credit. In: Septentrio Conference Series, no. 1 (2019). https://doi.org/10.7557/5.4970, https://doi.org/10.6084/m9.figshare.10011788.v2;
21. Woolley, J.P., et al.: Responsible sharing of biomedical data and biospecimens via the automatable discovery and access matrix (ADA-M). NPJ Genomic Med. **3**(1), 1–6 (2018). https://doi.org/10.1038/s41525-018-0057-4

Authenticated Multi-proxy Accumulation Schemes for Delegated Membership Proofs

Hannes Salin[1]([✉]), Dennis Fokin[1], and Alexander Johansson[2]

[1] Department of Information and Communication Technology, Swedish Transport Administration, Borlänge, Sweden
hannes.salin@trafikverket.se
[2] Saab AB, Stockholm, Sweden
alexander.johansson2@saab.com

Abstract. Proving ownership (or possibly non-ownership) of an attribute associated with an individual or device can be used in many different use cases. For a user to prove age, credibility, medical records or other type of attributes, cryptographic accumulators can be used. Also, in a federated authentication architecture, a user may prove such ownership via one or many proxies, e.g. a trusted party such as a bank or government institution. We propose an authenticated multi-proxy accumulation (AMPA) scheme for solving these types of scenarios without the need for encryption and still preserve privacy and remove data set leakage during set membership proving. We illustrate how an AMPA scheme easily can be constructed and present initial results from a proof of concept implementation.

Keywords: Proxy accumulator · Proxy signatures · Cryptography

1 Introduction

Cloud computing and distributed data sharing is growing more than ever; outsourcing data storage to popular cloud solutions such as Amazon Web Services (AWS), Microsoft Azure and Google Cloud, which are the current top service providers [7], is constantly growing. However, government agencies and parts of the public sector are still reluctant to adopt cloud based solutions to third party service providers due to legal reasons (CLOUD Act [13]), but also due to security related issues [11]. At the same time, many types of information sharing use cases for individuals and government institutions remain, e.g. medical journal sharing between patient and hospital, and sharing and verification of criminal records between police authority, potential employers and other institutions. In all cases, the information could be considered attributes associated with an individual, i.e. the data owner. It is therefore of mutual interest that both the data owner and the data storage provider, e.g. the hospital or police authority, are able to verify the authenticity and integrity of the same data. Moreover, in some

B. Luo et al. (Eds.): CRiSIS 2021, LNCS 13204, pp. 162–171, 2022.
https://doi.org/10.1007/978-3-031-02067-4_11

scenarios a (trusted) third party is the requester of verifying attribute data of a person, e.g. an employer needs to verify an applicant's (non-existent) criminal records thus requesting proof from the police authorities. Ideally, these type of scenarios would benefit from using a cloud infrastructure shared between institutions and agencies, streamlined for fast data sharing and efficient real-time validity proof checking. However, due to GDPR it is problematic to share personal attributes between institutions, thus a mechanism for secure proof checking without revealing explicit data is required.

1.1   Problem Statement

Many different real-world scenarios rely on manual verification for both users and institutions. One example is where a prover $\mathcal{P}$ is going through a security screening when applying for a classified role, e.g. within the military or government sector. A prover $\mathcal{P}$ needs to prove a set of attributes such as no criminal record, no medical history of certain diseases/injuries etc. In a national database these attributes could be proven to exist or similarly, be proven as a non-membership in order to prove the lack of attributes. Other government agencies or medical institutions may have subsets of these attributes, hence are able to act as proxies when requesting the (non)-membership proofs for $\mathcal{P}$ to a verifer $\mathcal{V}$.

Intelligent Transportation Systems (ITS) and connected railway infrastructure are still on the rise, and with that many security implications as well [8, 9]. Personal devices (vehicle on-board devices, smartphones) and equipment such as cameras and radar sensory devices in the infrastructure can all be connected. A secure and privacy-preserving layer of data knowledge sharing is thus needed where a single device can prove attribute (data) knowledge or association efficient and through (multiple) proxies, e.g. a vehicle may need to prove eligibility for entering certain areas, or sensory devices must prove its geographical boundaries.

The given scenarios requires a multi-party setup where possibly a set of proxies $\mathcal{AP}$ is needed for proving that certain attributes $y_1, ..., y_n$ belong to $\mathcal{P}$, by proving that $y_1, ...y_n$ are securely stored in a trusted database at some database owner $\mathcal{S}$. Furthermore, proof of identity of all parties, including $\mathcal{P}$ and $\mathcal{S}$, and signatures for all proofs are needed to ensure authenticity and integrity. The assumption is that $\mathcal{P}$ either cannot provide such proofs, or prefer to delegate the proving part to one or many proxies, e.g. trusted parties such as a bank, hospital or in the IoT case intermediate servers. Therefore, we address the problem of delegated (non)-membership proving.

1.2   Accumulators and Proxy Signatures

A one-way *accumulator* is an efficient solution for secure set-membership proof problems, i.e. determine if a certain element belongs to a given set without revealing the elements. One important property of an accumulator is that it can efficiently provide a fixed-size *witness* for any element in the accumulator, which is used for verification of an element's set (non)-membership. The notion of one-way accumulators was first proposed by Benaloh and de Mare [2]. Another type of cryptographic accumulators are constructions based on bilinear pairings and was first proposed by Nguyen [12]. Proxy signature protocols consists of three parties: *original signer*, *proxy signer* and *verifier*. A *warrant* is sent to the proxy, consisting of a predefined message space, a signature, identity of original signer etc. The warrant is used in combination with the proxy key to compute a secret proxy key for further signatures.

1.3   Related Work

For the given use cases, tangent solutions exist addressing the privacy needs. In [14] it is demonstrated how a *private set intersection* (PSI) approach can be used in a cloud environment to calculate the set intersection on outsourced and encrypted data between client and server. However, the solution relies on encryption. Another approach is multi-party PSI solutions, first introduced in [6], where multiple data owners can prove data intersections among each other without revealing the non-intersecting parts. On the other hand, these and more recent protocols [1,10] which also have the ability to make use of delegated private set intersection computations via proxies, still rely on encryption and does not use the proxies as intermediate verifiers. Hence, to our knowledge, there are no proposed protocols for using (multi) proxy signature schemes and accumulators as building blocks with merged key- and signature mechanisms in current literature.

1.4   Contribution

Our paper introduces the notion of *authenticated (multi) proxy accumulation* for solving both current and potentially new use cases. Our contribution consists of:

- Proposing a suitable explicit construction of combining a multi-proxy signature scheme with a dynamic accumulator scheme,
- proposing a general construction process for authenticated multi-proxy accumulation schemes,
- presents a security and correctness analysis for the proposed scheme,
- a performance analysis from our proof of concept implementation in Java and jPBC.

2   Preliminaries

A function $\mathcal{H} : \{0,1\}^* \to \mathbb{A}$ is a cryptographically secure hash function taking any binary string as input and produces an element of some set $\mathbb{A}$. Let $x_i \leftarrow_\$ X$ denote a randomized selection of x_i from a set X over a uniform distribution. A security parameter 1^λ determines parameter selection during initialization of a scheme, i.e. choosing suitable secure groups for a bilinear map, prime numbers and hash functions; thus λ corresponds to the provided n-bit security.

Definition 1 (Pairing). *Let* $\mathbb{G}_1$, $\mathbb{G}_2$, $\mathbb{G}_T$ *be groups with generators* g_1, g_2, g_T *respectively. Let* $q = |\langle g_1 \rangle| = |\langle g_2 \rangle| = |\langle g_T \rangle|$. *Let* $\hat{e} : \mathbb{G}_1 \times \mathbb{G}_2 \to \mathbb{G}_T$ *be a bilinear map with the following properties:*

1. *Bilinearity:* $\forall (a, b \in \mathbb{Z}_q, g_1 \in \mathbb{G}_1, g_2 \in \mathbb{G}_2)$: $\hat{e}(g_1^a, g_2^b) = \hat{e}(g_1, g_2)^{ab}$,
2. *Computability: Computing* $\hat{e}$ *is efficient,*
3. *Non-degeneracy:* $\exists (g_1 \in \mathbb{G}_1, g_2 \in \mathbb{G}_2) : \hat{e}(g_1, g_2) \neq 1$.

we then say that e *is a* pairing *over groups* $\mathbb{G}_1$, $\mathbb{G}_2$, $\mathbb{G}_T$.

If $\mathbb{G}_1 = \mathbb{G}_2$, the pairing function is called *symmetric*, otherwise *asymmetric*.

Our construction use the Boneh-Lynn-Shacham (BLS) short signatures scheme [3]. BLS is provably secure under the Computational Diffie-Hellman problem and based on pairings. The signature of m is produced as $\sigma = \mathcal{H}_g(m)^{\mathtt{sk}}$ where $\mathtt{sk}$ is the signer's secret key. Verification is against the public key $\mathtt{pk}$ and the pairing $\hat{e}(\sigma, g) \stackrel{?}{=} \hat{e}(\mathcal{H}(m), \mathtt{pk})$.

3   General Scheme Construction Methodology

The benefit of using a modular construction as described here, is that each component can easily be changed when needed; if a scheme component is enhanced in the same security model the new component should seamlessly be interchanged. We propose a general approach, using a construction-by-modules principle, for constructing an authenticated multi-proxy accumulation scheme as follows:

1. **Scheme selection:** choose a signature scheme $\mathtt{Sig}$, (multi)-proxy scheme $\mathtt{Proxy}$ and accumulator scheme $\mathtt{Acc}$ based on same cryptographic primitives (and possibly same hardness assumption), e.g. bilinear pairings.
2. **Hardness selection:** Make sure the hardness assumptions are compatible, e.g. for pairings, check that the underlying pairing schemes are all symmetric or asymmetric, to avoid mismatches during the security analysis.
3. **Re-usage:** Make sure $\mathtt{Sig}$ can be re-used for all steps in the $\mathtt{Proxy}$ protocol and does not rely on several different signature schemes.
4. **Extension:** Extend the $\mathtt{Proxy}$ protocol to use one additional round of signature generation/verifying, as described in Sect. 4.2 for the *request* and *proving* phases, i.e. the proxies first compute an intermediate round of signature checking with the set owner, and then the final signature round to the verifying party.
5. **Security Analysis:** Make sure the security of the merged parts of the scheme can be reduced to the security assumption of the $\mathtt{Sig}$ component.

In conclusion, the merge of $\mathtt{Sig}$, $\mathtt{Proxy}$ and $\mathtt{Acc}$ builds on the efficiency of using the same cryptographical primitives and the flexibility to easily add a second round of signature checking with the data owner to perform an intermediate proof checking step. Naturally, this scales linearly; for n proxies only $2n$ additional signature checks are needed.

4   Authenticated Multi-Proxy Accumulation Scheme

4.1   System Model

The model consists of four parties: set owner $\mathcal{S}$, accumulation proxy $\mathcal{AP}$, prover $\mathcal{P}$ and verifier $\mathcal{V}$. Set owner $\mathcal{S}$ has full control over a finite set $Y = \{y_1, ..., y_n\}$ for which prover $\mathcal{P}$ wants to prove membership of some element $y_i \in Y$ for verifer $\mathcal{V}$. In this particular setting, $\mathcal{P}$ must delegate the proving part to $\mathcal{AP}$ which in turn communicates the proof to verifier $\mathcal{V}$. This implies $\mathcal{V}$ to verify three things: the validity of the membership proof, that $\mathcal{P}$ is authenticated and thus implicitly the delegation of the proof from $\mathcal{P}$ to $\mathcal{AP}$ also follows.

4.2   Proposed Construction

We propose an *authenticated multi-proxy accumulation scheme* (AMPA). It involves a multi-party setup with a prover $\mathcal{P}$, a set of (at least one) accumulation proxies $\mathcal{AP} = \{AP_1, AP_2, ..., AP_n\}$, a set authority $\mathcal{S}$ and a verifier $\mathcal{V}$. An element $y_j \in Y$ is considered an attribute of $\mathcal{P}$ and stored securely. Moreover, y_j is committed to the set authority's database, i.e. $y_j \in S$ where set S is securely stored and handled by $\mathcal{S}$. Our scheme consists of 7 algorithms:

Setup$(1^\lambda, n) \rightarrow$ (par, $pk_S, sk_S, acc_0, state_0$): generates a tuple of bilinear pairing parameters and necessary secure hash functions par $= (q, \mathbb{G}_1, \mathbb{G}_2, g, \hat{e}, \mathcal{H}_1, \mathcal{H}_2)$ to publish, where $\hat{e} : \mathbb{G}_1 \times \mathbb{G}_1 \rightarrow \mathbb{G}_2$ is a bilinear map and $\mathcal{H}_1, \mathcal{H}_2$ are collision-resistant hash functions such that $\mathcal{H}_1 : \{0,1\}^* \rightarrow \mathbb{Z}_q^*$ and $\mathcal{H}_2 : \{0,1\}^* \rightarrow \mathbb{G}_1$. Next, signature key-pair (sk, pk) for set authority $\mathcal{S}$, is generated as $sk = x_0 \xleftarrow{\$} \mathbb{Z}_q^*$ and $pk = g^{x_0}$. Accumulator key-pair (sk_S, pk_S) for $\mathcal{S}$ is generated as key tuples $sk_S = (\gamma \xleftarrow{\$} \mathbb{Z}_q^*, sk)$ and $pk_S = (pk, \hat{e}(g, g)^{\gamma^{n+1}})$. Additionally, the accumulator $acc_0 = 1$ with state table $state_0$ initiated. Finally, the prover $\mathcal{P}$ generates a keypair as $sk_P = x_1 \xleftarrow{\$} \mathbb{Z}_q^*$ and $pk_P = g^{x_1}$.

KeyExtract$(\{1, 2, ..., l\}) \rightarrow L$: generates set of key-pairs for proxy signers $L = \{(pk_1, sk_1), (pk_2, sk_2), ..., (pk_l, sk_l)\}$. Either a suitable key agreement protocol can be used if there is a single node running this procedure, otherwise each proxy signer runs this procedure locally and broadcast the public key to all other parties.

ProxyKeyGen$(w, S_{O_w}) \rightarrow sk_{AP_i}$: given a warrant w and S_{O_w} issued and generated by original signer, the proxy $\mathcal{AP}_i$ invokes ProxyKeyGen and verifies that $e(S_{O_w}, g) == e(\mathcal{H}_2(w), pk_P)$. If valid then the proxy signing key is computed as $sk_{AP_i} = S_{O_w} + \mathcal{H}_2(w)^{sk_i}$. Note that $S_{O_w} = \mathcal{H}_2(w)^{x_0}$.

ProxyAccSignWitness$(m_1, w) \rightarrow \sigma_1$: The proxy generates $k_{AP_i} \xleftarrow{\$} \mathbb{Z}_p^*$ and computes $r_{AP_i} = \hat{e}(g, g)^{k_{AP_i}}$. Each r_{AP_i} is broadcast to all other $\mathcal{AP}_i$'s who computes $r_{AP} = \Pi_{i=1}^l r_{AP_i}$, $c_{AP} = \mathcal{H}_1(m_1 \| r_{AP})$ and $U_{AP_i} = (sk_{AP_i})^{c_{AP}} + g^{k_{AP_i}}$. One designated $\mathcal{AP}_i$, called the *clerk* verifies $r_{AP_i} = \hat{e}(U_{AP_i}, g)(\hat{e}(\mathcal{H}_2(w), pk + pk_i))^{-c_{AP}}$ for $i = 1, 2, .., l$, and if successful computes $U_{AP} = \Sigma_{i=1}^l U_{AP_i}$ and sends signature $\sigma_1 = (m_1, c_{AP}, U_{AP}, w)$ to $\mathcal{S}$. Message $m_1 = (\omega_1, acc_P, g\|y_j)$

where ω_1 is the witness of y_j from $\mathcal{P}$, $acc_\mathcal{P}$ the accumulator of $\mathcal{P}$ and $g\|y_j$ which is used during accumulation verification as in [4].

ProxyAccVerifyWitness(σ_1) $\rightarrow$ σ_2: $\mathcal{S}$ receives the witness and element for verification from $\mathcal{AP}$. Next, $\mathcal{S}$ verifies that $y_j \in Y$ using the witness and check that $c_{AP} = \mathcal{H}_1(m_1\|r_{AP})$; note that $r_{AP} = \hat{e}(U_{AP}, g)(\hat{e}(\mathcal{H}_2(w), pk + \Sigma_{i=1}^l pk_i))^{-c_{AP}}$. If so, $\mathcal{S}$ signs $m_2 = (\omega_{i_{AP}}, acc_\mathcal{P}, \omega_{i_\mathcal{S}}, acc_\mathcal{S})$ implying that $y_j \in S$. Signature procedure is same as in ProxyAccSignWitness but with $\mathcal{S}$ as only signer (hence clerk), and returns $\sigma_2 = (m_2, c_\mathcal{S}, U_\mathcal{S}, w)$.

ProxyAccSignProof(σ_2) $\rightarrow$ σ_3: All proxies runs ProxyAccSignWitness over σ_2 as message. Resulting signature is $\sigma_3 = (\sigma_2, c_{\mathcal{AP}}, U_{\mathcal{AP}}, w)$.

ProxyAccVerifyProof(σ_3) $\rightarrow$ $\{\bot, true\}$: $\mathcal{V}$ verifies σ_3 by computing $c_{\mathcal{AP}} = \mathcal{H}_1(\sigma_2\|r_{\mathcal{AP}})$. If correct then parse σ_2 and if needed checks membership of $y_j \in S$. Note that if the signature verifies correctly, $\mathcal{V}$ implicitly knows that $y_j \in Y, S$, that $\mathcal{AP}$ is a designated signer and $\mathcal{S}$ is a valid set authority.

Note that four more algorithms, AccAdd, AccUpdate, AccWitUpdate and AccVerify, are used just as they are stated in [4]. The complete protocol executes in phases described below: *setup, request* and *proving phases*. Note that we assume $\mathcal{S}$ is running a trusted environment.

Setup phase: $\mathcal{P}$ securely sends and commit set Y to set authority $\mathcal{S}$ who updates the complete set S such that $Y \subseteq S$. $\mathcal{S}$ then runs Setup and publishes all public parameters such as groups and pairing function, accumulator value $acc_\mathcal{S}$ and generates associated signature- and accumulator keys $sk_\mathcal{S}, pk_\mathcal{S}$. All proxies runs KeyExtract to get their own key-pairs (these has to be exchanged using a secure key exchange protocol). Finally, $\mathcal{P}$ sends a warrant w to the collection of proxy signers $\mathcal{AP}_1, ..., \mathcal{AP}_l$ who then runs ProxyKeyGen to generate specific proxy signature keys sk_{AP_i} associated to $\mathcal{P}$ and $\mathcal{S}$.

Request phase: Verifier $\mathcal{V}$ asks $\mathcal{P}$ to prove membership of $y_j \in S$. This triggers $\mathcal{P}$ to send $w, \omega_1, acc_\mathcal{P}, g\|y_j$, i.e. warrant, witness for $y_i \in Y$, accumulator value and the element concatenation needed for the membership proof, to all relevant proxies $\mathcal{AP}$ who in turn create a signature σ_1 over the tuple by invoking ProxyAccSignWitness. Next step is that $\mathcal{AP}$ sends σ_1 to $\mathcal{S}$ who responds with witness ω_2 if the signature can be verified using ProxyAccVerifyWitness and that accumulation membership proof of $y_j \in Y$ holds.

Proving phase: $\mathcal{AP}$ runs ProxyAccSignProof to generate a final proof σ_3 which is a signature over σ_2 and contains information such as membership proof (witness), delegation proof and authenticity proof of $\mathcal{P}, \mathcal{AP}$ and $\mathcal{S}$. Verifier $\mathcal{V}$ runs ProxyAccVerifyProof function that uses AccVerify as subroutine, to verify membership proof $y_j \in S$. $\mathcal{V}$ responds either *true* or error symbol $\bot$ to $\mathcal{P}$.

Accumulators $acc_\mathcal{P}$ and $acc_\mathcal{S}$ ($\mathcal{P}$'s and $\mathcal{S}$'s accumulators respectively) and their associated states $state_\mathcal{P}, state_\mathcal{S}$, are variables we do not consider in the scheme definition.

5   Security Analysis

5.1   Proof of Correctness

We note that ProxyAccVerifyWitness verifies correctly and computes signature σ_2 if and only if $y \in Y$ and $c_{AP} = \mathcal{H}_1(m_1 \| r_{AP})$ holds. Since $\mathcal{S}$ verifies $y \in Y$ accordingly to [4], then if successful, ProxyAccVerifyWitness procedure verifies $c_{AP} = \mathcal{H}_1(m_1 \| r_{AP})$. This is only possible if r_{AP} is correctly generated. Moreover, ProxyAccVerifyProof verifies σ_3 correctly if and only if $y \in Y$ and c_{AP} holds. The proof for that follows since we set $l = 1$ for the number of proxies, thereby only using one proxy instead of a full collection.

Theorem 1. ProxyAccVerifyWitness *verifies correctly and computes signature* σ_2 *if and only if* $y \in Y$ *and* $c_{AP} = \mathcal{H}_1(m_1 \| r_{AP})$ *holds.*

Proof. We note that $\sigma_1 = (m_1, c_{AP}, U_{AP}, w)$, thus c_{AP} is parsed. Also, $pk = g^{x_0}$ and $pk_i = g^{x_i}$. We denote $\mathcal{H}_2(w) = h_2$ for readability. Next, since

$$= \hat{e}(U_{AP}, g) \left(\hat{e}(h_2, pk + \sum_{i=1}^{l} pk_i) \right)^{-c_{AP}} \tag{1}$$

$$= \hat{e}(\sum_{i=1}^{l} (sk_{AP_i})^{c_{AP}} + g^{k_{AP_i}}, g) \left(\hat{e}(h_2, g^{x_0}) \prod_{i=1}^{l} \hat{e}(h_2, g^{x_i}) \right)^{-c_{AP}} \tag{2}$$

$$= \left(\prod_{i=1}^{l} \hat{e}(sk_{AP_i}, g)^{c_{AP}} \hat{e}(g, g)^{k_{AP_i}} \right) \left(\hat{e}(h_2, g^{x_0}) \prod_{i=1}^{l} \hat{e}(h_2, g^{x_i}) \right)^{-c_{AP}} \tag{3}$$

$$= \left(\prod_{i=1}^{l} \hat{e}(h_2^{x_0}, g)^{c_{AP}} \hat{e}(h_2^{x_i}, g)^{c_{AP}} \hat{e}(g, g)^{k_{AP_i}} \right) \left(\hat{e}(h_2, g^{x_0}) \prod_{i=1}^{l} \hat{e}(h_2, g^{x_i}) \right)^{-c_{AP}} \tag{4}$$

$$= \prod_{i=1}^{l} \hat{e}(g, g)^{k_{AP_i}} = r_{AP} \tag{5}$$

we can verify that $c_{AP} = \mathcal{H}_1(m_1 \| r_{AP})$. $\mathcal{S}$ verifies $y \in Y$ accordingly to [4], thus $\mathcal{S}$ can successfully generate σ_2 using same procedure as for σ_1 but with $m_2 = (y_i, \omega_{i_{AP}}, acc_P, g \| y_i, \omega_{i_S}, acc_S)$.   □

Theorem 2. ProxyAccVerifyProof *verifies correctly and computes signature* σ_3 *if and only if* $y \in Y$ *and* $c_{AP} = \mathcal{H}_1(m_2 \| r_{AP})$ *holds.*

Proof. Same as in Theorem 1 but for $l = 1$.   □

5.2   Security Model and Analysis

We consider a security experiment where forger $\mathcal{F}$ is allowed to query signatures σ_1, σ_2 and σ_3 given public parameters. Let $\mathcal{O}_{\mathsf{Sign}}(\alpha, m, i) \rightarrow \sigma_i$ be a signing oracle which returns a valid signature $\sigma_i, i \in \{1, 2, 3\}$, m a message and $\alpha = \{par, pk_1, pk_2, ...\}$ is the set of public parameters and all public keys necessary. Moreover, let $\mathcal{O}_{\mathsf{H}_1}(x) \to c$ be a random oracle which return elements $c \in \mathbb{Z}_q^*$, given some binary string x, thus emulating $\mathcal{H}_1$, and similarly $\mathcal{O}_{\mathsf{H}_2}(x) \to d$ where $d \in \mathbb{G}$.

Definition 2 (Security Experiment). *Let π be an AMPA scheme initialized with Setup$(1^\lambda, n)$ and all proxy signature keys generated. Next, let $\mathcal{F}$ be a polynomial-time forgery algorithm with the ability to query $\mathcal{O}_{\mathsf{Sign}}$, $\mathcal{O}_{\mathsf{H}_1}$ and $\mathcal{O}_{\mathsf{H}_2}$ a polynomial number of times (q times). After a maximum of q queries, $\mathcal{F}$ is able to generate a signature tuple $(\sigma_1^*, \sigma_2^*, \sigma_3^*)$ for messages m_1^*, m_2^* that has not been previously queried. We then say that π is secure if*

$$Pr[\mathcal{F}^{\mathcal{O}_{\mathsf{Sign}}, \mathcal{O}_{\mathsf{H}_1}, \mathcal{O}_{\mathsf{H}_2}}(\alpha) \to (\sigma_1^*, \sigma_2^*, \sigma_3^*, m_1^*, m_2^*) \wedge \mathsf{Verify}(\sigma_1^*, \sigma_2^*, \sigma_3^*) = 1] < \epsilon \quad (6)$$

where Verify returns 1 if and only if subroutines ProxyAccVerifyWitness$(\sigma_1^*) = \sigma_2^*$, ProxyAccSignProof$(\sigma_2^*) = \sigma_3^*$ and ProxyAccVerifyProof$(\sigma_3^*) = 1$, and ϵ is negligible.

Theorem 3 (Non-forgeability). *The proposed AMPA scheme is secure against forgery as defined in Definition 2.*

Proof (Sketch of proof). The security experiment initializes according to Def. 2 and $\mathbb{G}$ is a computationally secure Diffie-Hellman group. We consider two cases: (1) where forger $\mathcal{F}$ compute σ_3^* directly and (2) when $\mathcal{F}$ compute σ_2^* and use it for further computations to achieve σ_3^*. We omit a third case where σ_1^* is computed since the proof is same as case (1) since σ_1 and σ_3 only differs over which message to sign, i.e. either m_1 or σ_2.

Case 1: Assume forger $\mathcal{F}$ manages to compute a forged signature σ_3^*. We note that a signature $\sigma_3^* = (\sigma_2^*, c_{AP}^*, U_{AP}^*, w)$ where $\sigma_2^* = (m_2^*, c_S^*, U_S^*, w)$. In such forgery we get that $\mathcal{O}_{\mathsf{H}}(m_2) \to c'$ thus

$$U_{AP}^* = \sum_{i=1}^{l} \left((sk_{AP_i})^{c'} + g^{k_{AP_i}} \right) = \sum_{i=1}^{l} \left((S_{O_w} + \mathcal{H}_2(w)^{sk_i})^{c'} + g^{k_{AP_i}} \right) \quad (7)$$

$$= \sum_{i=1}^{l} \left((\mathcal{H}_2(w)^{x_0} + \mathcal{H}_2(w)^{x_i})^{c'} + g^{k_{AP_i}} \right) \quad (8)$$

Since σ_3^* is a forgery and validates correctly by ProxyAccVerifyProof, the signing oracle needs to be a BLS-oracle $\mathcal{O}_{\mathsf{BLS}}$ (using $\mathcal{O}_{\mathsf{H}_2}$ as a subroutine), i.e. returning valid BLS signatures $\mathcal{H}_2(w)^{x_0}$ and $\mathcal{H}_2(w)^{x_i}$ after at most q queries. Therefore, c' will not help $\mathcal{F}$ in breaking the scheme and

$$Pr[\mathcal{F}^{\mathcal{O}_{\mathsf{Sign}}, \mathcal{O}_{\mathsf{H}_1}, \mathcal{O}_{\mathsf{H}_2}}(\alpha)] \leq Pr[\mathcal{F}^{\mathcal{O}_{\mathsf{BLS}}}(\alpha)] \leq \epsilon \quad (9)$$

since BLS is provably secure in the random oracle model with a reduction to breaking the computational Diffie-Hellman problem [3].

Case 2: Assuming $\mathcal{F}$ manages to compute a forged signature σ_2^*, then similar to case (1) the forged signature contains $U_{\mathcal{S}}^* = (sk_{\mathcal{S}})^{c'} + g^{k_{\mathcal{S}}} = \left((\mathcal{H}_2(w)^{x_0} + \mathcal{H}_2(w)^{x_s})^{c'} + g^{k_{\mathcal{S}}} \right)$ where x_s is the secret key of $\mathcal{S}$ and $k_{\mathcal{S}} \in \mathbb{Z}_p^*$ chosen randomly by $\mathcal{S}$. Again, the forgery implies a BLS-oracle, hence the scheme is secure. □

6   Implementation

The Java Pairing-Based Cryptography library (jPBC) is a Java port of the PBC library written in C which provides the mathematical operations needed for pairing-based cryptosystems [5]. Computations were over a field of 318-bit modulo.

In order to better understand the efficiency of our protocol, a set of different operations and procedures went through a performance analysis, measuring the approximate time in milliseconds. Each operation and procedure was executed 1000 times on a MacBook Pro, 2017, with 2.3 GHz Dual-Core Intel Core i5, 16 GB 2133 MHz LPDDR3 on macOS Big Sur 11.2. The results are presented in Table 1. As expected, all procedures containing pairings were the slowest. We strongly expect our results to be much faster using a more efficient implementation of the hash-to-group algorithm. The scalability analysis consider running the ProxyAccSignWitness procedure with different number of proxies. It seems to scale linearly as expected, and for 1000 participating proxies the proxy signature- and verification procedure takes roughly 1 min.

Table 1. Performance analysis. Ops is number of operations.

Operation	Time(ms)	Ops.	Procedure	Time(ms)
$\mathbb{G}$: point addition	0.0003	4	ProxyAccSetup	31.04
$\mathbb{G}$: point multiplication	0.0006	3	ProxyAccKeyExtract	9.76
$\mathbb{Z}$: exponentiation	0.0310	10	ProxyAccProxyKeyGen	51.18
Hash to $\mathbb{G}$	21.5461	5	ProxyAccSignWitness	59.83
Pairing	5.5111	7	ProxyAccVerifyWitness	55.97
Proxies	**Time (ms)**		ProxyAccSignProof	59.57
10	728.72		ProxyAccVerifyProof	54.46
100	6591.15			
1000	63847.88		**Total run**	316.14

7   Conclusion

We provided a method for constructing AMPA schemes, illustrating how to combine them into a practical protocol along with a proof-of-concept implementation and performance analysis. We have also shown the validity of the intact security analysis covering the merge of two schemes, showing the correctness and non-forgeability. We conclude that important aspects to consider in our merge methodology is to choose an overlapping underlying hardness assumption for the combined schemes, utilizing the same key-pairs and reuse signature procedures as a second layer between proxies and database owner(s).

References

1. Abadi, A., Terzis, S., Dong, C.: VD-PSI: verifiable delegated private set intersection on outsourced private datasets. In: Grossklags, J., Preneel, B. (eds.) FC 2016. LNCS, vol. 9603, pp. 149–168. Springer, Heidelberg (2017). https://doi.org/10.1007/978-3-662-54970-4_9

2. Benaloh, J., de Mare, M.: One-way accumulators: a decentralized alternative to digital signatures. In: Helleseth, T. (ed.) EUROCRYPT 1993. LNCS, vol. 765, pp. 274–285. Springer, Heidelberg (1994). https://doi.org/10.1007/3-540-48285-7_24

3. Boneh, D., Lynn, B., Shacham, H.: Short signatures from the weil pairing. In: Boyd, C. (ed.) ASIACRYPT 2001. LNCS, vol. 2248, pp. 514–532. Springer, Heidelberg (2001). https://doi.org/10.1007/3-540-45682-1_30

4. Camenisch, J., Kohlweiss, M., Soriente, C.: An accumulator based on bilinear maps and efficient revocation for anonymous credentials. In: Jarecki, S., Tsudik, G. (eds.) PKC 2009. LNCS, vol. 5443, pp. 481–500. Springer, Heidelberg (2009). https://doi.org/10.1007/978-3-642-00468-1_27

5. De Caro, A., Iovino, V.: jPBC: java pairing based cryptography. In: Proceedings of the 16th IEEE Symposium on Computers and Communications, ISCC 2011, pp. 850–855. IEEE (2011). http://gas.dia.unisa.it/projects/jpbc/

6. Freedman, M.J., Nissim, K., Pinkas, B.: Efficient private matching and set intersection. In: Cachin, C., Camenisch, J.L. (eds.) EUROCRYPT 2004. LNCS, vol. 3027, pp. 1–19. Springer, Heidelberg (2004). https://doi.org/10.1007/978-3-540-24676-3_1

7. Graham, C., Gupta, N., Dsilva, V., Warrilow, M., Medford, B., Eschinger, C.: Forecast: public cloud services, worldwide, 2018–2024, 3q20 update (2020)

8. Hahn, D.A., Munir, A., Behzadan, V.: Security and privacy issues in intelligent transportation systems: classification and challenges. IEEE Intell. Transp. Syst. Mag. **13**(1), 181–196 (2021)

9. Lamssaggad, A., Benamar, N., Hafid, A.S., Msahli, M.: A survey on the current security landscape of intelligent transportation systems. IEEE Access **9**, 9180–9208 (2021). https://doi.org/10.1109/ACCESS.2021.3050038

10. Miyaji, A., Nishida, S.: A scalable multiparty private set intersection, pp. 376–385, November 2015. https://doi.org/10.1007/978-3-319-25645-0_26

11. Netwrix: 2021 cloud data security report. https://www.netwrix.com/2021_cloud_data_security_report.html. Accessed 20 Jun 2021

12. Nguyen, L.: Accumulators from bilinear pairings and applications. In: Menezes, A. (ed.) CT-RSA 2005. LNCS, vol. 3376, pp. 275–292. Springer, Heidelberg (2005). https://doi.org/10.1007/978-3-540-30574-3_19

13. Rojszczak, M.: Cloud act agreements from an EU perspective. Comput. Law Secur. Rev. **38**, 105442 (2020). https://doi.org/10.1016/j.clsr.2020.105442

14. Zheng, Q., Xu, S.: Verifiable delegated set intersection operations on outsourced encrypted data. In: 2015 IEEE International Conference on Cloud Engineering, pp. 175–184 (2015). https://doi.org/10.1109/IC2E.2015.38

Extending the Exposure Score of Web Browsers by Incorporating CVSS

Fadi Mohsen[1]() , Adel Shtayyeh[2], Riham Naser[2], Lena Mohammad[2], and Marten Struijk[1]

[1] Information Systems Group, Bernoulli Institute for Mathematics, Computer Science and Artificial Intelligence, University of Groningen, Groningen, The Netherlands
f.f.m.mohsen@rug.nl
[2] An-Najah National University, Nablus, Palestine

Abstract. When browsing the Internet, HTTP headers enable both clients and servers send extra data in their requests or responses such as the User-Agent string. This string contains information related to the sender's device, browser, and operating system. Yet its content differs from one browser to another. Despite the privacy and security risks of User-Agent strings, very few works have tackled this problem. Our previous work proposed giving Internet browsers exposure relative scores to aid users to choose less intrusive ones. Thus, the objective of this work is to extend our previous work through: first, conducting a user study to identify its limitations. Second, extending the exposure score via incorporating data from the NVD. Third, providing a full implementation, instead of a limited prototype. The proposed system: assigns scores to users' browsers upon visiting our website. It also suggests alternative safe browsers, and finally it allows updating the back-end database with a click of a button. We applied our method to a data set of more than 52 thousand unique browsers. Our performance and validation analysis show that our solution is accurate and efficient. The source code and data set are publicly available here [4].

1 Introduction

Web browsers are programs that allow you to search for and view the content of the World Wide Web [7]. Though, these browsers do more than just simply rendering HTML (Hypertext Markup Language) pages and displaying the results. They enable users to use search engines, make online purchases, communicate with each other using social media sites, and much more [19]. However, there are issues related to maintaining the privacy of users and the security of their devices while surfing the web using these programs. These issues can possible result in compromising user's devices and access their personal data such as browser history and auto-fill information [2,14]. For instance, vulnerable browsers could give attackers the opportunity to exploit their security gaps to steal information, delete files, and other malicious activities [21]. Though, executing such attacks is normally proceeded by collecting detailed information about the target. For

© The Author(s), under exclusive license to Springer Nature Switzerland AG 2022
B. Luo et al. (Eds.): CRiSIS 2021, LNCS 13204, pp. 172–182, 2022.
https://doi.org/10.1007/978-3-031-02067-4_12

example, the version of the operating system, the version of the hardware, and browsing software type. In fact, each browser has its own distinctive User-Agent request header [9]. The User-Agent request header exposes information about the software being used, the operating system and the installation of certain plugins [15]. This information can also be leveraged to track user activities on the web via a process called fingerprinting [12]. Fingerprinting is the process where the combination of fields exposed by the browser leads to an (almost) unique combination [3]. Although most people are aware of the role of cookies in fingerprinting and tracking users across the internet, the use of the User-Agent request header is relatively unknown. Users are not even asked to share this information. Our previous work Mohsen et al. [15] pointed out the privacy and security risks of User-Agent request header because of the amount and the sensitivity of the information it exposes. We proposed a new technique to quantify the exposure of Internet browsers. The technique is merely based on the information items that exist in the User-Agent request header. As a proof of concept, we implemented a simple prototype to demonstrate how such a technique could be useful in protecting the privacy of users. Thus, in this work, we are primarily extending that technique by incorporating the Common Vulnerabilities and Exposures (CVE) of a browser. CVE is a list of publicly disclosed computer security flaws. We rely on the Common Vulnerability Scoring System (CVSS) to calculate the severity score of each CVE record [1]. We then aggregate the severity scores of all CVE records of a browser. The resulting severity score and the relative score Mohsen et al. [15] are then merged together. The resulting score is the final exposure score of the browser. The following are the research contributions:

– Conducting a user study to explore the limitation of an existing method for quantifying the exposures of web browsers.
– Extending the technique that we previously proposed Mohsen et al. [15] to calculate new exposure score for Internet browsers.
– Providing a full implementation - online tool that uses the resulting exposure scores to suggest alternative privacy-preserving Internet browsers. The PHP source code, the database schema, and the final data set are publicly available here [4].
– Conducting an evaluation and validation studies on our tool.

The rest of the paper is organized as follows. In Sect. 2 we discuss the design and the results of the user study. In Sect. 3 we go briefly over the methodology of the previous technique then we move to talk about our extension. In Sect. 4 we discuss the implementation details. In Sect. 5 we go over the related works. Finally, we conclude the paper with Sect. 6.

2   User Study

The aim of this user study is to study whether the tool that we previously proposed [15] is appealing to the end users, and if not, obtain the list of new features that need to be added to the tool. As such, this study raises three main research questions: (i) Are users aware of the data that is being exposed by their browsers?. (ii) How likely are they willing to use such a score-based system?. (iii) Are there any vital features missing this system?.

2.1 Survey Design

We created a custom survey that prompts participants to answer a set of questions before and after showing them the exposure scores of their browsers. The custom survey collects also the User-agent strings of participants after taking their consent. The survey's questions were also split into multiple pages to make participation less overwhelming. The survey starts with an introduction followed by the demographic questions. After that comes in a set of questions concerning information privacy and Internet browsers. The exposure score report is then shown to the user alongside questions pertaining the exiting scoring system and ideas to improve it. During the survey, participants get to see their parsed User-agent string and the exposure score of their browsers, a list of alternative browsers, and a unique token. The unique token is connected to their survey answers in case they decided to have them removed from the data set.

2.2 Demographics

Nearly, half of the users who visited the study URL managed to complete it. In total, 115 participants has answered all the questions successfully. The average time of completing the survey was eight minutes. More than 85% of participants were aged between 15 and 25: 15–20 (29.6%) and 20–25 (55.8%). About 32.2% of participants were female and 67.0% were male. The education and technical experience of the participants can be noted as relatively high. The distribution of participants over the age groups, education, and technical skills should be taken in consideration before generalizing the results.

2.3 User Awareness

The majority of participants disagreed with the statement that their browser did not share any data about them. However, they indicated not to know what data their browser shared. After showing them their parsed User-agent strings, participants were asked if they were aware such data was being exposed. Our analysis showed that the technical skills of a participant plays an important role in her awareness of the data exposure. Participants with high technical skills were less surprised by the exposed data in comparison to participants with low technical skills.

2.4 Likely to Use

The results show that users are not very likely to use the current score-based system. Yet, there seems to be no overwhelming majority for either side, which gives us a window to improve the current system. Moreover, some participants find that the current score-based system uses technical terms that is hard for some users to understand. Others have stressed the need to add more information as to how the score is calculated.

2.5   Key Features

Our analysis shows that the browser UI and page loading speed are the most important features for users when choosing a browser. The plugin support, startup speed and privacy comes after that. The Least important feature was if a browser was pre-installed on the machine. Although people do consider privacy, it is not the most important feature that people will base their browser choice on.

2.6   Identifiable

Out of the 115 User-agent strings that we collected from participants, 53% of the users had a unique User-agent string. The User-agent string that appeared the most was generated by Chrome browsers running on windows 10. They appeared 19 times. Closely followed by Safari running on iOS 14.4.2 and Firefox on windows. They both appeared 11 times. A closer look at the collected User-agent strings, we could make a number of observations. First, we noticed that Android devices add the product code of the device to the User-agent string. Second, IPhone devices generally generate the same User-Agent string regardless of the phone's type as long as they are on the same iOS version and use Safari. Instagram and other mobile apps use an in-app browser with a custom User-agent header (for both iOS and Android).

3   Methodology

In this section, we will discuss our methodology in generating a final exposure score for Internet browsers. The final score is a combination of two scores; thus, we will start by briefly talking about the first one, the relative score. After that, we will discuss the second score, the CVSS score.

3.1   The Relative Score

In our previous work Mohsen et al. [15], we devised a formula to calculate a relative score for browsers. The score is based on the amount of information that are revealed by the browser's User-agent string in relative to the other browsers in the data set. The equation shown in Eq. 3 shows the exposure score of browser i based on all j's, the attributes that were contained in the User-agent string. For each element j, the sensitivity and visibility scores and constants are calculated based on other equations, which we do not show here. For further information about this equation, we refer you to [15].

$$EXP(i) = \sum_j EXP(i,j) = \sum_j (S(j) + S_j) \times (V(i,j) + V_j) \qquad (1)$$

$$CVSS\_FinalScore(browser) = (\sum_{vuln} CVSS\_BaseScore(vuln))/N \qquad (2)$$

$$CVSS\_BaseScore(vuln) = [AVG(CVSS2(vuln), CVSS3(vuln))|(CVSS2(vuln))] \qquad (3)$$

3.2 The CVSS Score

The National Vulnerability Database (NVD) is currently supporting CVSS Version 3.x [17] and CVSS Version 2.0 [18]. Thus, a particular vulnerability can have at most two scores. However, since the CVSS 3.0 is not yet complete, many vulnerabilities will only have one score, the CVSS version 2.0. As such, we decided that the CVSS score of a vulnerability is the average of two scores if both existed, otherwise, it is the CVSS 2.0 score.

3.3 Final Exposure Score

In Eq. 4 we show our methodology in calculating the final exposure score for a browsing software. The final exposure score equals the normalized relative score plus the CVSS score divided by 2. The CVSS score is the average of the two scores. In case the CVSS version 3.x is missing, the CVSS score becomes the CVSS 2.0 score. Originally, the relative score has no maximum value. In order to combine it with the CVSS score, we had first to normalize it.

$$FIN\_SCORE(i) = NORM(REL\_SCORE(i)) + CVSS\_FinalScore(i) \qquad (4)$$

3.4 Dataset

We used the data set of [15], which contained over a million User-agent string. Our evaluation of this data set revealed two important points. First, the data set contained a lot of duplicated records. Second, a good number of these records were for old browser versions. Thus, we removed all duplicates and then looked online for newer data sets, that contain more recent versions of the existing browsers. The result is a new data set, that contains 52,000 unique browsers. Each record in the final data set is composed of 51 columns. Forty-seven columns are for the different attributes that we retrieved from the User-agent string. Two columns are for the CVSS and the relative scores. The last two columns are for keeping track of when were the two scores last updated.

3.5   Final Data Set Summary

Nearly, 89% of the User-Agent strings were coming from a browser, the other 11% are divided among other browsing software types such as Application 6%, Bot/Crawler 3%, Email Client 2%. As per the device types, 45% were mobile phones, 33% desktop, 19% tablets, and the remaining 3% were unknown devices. Regarding the distribution of the platform makers, it comes as no surprise that the top three most used platforms were Google, Microsoft and Apple, since 45% of the devices were mobile phones. Finally, the distribution of the used rendering engines shows that Blink was the most used, with 54% share, WebKit 19%, Gecko 13%, Trident 3%, on Presto Opera 3%, and UCWeb 3%.

Fig. 1. A snippet of an NVD Json file. It contains the number of vulnerabilities, and the CVE id of each vulnerability and its CVSS score.

4   Implementation

As a first step, we calculated the relative scores for all the records in the final data set according to [15]. We then calculated the CVSS scores, which took a lot of time because we had to crawl the information from the NVD website. Finally, the final score, exposure score, is derived from the previous two scores. In this section, we will give an overview of the score-based system that we developed. It uses the aforementioned scores to recommend safer browsing options to the users. The system first extracts then processes the requester's User-agent string. After that, it calculates both scores. Then, it displays a report to the user. Finally, it updates the database accordingly. We will go over these steps in significant detail below.

Extracting and Processing the User-agent String. In this step, the User-agent string is extracted from the requests coming into our system. Then, the User-agent string is parsed to extract the 47 features [15]. Next, the final data set is searched to find a match based on the 47 features. The result of this search can be summarized in three cases: Best-case, Average-case, and Worst-case. In the former, a match is found and both scores are present and up to date. In the Average-case, a match is found, but one of the scores is missing. In the latter, a match is not found.

Calculating a Relative Score. This step is needed in the worst-case scenario. It is also needed in the average-case scenario when the relative score is missing. For the latter case, the relative score is calculated and the browser's record in the database is updated accordingly. However, calculating the relative score for a new browser is a quite cumbersome process. This is because it depends on all browsers in the database. It entails updating some of the terms and constants in the original equation [15] such as n and $|R^j|$. Moreover, it requires updating the relative scores of all browsers in the database. For simplicity and efficiency reasons, the current score-system updates the terms and constants temporarily to calculate the relative score of the new browser. The relative scores of all existing browsers are not updated at this stage. After the relative and CVSS scores are calculated for the new browser, a new record will be inserted into the database.

Calculating the CVSS Score. This step is needed in the worst-case scenario. It is also needed in the average-case scenario when the CVSS score is missing. The CVSS score is calculated by first searching the NVD website for associated vulnerabilities. The search is conducted based on three keys: the browser name, the browser version, and the platform. The NVD website sends back the results as a JSON file. The file contains several information, most notably the number of vulnerabilities, the ID of each vulnerability and the base metric that contains the CVSS score in its two versions. The file shown in Fig. 1 was returned after searching for the following keys: Chrome, 90.0, and Win10. It shows that there are 46 distinct vulnerabilities linked to this particular browser. The CVSS scores for one of these vulnerabilities are highlighted. The Json file is then parsed into two-dimensional array. For each vulnerability, the final CVSS score is calculated by either averaging both scores or considering one of them if the other is missing. The final CVSS score of a browser would then be the average CVSS score of all its vulnerabilities.

Calculating the Final Exposure Score. The final exposure score for each browsing software in our final data set is calculated using Eq. 4 of Sect. 3.3. The maximum possible value for this score is 20. The relative and CVSS scores contributes evenly to this score with 10 each. Browsers with lower scores are better for users because they reveal less information and has less vulnerabilities. In order to understand the relationship between the CVSS score and the relative score of a browser, we calculated the correlation coefficient between the two scores. It meant to measure the degree of linear association between the two continuous variables. The correlation value was 0.18, which is considered weak. Thus, merging these two scores is considered advantageous as it gives us a better representative score. Otherwise, one of these scores would've been enough.

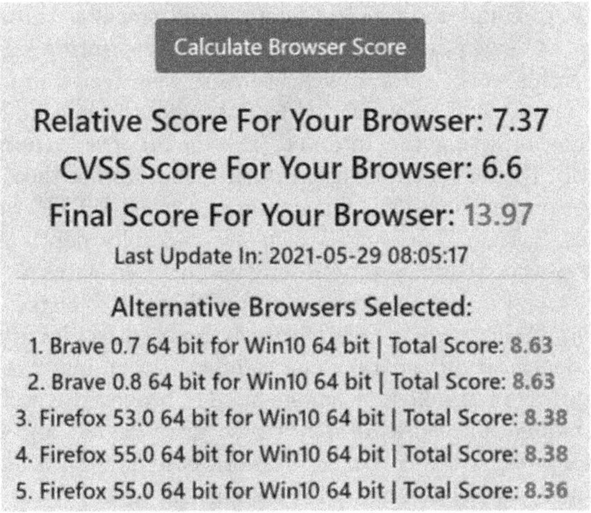

Fig. 2. The current implementation returns a list of alternative browsers with lower final exposure scores that also fit the user's device specifications. Due to the space limit, we could not show the entire GUI.

Displaying Scores and Suggestions. In this step, a report is displayed to the user pertaining her browsing software. The report contains information such as the relative and the CVSS scores, the final score, the last update, and alternative browsers. It also shows all the attributes that the current browser reveals. Additionally, it provides a description of the scores and their privacy implications. In Fig. 2, the final exposure score of the user's browser, which is *Chrome 90.0 on Windows 10 64bit*, is 13.97 out of 20, the relative score is 7.37 out of 10, and the CVSS score is 6.6 out of 10. The browsing software reveals numerous attributes such as the platform, the device type and the device name.

Update: Admin Portal. The Admin Portal is used to add new User-Agent strings to the database and update the privacy scores of existing ones.

5 Related Works

Our work is considered an improvement over our earlier work Mohsen et al. [15]. In that work, a new formula was introduced to measure the privacy exposure of web browsers. The formula considered only the information that are included in the User-agent string. In addition, the implementation was meant as a proof of concept rather than a complete tool. Finally, the seed data set that we used contained numerous duplicate entries. Thus, in this work, we first extended the exposure formula by considering the browsers' vulnerabilities, cleaned the data set and added new records, and provided full implementation. The goal of both works though is to counter user identification and tracking through numerous techniques such as device fingerprinting. Device fingerprinting was first studied by Peter's [3]. In his work, modern web browsers were tested in order to determine whether they can be fingerprinted or not using the information that they disseminate while browsing the Internet. Takeda proposed a number of techniques to identify the owner of a digital device [20]. One of these techniques is based on analyzing the browsers' fingerprints such as: HTTP Accept Header, Browser Plugins, System Fonts and Screen size and color depth. Yen et al. [22] carried on a large-scale study on month-long anonymized datasets that were collected by the Hotmail web-mail service and the Bing search engine. Their results showed that User-Agent strings can effectively be used to identify hosts on the Internet. The identification accuracy can significantly be improved if combined with the IP address of the host. Kaur et al. [11] proposed a web browser fingerprinting technique that works despite the security devices and measures that are normally deployed at the corporate network boundary such as VPNs, proxy servers and NAT. Laperdrix et al. [13] demonstrated the effect of the recent innovations in HTML5 on increasing the accuracy of fingerprinting. They also showed that browser fingerprinting on mobile devices is highly possible and effective similar to personal computers. On the contrary, Hupperich et al. [10] found that existing tracking techniques do not perform well on mobile devices; thus, they proposed several features that tracking systems could leverage to fingerprint mobile devices. Martin et al. [16] was able to identify web browsers using the underlying JavaScript engine. As far as the preventive measures, Laperdrix et al. [13] explained different ways to reduce the possibility of fingerprinting, such as removing plugins and using regular HTTP headers. Martin et al. [16] leveraged their proposed browser fingerprinting technique to prevent session hijacking attacks. In addition, there were a number of proposals to counter the privacy threat of browser fingerprinting and tracking users [5,6,8]

6   Conclusion and Future Work

In this paper, we first conducted a user study to identify the limitations of an existing method for quantifying the privacy exposure of web browsers. We then extended the method by incorporating the browser's vulnerability records that are extracted from the National Vulnerability Database (NVD). We also provided a full web implementation for our approach, in which the relative exposure score of the user's browser is calculated on the fly, then a list of alternative safe browsers is shown to the user. Our implementation is based on a seed data set of over 52 thousand unique browsers along with their parsed user-agent strings and vulnerability records. Furthermore, the data set is constantly changing based on users' requests and the updates that happen on the NVD records. Our validation and performance analysis of our approach showed that it is accurate and efficient. For instance, the time needed to answer a user request is 0.85 s in case the request's browser exists in our database. In case it is a new browser, the request will be answered in it 6.16, which entails retrieving the vulnerabilities and calculating the final score. On the other hand, a complete update to the data set needs only 1.82 min. As a future work, we plan to improve our method by incorporating the CVSS temporal and environmental metrics. The PHP source code, the database schema, and the final data set are publicly available here [4].

References

1. Aksu, M.U., et al.: A quantitative CVSS-based cyber security risk assessment methodology for it systems. In: 2017 International Carnahan Conference on Security Technology (ICCST), pp. 1–2 (2017). https://doi.org/10.1109/CCST.2017.8167819
2. Barona, R., Anita, E.A.M.: A survey on data breach challenges in cloud computing security: issues and threats. In: 2017 International Conference on Circuit, Power and Computing Technologies (ICCPCT), pp. 1–8 (2017). https://doi.org/10.1109/ICCPCT.2017.8074287
3. Eckersley, P.: How unique is your web browser? In: Atallah, M.J., Hopper, N.J. (eds.) PETS 2010. LNCS, vol. 6205, pp. 1–18. Springer, Heidelberg (2010). https://doi.org/10.1007/978-3-642-14527-8_1
4. Mohsen, F., Adel Shtayyeh, R.N., Mohammad, L.: 52k+ User-agent strings and their exposure scores. V1, Dataversed (2021). https://doi.org/10.34894/2SVOIE
5. FaizKhademi, A., Zulkernine, M., Weldemariam, K.: FPGuard: detection and prevention of browser fingerprinting. In: Samarati, P. (ed.) DBSec 2015. LNCS, vol. 9149, pp. 293–308. Springer, Cham (2015). https://doi.org/10.1007/978-3-319-20810-7_21
6. Fiore, U., Castiglione, A., Santis, A.D., Palmieri, F.: Countering browser fingerprinting techniques: constructing a fake profile with google chrome. In: 2014 17th International Conference on Network-Based Information Systems, pp. 355–360, September 2014. https://doi.org/10.1109/NBiS.2014.102
7. GCFGlobal: Internet basics - using a web browser. https://edu.gcfglobal.org/en/internetbasics/using-a-web-browser/1/
8. Gómez-Boix, A., Frey, D., Bromberg, Y.D., Baudry, B.: A collaborative strategy for mitigating tracking through browser fingerprinting. In: MTD 2019–6th ACM Workshop on Moving Target Defense, pp. 1–12. London, United Kingdom, November 2019. https://doi.org/10.1145/3338468.3356828,https://hal.inria.fr/hal-02282591
9. Hoffman, C.: What is a browser's user agent? https://cutt.ly/DW77C6v
10. Hupperich, T., Maiorca, D., Kührer, M., Holz, T., Giacinto, G.: On the robustness of mobile device fingerprinting: can mobile users escape modern web-tracking mechanisms? In: Proceedings of the 31st Annual Computer Security Applications Conference, pp. 191–200 (2015)
11. Kaur, H., Zavarsky, P., Jaafar, F.: Unauthorised data leakage from corporate networks through web browser fingerprinting vulnerability. In: World Congress on Internet Security (WorldCIS-2017), pp. 55–61 (2017)
12. Laperdrix, P., Bielova, N., Baudry, B., Avoine, G.: Browser fingerprinting: a survey. CoRR abs/1905.01051 (2019). http://arxiv.org/abs/1905.01051
13. Laperdrix, P., Rudametkin, W., Baudry, B.: Beauty and the beast: Diverting modern web browsers to build unique browser fingerprints. In: 2016 IEEE Symposium on Security and Privacy (SP), pp. 878–894. IEEE (2016)
14. Matteson, S.: 5 common browser security threats, and how to handle them. https://www.techrepublic.com/article/5-common-browser-security-threats-and-how-to-handle-them/

15. Mohsen, F., Shehab, M., Lange, M., Karastoyanova, D.: Quantifying information exposure by web browsers. In: Arai, K., Kapoor, S., Bhatia, R. (eds.) FTC 2020. AISC, vol. 1290, pp. 648–667. Springer, Cham (2021). https://doi.org/10.1007/978-3-030-63092-8_44

16. Mulazzani, M., et al.: Fast and reliable browser identification with javascript engine fingerprinting. In: Web 2.0 Workshop on Security and Privacy (W2SP), vol. 5. Citeseer (2013)

17. NIST: nvd.nist.gov. https://nvd.nist.gov/vuln-metrics/cvss/v3-calculator

18. NIST: nvd.nist.gov. https://nvd.nist.gov/vuln-metrics/cvss/v2-calculator

19. Scientific, F.: Introduction to browsing the web. https://www.freedomscientific.com/SurfsUp/Introduction.htm

20. Takeda, K.: User identification and tracking with online device fingerprints fusion, pp. 163–167, October 2012. https://doi.org/10.1109/CCST.2012.6393552

21. Wikipedia: Web browser. https://en.wikipedia.org/wiki/Web_browser

22. Yen, T.F., Xie, Y., Yu, F., Yu, R.P., Abadi, M.: Host fingerprinting and tracking on the web: Privacy and security implications. In: NDSS, vol. 62, p. 66 (2012)

Author Index

CPSIA information can be obtained
at www.ICGtesting.com
Printed in the USA
LVHW050224140422
716101LV00004B/58

9 783031 020667